BECOMING
VISIBLE IN
IRAN

BECOMING VISIBLE IN
IRAN

WOMEN IN CONTEMPORARY
IRANIAN SOCIETY

MEHRI HONARBIN-HOLLIDAY

I.B. TAURIS
LONDON · NEW YORK

New edition published in 2013 by I.B.Tauris & Co Ltd
6 Salem Road, London W2 4BU
175 Fifth Avenue, New York NY 10010
www.ibtauris.com

Distributed in the United States and Canada Exclusively by Palgrave Macmillan
175 Fifth Avenue, New York NY 10010

First published in 2008 by Tauris Academic Studies, an imprint of I.B.Tauris & Co Ltd
Copyright © Mehri Honarbin-Holliday, 2008, 2013

ISBN: 978 1 78076 086 5

A full CIP record for this book is available from the British Library
A full CIP record for this book is available from the Library of Congress

Library of Congress Catalog Card Number: available

Printed and bound by CPI Group (UK) Ltd, Croydon, CR0 4YY
from camera-ready copy edited and supplied by the author

For my grandmother, my mother and my daughter

Contents

List of Illustrations

Acknowledgements

I am profoundly indebted to the women whose interviews and specific conversations are represented in this book. Their accounts of their lives as grandmothers, mothers, and young women engaged in re-defining identities and effecting change have been most inspiring. They know who they are, and how invaluable their presence and the knowledge of both themselves and their socio-political location have been to the message of this book. I am grateful for their trust, for allowing me into their spaces, and for giving me the opportunity to inform others of their achievements. This book would not have been possible without their thoughtful and generous contributions.

My gratitude is extended to colleagues in Tehran for inviting me to their academic institutions and campuses. Valuable data have emerged as the result of such collaborations.

I am grateful to Dr Marjaneh Halati for facilitating an interview with Naazila.

I first discussed my ideas with Professors Yvonna Lincoln and Christine Skelton. I am indebted to both for their encouragement, and appreciation of the interdisciplinary and intergenerational nature of my work.

My gratitude goes to Professor Diana Leonard for prompting me to write in the same way I create my art. I thank her for her enthusiasm and appreciating the 'colour' in my writing.

I am profoundly indebted to Dr Elahe Rostami-Povey for her intellectual support. She has read and critically addressed the entire book. Her knowledge of women's development regionally in the Middle East, and Iranian women's socio-political activisms have been illuminating and have energized my own voice.

I am most grateful to Dr Nadje Al-Ali for reading the Texts and for being at once critical and enthusiastic. I very much hope she will find the finished product as 'fresh' as she did the draft.

I thank the Institute of the Advanced Studies in Anthropology, in Oaxaca, Mexico, for inviting me to discuss my ideas about young women in Iran and their forms of resistance. I benefited enormously from discussions with their international audience of academics, writers, gender specialists, artists, and anthropologist.

I thank my daughter Shabnam Jane, now Dr Holliday, for reading the final draft, but above all for embracing her Iranian cultural heritage and continuing to improve her Farsi.

I am profoundly indebted to my friend for life-and-after and my husband, Professor Adrian Holliday, for his complete understanding of my ideas, for his love of Iran, and for reading and commenting on the Texts. He deserves a medal for tolerating my Proustian style of authorship with multiple sensitivities, writing between migraines, and especially when 'A change in the weather is sufficient to recreate the world and ourselves'.

In Tehran I was given shelter by a number of people. I thank Mr Mori Alavi and Mrs Manzar Alavi for their kindness. I am enormously grateful to Ms Fereshteh Honarbin, Mrs Akram Golmohamadi, Ms Maryam Salour, and Ms Lily Farhadpour for giving me shelter when I most needed it during the challenging processes of research.

I thank Mr Paul Hepworth for being a great friend and for our on-going dialogue in the past decades about art, life, and Western Imperialism, whether in Damascus, Cairo, New York, Baltimore, Istanbul, or Canterbury.

I am grateful to Mansour Nasiri for the two images of young women protesting in front of Azadi Sport Stadium in Text Four, and Fictionville Studio for Naazila's photograph in the same Text.

Preface

Iranian women have been at the forefront of the civil society debates in Iran, insisting particularly in recent decades on being visibly active in all aspects of life. Equipped with increasing self-knowledge and self-confidence through education, they have engaged in a battle of ideas with passion and dynamic methodologies, aiming to effect cultural change, reform in the legal system and a more developed democracy which safeguards women's rights as well as men's. This was demonstrated to the world in the aftermath of the disputed presidential elections in the summer of 2009 and the birth of the Green Movement. Millions of Iranian women, young and old, marched in the public space, shoulder to shoulder with their male counterparts and their families, in a mass display of civic resistance, enquiring after the plight of their uncounted votes. In reporting these events, the world media showed an unexpected face of Muslim Iran. The narratives in this book illuminate, through a detailed and personal exploration of life experiences, the ways in which Iranian women endeavour to re-define identities and construct the building blocks of a just society based on the rights of all citizens.

The interviews for *Becoming Visible in Iran* were conducted in 2007. However, my interest in Iranian women's expressions of identity began in 1998 when I returned to Iran for eight weeks after a considerable period of absence. I had kept in touch with my cultural heritage and history through reading Persian poetry, holding poetry evenings and regularly viewing Iranian art in museums and galleries around the world. I had kept company with Iran through the iconic 1,000 year-old epic of the kings, the *Shah Nameh* of Hakim Abolghasem Ferdowsi Toosi, the 800 year-old school of love poetry of Mowlana Jalaledin Mohammad of Balkh known also as Rumi, in his *Divan-e Shams*, as well as the vital modern poems of Forough Farokhzad and Ahmad Shamloo.

During the eight weeks in Iran I created a routine of attending and reading at the Reza Abbasi Museum library, mindful of developing new understandings and relationships with verbal and visual texts of exquisite beauty and historic significance. While walking to the museum I encountered several newspaper kiosks and observed the impressive range of a dynamic and generative media which included numerous women columnists, editors and writers. I further observed the enthusiasm and anticipation with which young people regularly bought daily newspapers and periodicals in order to speculate, examine and debate the latest disclosed and undisclosed political news.

Returning to England and seeing Ziba Mir-Hosseini and Kim Longinotto's award-winning documentary, *Divorce Iranian Style*, I was gripped by their vision as researchers, the sensitivity of their visual execution of complex ideas, and above all the pragmatism of the women they depicted. Seemingly of low education, and despite limitations in legal rights, these women fought for divorce or custody of their children with probity, relating narratives of courage, imagination and perseverance. Moved and alerted, I subsequently found meaning in Elaheh Rostami-Povey's book, *Women, Work and Islamism*.

About the same time and as part of world cinema studies I was able to teach, in a British university, the internationally acclaimed cinema of Abbas Kiarostami and Samira Makhmalbaf. Kiarostami's *Through the Olive Trees* narrated the story of a young man's love for a young woman in the rural north devastated by earthquake. The 15-year-old heroine displayed strong presence and determination to remain autonomous. Reluctant to undermine her identity, she resisted the choice of dress prescribed for her by the director because it did not befit someone who was 'in education'. Between Kiarostami's fiction and Samira Makhmalbaf's award-winning critical real-life filmmaking at the age of 17, creating visual lyricism at once about neglected young girls and high art, I was convinced to engage in an in-depth study of Iranian women. This in turn led to the focus of this book where I take the reader with me on a journey to spaces of transition and continuity, and contradiction and paradox – to homes where male relatives are challenged, and classrooms, parks, metros, taxis and cafes where social and political debates persist and women speak their minds. This emerging cartography is the continued testament to Iranian women's march for self-realisation and the sustained development of civil society.

Introduction

To determine the meaning of concepts such as identity, autonomy, and agency, we increasingly refer back to the experiences of individuals. Similarly, in identifying the shape of the bigger picture in society we examine the condition of the personal. This book creates a space to relate the lived experience of individual women in contemporary society in Iran, and how they resist the limitations placed upon them. The book presents narratives which project continuities in women's social history and engages with their activism in demanding change.

The narratives provide glimpses into lives; they represent those lives, and register histories of struggles, triumphs, and certainties as well as uncertainties. While the narratives are selected for their power and expression of autonomy, their relevance to the current discussions on gender and politics, both locally and globally, is multi-fold. They illuminate layered and complex experiences of women living in Muslim majority Iran at a significant time in the history of the country. They create an opportunity to engage with developments in forms of *being* amongst young women, and the ways in which they critically reflect on their selves and endeavour to widen discussions to influence change in Iran's social and legal systems. Ultimately the narratives create the much needed knowledge and context to contemplate the interrelationships between particularity and universality in existences within the global community at the beginning of the twenty-first century.

My interests in conducting research in Iran precede and overlap with the data presented in this book. Earlier work focused on investigating the developments in teaching, learning, and practising art in formal university settings after the 1979 Revolution with myself as a participant researching-artist. I subsequently realized however, that the power and connectedness of the social acts and personal conduct of young urban women demanded a sharper focus. I found them highly persuasive if also subtle at times. This, I discovered, was due to their circumstances. As if regulating a well-worn item of curiosity, they seemed to fine-tune their actions on a daily basis, listening and watching for the uneven turn of political events. Then, a little here and a lot there, they would re-define those actions and locate new trajectories for change accordingly, and take others with them.

The material presented here is the result of fieldwork in Tehran during six visits between 2004 and 2007. It has revealed a chain of interrelated themes and ideas illuminating the young women's intent and persistence in expressing desire for being visible and at large as active citizens in society, performing complex and fluid identities, and engaging in critical explorations of socio-political concepts. As we shall see, at the centre of these themes and ideas there exist strategies for developing self, society, and the notion of a collective voice based on reason and legal entitlements. Adopting intellectual, social, and cultural capital, and employing their bodies as well as their minds, and in most cases regardless of socio-economic conditions, these young women seem to want nothing that does not resist restrictions. Their demand for shifts in attitudes and legal perspectives, at home in relation to male relatives, and outside in relation to patriarchy, is compelling. Indeed, their adopted methods of activism indicate a movement from the grassroots to fulfil collective aspirations for a more developed and pluralistic democracy in Iran.

Local perceptions and Western misperceptions

At the same time as carrying out fieldwork in Iran, my experiences in the West continue to indicate profound knowledge deficiency and confused imagination regarding Muslim women and their efforts to challenge and overcome socio-political discrepancies. There seems to be little understanding of the degrees of diversity in spiritual, political, and cultural practices and existences amongst Muslims and Muslim nations, let alone Muslim women. It is a vastly misunderstood and neglected fact that although Islam has a unified source, it is also fluid and giving, capable of multiple interpretations which often take the colour and texture of the locale, and project complex perspectives. This lack of knowledge is currently acutely exacerbated by a mixture of political and media misinformation in the West. This has become particularly dangerous because of the United States' expansionist neo-conservatism and shameless neo-imperialist policies in the Middle East. The fact is that the occupation of Iraq in 2003, and the invasion-occupation-bombing campaigns in Afghanistan by the United States and British military forces, and the sustained proxy war against Palestine, have profoundly undermined the development, integrity, identity, and humanity of the Palestinian, Iraqi and Afghan nations, including their women.[1] Further, the highly ignorant and damaging rhetoric extended towards Iran, with a promise of military attack, has suggested, amongst other things, that military intervention will bring liberation for the Iranian nation and its female citizens. This shameless discourse of 'we want to liberate you, but have to bomb you first' and the construction of the idea that the women of the region are subjects needy of this particular brand of liberation by the military forces from the West, are profoundly deluded.[2] I believe that the narratives presented here will demonstrate how able Iranian women are in pursuing their interests despite the uneven terrains before them, and how the only legacy Western military meddling in the region can wish for is profound resentment and abhorrence creating irreparable political damage globally.

At its most banal, the discourse of liberation by military force creates profound misperceptions with a ripple effect especially within Western communities. They add to the longstanding themes of arrogance and ignorance, and sustain the misguided perceptions about the superiority of Western thought. Apparent government-to-government rhetoric in the media thus becomes a destructive simplification and rejection of non-Western individuals and communities. During an exchange of ideas about current trajectories in the literature on gender, a research student in the West asks whether Iranian women, because of their religion and their government, are permitted to leave their homes. Further, when attending an international conference in Manchester, an art and media research student from Tehran is told how unexpected it is to see an abstract from Muslim Iran discussing current developments in the psychology of art, and how unimaginable it is that a young woman speaker from an art university in Tehran can deliver her paper in English. The image of Iranian woman being kept indoors, in the first example, and lacking in both personal ability and collective socio-cultural aptitude because of religion, in the second example, could not be in sharper contrast to the realities and self-perceptions of the predominant majority of Iranian women. Such widely held misplaced and miss-imagined perceptions of Muslim women, even amongst the well-educated in the West, overlooks Iranian women's activism in the last hundred years supported by a rich body of academic research. It demonstrates the persistent Western political agenda which has never been liberating, even at its best during times of peace. This agenda has sought increasing economic gain to feed its greed machinery, sustained political power and exceptionalist policies, and cultural dominance which nurtures at its very core unforgotten colonial values.[3] It is sadly a devouring essentialist agenda which simplifies Others, and in order to dominate, it ignores or fails to grasp the entirety of their existences.

Women in Iran, regardless of their locale, take part and can have an input in vast arrays of outdoor social life. This is not to deny restrictions, and at times profound injustices which have also existed during more secular periods in the country's recent and distant past, as indeed has been the case in the West. Although the social conduct and professional development of many women in Iran, individually and collectively, are routinely undermined, the women themselves have proved difficult to stop and have become a visible political force. As they continue to develop themselves they aspire to and in many cases succeed in engaging others in discourses of change. Whether urban or rural, and whether in the capital city of Tehran, as the seat of government, centre of art, culture, and urban opportunities, or in the small clerical city of Qom, as the centre of conservative Shi'ite Islam, second only to Najaf in Iraq, and the site of university campuses, women are becoming visible more than ever before.[4] Limitations and restrictions on women are not necessarily required or designed by Islamic thought, rather, they are constructed over centuries of patriarchy in the name of Islam. Islam advocates learning and voice for both men and women. Women's vulnerabilities in Iran, and globally, including the Christian world, are primarily connected to age-old gender hierarchies, gendered politics, economic and educational shortcoming and constraints, accumulated socio-cultural misperceptions, and familial circumstances. Religious interpretation is just one link in the chain of the causes of women being vulnerable.

The title, 'Becoming Visible'

My understanding of the term 'Becoming Visible' is multi-fold. Firstly, the term embodies the chain of ideas and actions generated by the women over time and during the processes of data collection. These ideas and actions have communicated meaningful and complex visibilities to me as the Iranian-born researcher, art maker, and writer residing in Britain who visits Iran frequently. I have identified with the essence of the women's ideas and actions and have engaged with their intellectual and highly reflexive and critical stance. While such essence sustains and projects the aspirations of individuals, it keeps alive a multi-dimensional debate and hope for the country's journey towards a more developed democratic and egalitarian civil society. The visual dimension, despite Islamization, possessed particular power with an emphasis on the language of the body, which matches the power of the women's words and verbal eloquence. Body presence, knowledge, ownership, and representation have been at the centre of such visibilities. As if regulated through a sensitive lens, the women and their actions moved into sharper focus as the research progressed. One by one, statement after statement, and headscarf after colourful headscarf, they declared their positions with probity, precision, and with clarity of purpose.

Secondly but most vitally, I believe the new generation of Iranian women have become visible to themselves collectively through the power of their ideas. Notwithstanding the challenging paradox of their socio-political environment, and both familial and political systems, they have continued to communicate their critical position through forms of education and activism. The knowledge of both their location as citizens and the condition of their selves and society has provided the women with tools with which to posit the idea of 'who' and 'how' they wish to be. As we shall see in Texts Two, Three, and Four, they have set out to construct the scaffolding for new perspectives and beginnings, questioning their individual as well as collective status in the legal system. Though legal constitutionally, the right of assembly other than for prayer is made problematic by the ruling elite within the government. Women, however, have continued to assemble in solidarity and non-violent resistance even though many have been arrested for doing so.[5] Ideas however are not lockable, they can only grow.

Whilst such endeavours cannot be seen as a unified and synchronized mass movement yet, they must be recognised and acknowledged as a mobilizing force which is gathering pace, and as a highly significant current socio-political phenomenon. Perhaps it would not be a gross exaggeration to suggest that the future is female in Iran. Despite gender hierarchies, the gender gap in education has fallen and currently over 67 per cent of the three million strong student body in higher education is female.[6] There is a further remarkable narrowing of the gender gap in education between rural and urban areas.[7] Enrolment for girls in 2002 in upper secondary school overtook boys' and reached 82.6 percent.[8] Indeed the government has succeeded in increasing literacy, with a rate of 85.2 percent in 2005,[9] and predictions of 92.1 percent for 2015.[10]

Not only do the millions of young women turn to education hoping for economic independence and broader personal development, they rely on education as a political tool to be seen at large and in search of means to penetrate and regulate systems of patriarchy and hierarchy. Such adjustment and regulating of the interface of self and society further reflects their collective desire and ability in electing and applying unfixed and fluid gender boundaries. This has become evident in cases where women's groups have proceeded to openly declare their support for student, teacher, and trade unionist movements regardless of gender, and participating in joint demonstrations to strengthen the forces necessary for a more developed democracy in the country.

It is crucial to view the above in relation to and in the context of the historic developments in the women's movement and activism globally as well as locally since the last decade of the nineteenth century prior to Iran's Constitutional Revolution (1906-1911). The complexity of the latter continues to be revisited and debated by scholars especially with regard to the role of women in the 1979 Revolution.[11] Vast numbers of Iranian women from all walks of life, whether students, intellectuals, professionals, from grassroots labour communities, and from the religious classes with particular allegiances with the regime, supported the 1979 Revolution.

Out of the internal consequences of the 1979 Revolution, two interconnecting forces have prevailed. On the one hand the Revolution enabled the emergence into a position of power of a hitherto religious, political, and economic underclass, as well as illuminating perspectives from the marginalized intellectuals and libertarians from the middle and upper classes.[12] On the other hand, this regeneration cost the previously politically and economically influential classes who were perceived to be increasingly out of touch with the suffering of the grassroots their place in society. This was because of their allegedly, though by no means always the case, 'secular', 'monarchist' and 'Westernized' lifestyles.[13] Thus polarized, significant numbers fled and the country has been in the midst of ongoing processes of restructuring, contemplating problems and solutions of systems of governance according to Islamic Law and its interpretations.

Externally the Revolution has meant a prolonged period of aggression against Iran by the United States of America. With a combination of a sustained policy of Iranophobia and demonization against the regime, and relentless unilateral and multilateral economic sanctions, the United States has isolated and alienated Iran in its entirety.[14] Fur-

ther, encouraged by the United States and Britain and acting as their
agent, from 1980 to 1988 Saddam Hossein, armed also with chemical
weapons provided by the US, attacked Iran aiming to damage Iran's
political system, infrastructure, and nation. This imposed eight year
war was at once savage and pointless, with catastrophic consequences
and a tragic loss of one million lives. Neither Britain nor the United
States have yet to acknowledge the suffering they have caused with
their greed for oil and geopolitical power agenda. The war left Iran
economically and emotionally devastated, with many women displaced
and in mourning for husbands and sons, and many more failing to
secure potential life and economic partners. Indeed, women have been
the invisible victims of this war, and the processes of repair are ongoing today. As a well-known professor at Tehran University pointed out
to me, it took Europe forty years to find its feet again in the aftermath
of the Second World War, and that was with the help and support of
the United States, rather than facing its imposed sanctions, isolation,
and demonization.

The title 'Becoming Visible' thus relates a knowledge of the experiences and meanings in the lives of groups of women in Muslim
majority Iran in the light of the above circumstances. Even as fragments, their narratives are a world apart from the stereotyped
propaganda and misplaced imagination of the West. Rather, they suggest patterns in thought and courageous behaviour which push
boundaries and resist forms of subordination.

'Becoming Visible' might also be an indicator of existences of millions of women outside Iran, whether in the Middle East or other parts
of the world, illuminating the complexities of perceptions and practices
amongst Muslims. It might resonate symbolically, regardless of gender
and geographical location, with those who wish to contemplate their
own particular version of becoming visible in relation to class, race,
and ethnicity – those who seek the clarification of unjust laws in their
communities, and finally those who succeed in juxtaposing *difference*
with *similarities* when contemplating human condition.

'Becoming Visible' is an effort on my behalf to resist simplification
and trivialization of the Other, and to recognize and register particular
gendered existences from the non-Western world and place them
firmly at the centre of global discourses on gender, only a small por-
tion of which is Western.

The site of research

The site of my enquiries is the metropolis of Tehran, the capital city of Iran. The capital moved from Isfahan to Tehran in 1786 in the second year of the foundation of the Qajar dynasty (1785-1925).[15] With its population estimated at over twelve million, Tehran is the centre of the government, a centre for art and culture nationally as well as in the Middle East, and a centre for education and industry. It accommodates a variety of life styles from the highly economically vulnerable to the opulent. While most of the participants in my study live in Tehran now, the majority of them have migrated from other regions of Iran. They bring with them multi-ethnicities and diverse cultural perspectives, languages, and religious practices. Tehran has continued to grow steadily since the mid-1920s when a comprehensive modernizing programme began.[16] The mass urbanization which took effect between the 1930s to the 1950s has continued to much higher proportions after the 1979 Revolution with an influx of cadres sympathetic to the Islamic regime. This population movement further intensified as a consequence of the eight year war with Iraq, when the fleeing and the war-damaged were attracted to the capital.[17] Notwithstanding the harsh economic realities and vulnerability of the displaced millions, Tehran has developed vastly. It has become an intra-national melting pot much greater than previously imagined. Whereas early migrants were unskilled workers seeking livelihoods in the decades before the 1979 Revolution,[18] the post Iran-Iraq war reconstruction programmes, the development of new political and economic trajectories in the 1990s, the exposure of Iranians to cyberspace, and the socio-economic reformist ambitions of Seyyed Mohammad Khatami's presidency (1997-2005), have attracted the urban rich from the regions, and have caused Tehran to become a complex modern centre for diverse cultural and entrepreneurial behaviours. Women maintain a strong presence in the latter while struggling to regain high visibility in the political and judicial systems.

Although possessing a multi-millennia heritage and history, Iran finds itself with a young face at the beginning of the twenty-first century with two-thirds of its population under the age of 30,[19] and over three million in higher education.[20] Whilst it would be a mistake to expect a homogeneous and unified set of behaviours on the part of the three million students, the cross-disciplinary nature of the national university entrance examinations, student selection and placement procedures particularly, create unprecedented educational and social dynamics across the country. These processes bring together young people from different regions, disciplines, and socio-economic and cultural backgrounds. Just as the first year male and female university students from Tehran might end up studying in cities such as Isfahan in the centre, Tabriz in the northwest, Kerman in the east, or Yazd towards southeast, large numbers of students from the provinces end up in the universities in the capital and across regions. To begin to understand the dimensions of such cosmopolitanism, one needs to imagine three million students on the move, coming together for the first time, passing one another in the public sphere, curious about each other's ideas and expressions, and consequently forming new dynamics of socialization and interaction not experienced or imagined by their elders. The public sphere in Tehran, comprising various corners of the city, university campuses and public transport, underground and overland trains and buses, assumes different and new spatial meanings. The exchange of ideas and behaviours, and the rapid development of particular youth cultures become inevitable. Whilst I appreciate the limitations of the data collected in Tehran and presented here, and caution myself against over-generalizing, I cannot but help to contemplate the significance of such mobilization and its dynamics, and the potentially imminent multi-dimensional shifts in socio-political perspectives.

Structure

I recognise the contention that social acts of being in the world are text-analogous.[21] I would suggest that routinely and intentionally, in our layered, multi-truth, multi-identitied existences, we select ranges of behaviours which are at once significant and meaningful to us, help us make sense of the world, and communicate to others how we perceive ourselves. Similar to word texts, the behaviours we consider, select, order, perform, and present to others are bodies of ideas which possess layers of significant meaning. We thus become sources of meaning which in turn could be contemplated, deciphered, and understood by others. The material presented here is viewed and presented in this light. It is perceived as Texts of human experience and existence.

As sites of expression and narration, these Texts relate observed realities in the lives and spatiotemporal circumstances of groups of women in Iran. Whilst I do not claim homogeneity which represents the whole population, I believe the Texts posit significant emergent structures and patterns in society which indicate a growing socio-political movement. Whether given in formally structured interviews or discussed more fluidly in conversations, the processes of creating the Texts have highlighted a shared sense of understanding and belonging between the researched bodies and myself regardless of our geographies. The narratives and the Texts are thus co-constructions and project our interconnected collective histories, acquired as well as contested identities, and socio-political experience and location.

Texts can be embellished in their margins; they might be marked by seals, an illumination, an additional illustration, or a narrative within a narrative. This is particularly relevant to the heritage of manuscript writing-painting, the ancient tradition of the arts of the book and decree presentation in Iran. In this heritage the margins of texts might simultaneously reaffirm what has been discussed, in song, in pen and ink, or through ornament and pattern in colour and gold. The scribes and illuminators would thus collaborate to sustain the act of narrating in order to promote deeper understanding and maintain continuity. They might also recommend the consolidation of the body of ideas in the narratives with new possibilities by entering a visual world. Whichever the method, making spatial shifts to the margins of texts, and offering additional verbal and visual illuminations would provide deeper engagement with form, content, and meaning.

Inspired by these ideas I have determined to present the continuum of the narratives and discussions in this book through five Texts with Margins, producing a network of interconnected themes. The Margins will be presented at the end of each Text, except in Text Five where there is a shift to the beginning of the Text in order to mark new arrivals. The sources for the Margins will be the bank of undisclosed material from the field in and around the educational institutions in Tehran, as well as the views and observations from the interiors of taxis. Tehran is a crowded city which struggles with serious traffic and pollution. The debilitating traffic brings with it much time spent in the interiors of taxis. These are spaces on the move; seemingly a gap or a non-place departed from one point and not yet arrived at another. As they weave through the arteries of the city, the taxi drivers provide links, another socio-cultural perspective or political view, and oral social histories. I have looked upon these as metaphors, expressing transitions and much appreciated vernacular expressions from the heart of society, signifying patterns of thought in association with the body of ideas discussed in the book.

Due to their particular significance the central position in the book is allocated to the three Texts which assemble the thoughts and actions of the young generation of urban women. These are Texts Two, Three, and Four. Text One will provide narratives given by two grandmothers, a historic context, indicating at critical political incidents, means of education, and subjective presence. I consider these women as my elders and the source for much of the social and cultural capital I possess. Text Five will reflect on the continuum of my methods and thoughts authoring the narratives from Tehran, both arriving at and departing from concepts. The Text will also introduce short but poignant statements by the middle generation of women in the book.

A number of the narratives presented are unusually long and I am reluctant to break them up, fragmenting them further for the sake of orthodox methods of analysis. I believe the disclosed views and ideas in the narratives have both the strength and power to communicate with the reader. I resist re-interpretation. I believe the act of telling is itself a deconstructive act and firmly trust in the reader's willingness to wish to enter the spaces of narration without interruptions, and to deconstruct-reconstruct the narratives autonomously regardless of their length. I have no doubt this process can reveal wider meanings and epistemologies beyond the researcher's purposes. Further, the five Texts possess intertextuality. This allows for an inbuilt system of understanding. Indeed, it would be desirable for the reader to juxtapose, reposition, and compare the narratives beyond the limits of the book, locating and defining interrelationships with other experiences, other locations globally.

The Texts

Text One: Histories, Transitions and Continuity. This Text contextualizes the ideas in the book through the narratives of two grandmothers. Forms of literacy and know-how amongst the elders born in the nineteenth century, interruptions in the history of women becoming visible in the urban space in Iran, and the roots of personal struggles for intellectual and economic independence are illuminated. The lived experiences of these two women will interconnect with the circumstances of the young generation central to the book's thesis.

Text Two: Making Meaning, Acquiring Identities. I believe the entire book might be considered as a forum for expressing diverse and composite identities whether personal or collective. Here however, I provide glimpses into a selection of events in private and public spaces and show how layers in identities are acquired involving minds and bodies. The Text illuminates some of the building blocks and tools adopted by the participants in order to shape, re-define, construct, and express meaningful ways of being who they are.

Text Three: Presences. In this Text I will draw on a selection of narratives which demonstrate how the young women persistently and routinely sustain noteworthy and active presence in daily living. While doing so they problematize the expected norms, propose change, and carve out new and vital personal spaces within the family, in the public sphere, and inter-personally with males, where bodies and minds perform to produce new forms of dialogue.

Text Four: Visions of a Civil Society. This Text will relate the young women's visions of a civil society. It will elucidate just some of the ways in which they actively seek legal solutions to unjust laws. Whether campaigning for peace, or for the right to entry and share sport stadiums, or engaging in bringing about change in punishment for adultery by married women, the Text demonstrates the young women's activism in changing laws.

Text Five: Departures and Arrivals. This Text will reflect on the continuum of the author's methods and ideas, both arriving at and departing from concepts. It will discuss some of the sources of strength and motivation, social know-how, and cultural capital of the young women.

Text One: Histories, Transitions and Continuities

In this opening Text I will introduce two women born in Tehran in 1930, and will draw on their lived experiences to provide the context for the body of ideas presented in the subsequent Texts. Their narratives can only be fragments of much richer and complex life histories, and belong only to those who were able to access and take advantage of the systems of education as they became available to larger groups in society. Nevertheless, they indicate and highlight a number of significant developments in Iranian women's collective histories which are beyond these fragments. As a nurse and a teacher, the two women belong to groups of tens of thousands who were elemental in the architecture of modern urban life in Iran in the first half of the twentieth century. Their memories, whether of a childhood home, early years education, struggles for accessing professional training, achieving economic independence, or of becoming politically alert and active, are markers of shifts in societal structures.

Key in deconstructing the above are the elements of veiling and education, both of which have remained locked into patriarchal interests in the politics of power in the name of governance and religion. Education has always been valued by Iranians; this is evident and reflected in the country's written literary heritage from over a thousand years ago. In the absence of mandatory state education until the turn of the twentieth century, however, the tradition of *maktab*, or small scale elementary school, offered a non-governmental educational system which was a programme of reading and writing and Qoranic knowledge. This could of course lead to developing skills in interpretation of the Qoran, and most forms of judicial and legal discourses for male students.[22] In the case of girls, maktab schooling seldom offered adequate writing skills, limiting itself to sight reading and Qoranic recitation by rote.[23] Aristocratic women and their milieu were different however, and for centuries were routinely educated by scholars in the interiors of their homes; and many became educators, writers, musicians, and poets.[24] Further, in the latter part of the nineteenth century there were numerous missionary schools in Tehran and other major cities where young Muslim women were educated alongside the Christian minorities. Around the same time however there grew concerns amongst forward-looking women, as well as men, about the condition of women other than the privileged classes, particularly with regard to their education and their wider social participation as visible members in society. These concerns had been to some degree part of a demand for greater socio-political change in the country with particular focus on education, polygamy, and marriage and divorce laws.

During the constitutional movement, and subsequently the Constitutional Revolution (1906-1911), women activists established numerous women's societies, published women's newspapers and periodicals, and organized public debates and discussed women's issues in their homes with invited speakers.[25] Whilst unveiling had been found disagreeable, particularly by the majority of the cleric elite who oversaw the legal system, discussions about women's education gained some momentum in the years of 1906-1908. As a consequence, on January 20, 1907, a women's meeting was held in Tehran where establishing girls' schools were amongst the resolutions adopted.[26] Two schools were opened in Tehran, *Effatiyeh*, or The House of Chastity, and *Namus*, or Honour, which opened several branches subsequently.[27] Despite women's contributions to the constitutional revolution however, the conflict of ideologies between the religious elite, the monarch, the intellectual revolutionaries, and the designers of the newly established national parliament, resulted in women's issues being profoundly neglected if not totally forgotten. More widespread public education for girls took two more decades to arrive at the national level, and women's right to vote was not secured until five decades later. However, women's consciousness of their location in society, and of their contributions to extending the debates about women's education and role in society one hundred years ago during the Constitutional Revolution placed them firmly in the national political psyche. It instigated a process of gendered critique and reflection on women's issues by the women themselves.

Here, We meet Akram. Her early life history provides, amongst other topics, glimpses into a household shared by several industrious women born in the nineteenth century. With little or no formal education the latter draw on other literacies fundamental to managing their household. We will then meet Naaztaab who points the reader, amongst other things, to the recurring theme of local interpretations of Islam by the clerics and their opposition to mixed schooling for boys and girls. The Text will conclude with short narratives from taxis, transporting the reader to the streets of contemporary Tehran.

Meet Akram

Akram, also known as Aki Joon to the circle of her family and friends, is a retired senior nurse. At seventy-eight, she is well-built and tall, with shiny white-silver hair cut short to below the ears and held back with combs. She is an ordinary Iranian citizen, one of many millions of her age and socio-economic circumstance, who could also belong to similar urban spaces anywhere around the world. Her autonomous manner is cool and considered, both in her choice of words and the subjects she chooses to discuss. Her eyes exude a calm sense of knowing and kindness, and sparkle unexpectedly with joy when she recalls memories of her female elders. She addresses them as 'the angels' who worked for and nurtured others unquestioningly. Akram is a practising Muslim and has prayed five times daily since childhood. She considers her faith as the centre to her spiritual life and oneness with humanity, and above all fundamentally free from conflict with the world. She suggests that humanity confuses spirituality, whatever its source may be, with the notions of seeking power and domination over others in the name of religion.

Aki Joon is a firm believer in the necessity of daily exercise for the body and the mind. Her library of several shelves houses dozens of articles on health, hundreds of novels, dozens of philosophical and Qoranic texts, and stacks of recent newspapers and periodicals not yet finished with. On a chest of drawers near her bed, Aki Joon keeps several volumes of the Qoran, and a collection of articles and books by the late sociologist and interpreter of the historical context and philosophical perspectives in Islam, Dr Ali Shariati.[28] One of her Qorans is entirely in Farsi, and one is in Arabic with translations and interpretations in the margins. She says she could not recommend the volume in Farsi highly enough simply because people could read it themselves rather than relying on the interpretive fragments by some clergy. She further explains that understanding the text in its historic context at the time it was written is crucial. She admits however that the sound and poetic rhythms in the Arabic Qoran are beautiful to the ear and for many transcendental. She reads her Qorans after her noon prayers on most days.

To keep her body agile, Aki Joon carries out stretching exercises influenced by yoga every morning. She also rigorously paces up and down the apartment for thirty minutes 'to warm up her bones' when the weather is bad with snow or dangerously polluted in winter. When the weather is agreeable she celebrates the outdoors in long walks and visits to the nearby parks reminding herself, and promising others, that she will not carry heavy groceries on the way back home because of her aching shoulders and weak neck. She smiles and says that fifty years of enthusiastic knitting of all manners of garments for the family has taken its toll on the body.

Akram in front of her library

I meet Aki Joon three times to conduct the interview. The first day is a snowy winter's day in Tehran and we sit in the warmth of Aki Joon's recently redesigned, ultra modern, open-plan kitchen joining the large sitting rooms with armchairs, plants, and family photographs. This is a large two bedroom apartment in a pleasant block in northeast Tehran. This residence is the result of the life-long work of three people, hers, her late husband's, and her eldest daughter's, who has patiently and cleverly developed a career as a high ranking civil servant in the last three decades, despite the socio-political difficulties. This daughter has remained single and financially and intellectually independent.

In her personal narrative starting with 'the household', Aki Joon takes us through her early life, which coincides with the history of social reform in Iran in the 1930s, which took place during the reign of Reza Shah, from 1925 when he overthrew the last king of the Qajar dynasty to 1941 when he was forced to abdicate as a result of the invasion of Iran by the Anglo-Soviet forces. Specifically addressed at women, these reforms included mass education for girls, as it had previously been the case for boys, with a national curriculum, the process of unveiling women which started in 1934-35 and became law in 1937-38, and the marriage and divorce law as part of the Civil Code in 1931 and Marriage Act of 1937.[29] Although the latter did not nearly go far enough, it made some difference to Akram's and her mother's lives, as one got married and the other divorced at the notary public offices rather than following traditional religious procedures. In the accounts of 'the household' we are introduced to the range of competencies the elders display in managing the day-to-day affairs of a crowded household, creating private spaces to teach and sew to create income, hold religious consultancies, display sophisticated cooking and preserving skills, and dispense medicinal remedies. It becomes clear that the women had their own systems of management and knowledge construction. The following sections are Akram's accounts of her life as a child and young women.

The household

One of my earliest childhood memories takes me back to when I was being carried on my father's shoulders in the streets of Tehran. It was crowded, and my parents later told me that they were going to see the great singer Ghamar-ol Molouk-e Vaziri perform for the first time to a mixed male and female audience in the Laaleh Zaar quarter in Tehran.[30] My parents must have been amongst the first ordinary young families to become visible in the public social arena attending the theatre together as a consequence of the newly introduced unveiling laws.[31] Although appearing unveiled in certain public spaces had been adopted by women amongst the aristocracy and the highly educated in the late 1920s, unveiling was discussed with women from the teacher training college in 1935 and was subsequently made compulsory by law in 1937.

I was born in 1930 and was raised around my grandmother who was born in the latter part of the nineteenth century. My mother was only 13 when she was married to my father ten years older than her, in a way I am pleased he was not 13 too. By the time I started school my mother was working and training nearby in a tailor's shop to become a seamstress, she was the first member of the Labbaf family to take advantage of the unveiling laws and go to work. There was a great demand for outdoor dress during this early period of unveiling, and becoming an able seamstress would have been financially rewarding.[32] My father, who was of Turkish descent from the northwest, had come to Tehran with his capital and had opened a grocery shop. Neither he nor my mother had much education it appears, but were ready to join and enjoy what social public life was available to them and went to the newly opened movie houses.

The Labbaf household including several of my grandmother's six sisters and two brothers lived in a large house in one of the oldest quarters of Tehran near the Bazar. The only men in the house, Haj Da'ee and Agha Sheikh Abdolah, had inherited their business and were small merchants in the Bazar in the weaving industry. Asheikh Abdolah was also the gofer in the household who brought the groceries, and often travelled to the villages nearby, such as Kan, to bring supplies of dried fruits, dried village bread, whey, and even fresh meat. He had a speech impediment and would elongate his words, sometimes on purpose, to make everyone laugh. He had a great sense of humour and created much laughter with his gestures in our play area around the *hoze* [water pool] in the garden. He teased us children when we were little and lifted us high in the sky. My most significant memory of the two men is when I saw them carrying two hide sacks of money to one of the rooms in the house, I followed them and saw them counting. I suppose traditionally merchants kept the bulk of their money in chests in their homes, banks were a new development.[33]

Although the centre of my world was my grandmother, I also spent a lot of time around her sisters. They were authoritative women who together managed the affairs of the household and took the practice of rituals and religious traditions to heart. Husbands being scarce for all seven, some had looked for means of earning money as soon as they could, or let themselves be wives to older widowed men as both a companion and a helper. So, there were always, always some half-sisters or brothers, and step-children, around the household women. These women were working women really, they would get up at dawn to pray first and then make tea. They would be busy thereafter doing every-thing themselves – cook, clean, sew, care for their own children as well as those belonging to others. Ear ache, bad coughs and bowels, and fever seemed to be common with the children. The women would administer home-made ointments, drinks made with a variety seeds and herbs, and or force-feed them with tiny spoons of seed and nut oils to make them better.

One of my great aunts was married to a well-known high ranking cleric residing in one of those houses with three separate inner and outer living quarters. The *andaruni* [private interiors] were kept for the women and their visitors; they would keep them-selves invisible to male guests and non-blood relatives. They would of course go out visiting, to the Bazar, the public baths, and the shrines. The *biruni* [the exterior space] was the apart-ments kept for my great aunt's husband to receive male guests and any enquiries from the members of public, or merchants, about religious matters.[34] My great aunt Shari'at, we called her by the shortened form of her husband's name, was his personal carer as well as housekeeper. So she had a full time job. Whether he was ill or not he needed someone to accompany him to the bathroom to assist him with his ablutions. Even though she was completely worn down and consumed by such duties at times, water jug in one hand and towel in the other she would serve him with a smile. It is her smile I remember as a child when we visited, and the delicious lunches she served us. Two other sisters had returned to the household within a decade of getting mar-ried, with their young having lost their husbands. I think men used to die younger or more frequently then. If there was any in-heritance it was always lost. According to familial tradition it was handed to the older brother Haj Da'ee to invest in *halal*[35] [in line with Islam] transactions, and subsequently mismanaged, with no explanation given. Perhaps the sisters should have taken over the affairs of the Bazar too, managing both the inside and the out-side.

Except for Aunt Shari'at, we did not address my great aunts by name. Well, we did not know their names; they were addressed by their titles which could be indicative of their rank and seniority. The eldest for example was addressed as *Khanoom Aqa*,[36] and the second in line was *Mirza Khanoom*, or *Miz Khanoom* for short, which implied a degree of literacy as well as seniority. She and a younger sister known to us as Aunt Aziz, and to others as *Aziz Aqa*, were Qoranic scholars. They shared students between them and taught recitation and diction, specific prayers for festivals, rituals, and shrines, as well as Islamic principles in daily conduct. Amongst these were important rationalized consultations and argumentations about concepts of *wajeb* acts [necessary and obligatory], *qabih* acts [impure, wicked, or vulgar], or *mostahab* and *hasan* behaviours [recommended and worthy]. My great aunts not only provided these guidelines, but elaborated with anecdotal references. Approaches to women's bodily cleansing and ablutions at puberty, in marriage, and childbirth, were at the centre of the consultations given.[37]

Aunt Aziz had a further responsibility in the household, the affairs of the Kitchen. Someone had to be in charge of the quantities of food managed and prepared daily. Often, just the immediate family of over 20 sat around the *sofreh* cloth to lunch. The Bazar was nearby and men came home to eat and nap. In the cities, bread was mostly fetched in, but the many grains, herbs and greens used in Persian food must have taken hours to prepare prior to cooking and serving daily. Aunt Aziz was also known for her preserves, vinegars and pickles which she prepared every autumn. When the delivery of the vast quantities of little pink onions arrived, everyone sat around the sofreh to peel off their paper thin golden skins so that Aunt Aziz could make them into pickles or caramelize them. She made everything with exactitude and passion, making sure that the processes of soaking and developing the grapes or raisins into vinegar were followed accurately in order not to render forbidden wine or spirits instead. I believe many households also made alcohol for men to drink; they claimed these were for medicinal purposes only. By the beginning of the cold season there were lines of very large thick green glass bottles of vinegar, and green glazed pots of pickles, in the kitchen corner of the garden. She also melted quantities of sheep fat for cooking.

I have only understood the significance of these things as an adult, realizing what incredible knowledge one needs to have to perform these extraordinary tasks. On festive occasions, with a *chador*[38] on her head and another wrapped over it around her waist, our tall, thin and nimble Aunt Aziz hovered over outdoor wood burning stoves. The numerous large copper pans, whitened on the inside with tin and covered on the outside with a thick layer of mud to regulate the heat, held the promise of culinary creations of legendary exactitude in flavour, colour and scent. One might say she had at least two professions: a tutor and a chef. Oh, she also performed 'vacuum cupping' which is an ancient medical technique for releasing muscle spasms and pain by placing heated glass cups upside down on the area of pain.

As a child of a working mother I was a frequent visitor to this household to be with my grandmother *Khanoom Bozorg*.[39] I can recall vividly their alley, and the double-sided wooden doors to the house with stone seats on each side. The double doors were decorated with rows of large round button-like metal studs, and had two round metal door knockers the size of one's palm. I understood later that the door knockers made distinctly different sounds so the women would know whether the visitor was male or female. The sense of pleasure to reach and touch those door knockers is still with me at the age of seventy-eight. The joy, warmth and laughter of my Khanoom Bozorg, and the permission to hug her and bury my face in her generous bosom I remember with much gratitude.

Through the door you entered into the *hashti*, a large rectangle with a vaulted ceiling and small windows. We were not allowed to climb the steps to the hashti's open roof, but I remember light pouring in from its side windows. The hashti had steps from two sides into other large rooms, and the steps in the centre took you into the garden with a hoze, or water pool, connected to the water cellar by a hand pump. The hoze provided for ablutions and the ritual of rinsing clothes and crockery to render them symbolic purity. At the end of this garden there were the kitchens both indoor and outdoor for wood-burning stoves to cook large quantities, and built-in alcoves and shelves for all manner of storage. There was a lavatory down a few steps as was the *pashir*, or the cool room, next to the water cellar. There were several small and large rooms above the kitchens. My Khanoom Bozorg lived in two rooms up a narrow staircase in the southern corner of the garden. She was the cleverest amongst her sisters in sewing by hand, and always had a couple of young girls as apprentices. She was often commissioned to create trousseaux, and sewed simple dresses to order all through her life. She also took orders for cotton indoor chadors in pretty patterns, outdoor thick black chadors, and embroidered cloths and bedding for weddings. This is how she had paid her way since becoming a widow 'two years before my twentieth' as she put it, bringing up her three girls.

I believe Khanoom Bozorg was illiterate. Well I never saw her write anything down. Education for girls when she was little was mostly oral at the *maktab khaneh* [Qoranic schools], where writing skills, for girls specifically, were considered unnecessary and corruptive. They used to say if girls learn to write they will send love letters to men! Apart from the maktab, very few girls were educated either at home with different degrees of secular education, learning reading properly and prose more than writing, or they were sent to the very few private schools in big cities sponsored and taught by aristocratic women. Many of these aristocratic women from the *thousand families*[40] were themselves the offspring of brides from various regional families or tribes whose newly acquired rank and status brought educational training.[41]

The daughter of my great Aunt Aziz, Fahimeh Azam, who was much older than me, went to a maktab initially and had a teacher at home for a few years before she was married off at the age of 13 to the 18 year-old son of the well known land and caravanserai owner Mirza Ibrahim Khan. I believe she learned reading and writing through the prose and poetry of Sa'di, the thirteenth century poet[42]; she also learned Qoranic recitation and embroidery. She and my mother were the first women in the family to ask for divorce; they were helped by the second round of the divorce laws legislated in 1937. Fahimeh Azam did it because her young husband was useless professionally, spent all his time on the roof feeding and training pigeons, and she did not love him. My mother did it because she did not love my father. The idea of a divorce because you don't 'love' your husband, must have been revolutionary in the Labbaf household, and in the country. Obviously the two cousins were avant-garde in their ideas and did not wish to wait for 'fate' to guide their lives.

The unveiling laws had come about before I started primary school, but I remember several in the household resented the undermining of their Islamic identity and tradition, feeling shame at being exposed to the world outside the intimate circle of their families. So they chose to decline from appearing in public as much as they could and moved around in carriages and visited the public baths at dawn in order not be seen and recognised. The new laws must have been truly shocking for these ladies born in nineteenth century Tehran and guided by religion. They were supported by the clergy who severely and openly opposed the new law. I also remember my grandmother taking me shopping in the Bazar one day and the shopkeeper pointed to her long shawl and said 'cut a piece of this off and put it on the girl's head'. I was scared, but my grandmother just held my hand firmly and walked away from the Bazar. So she had accepted unveiling. I don't remember my elders ever suggesting that I should dress differently to what I wore at home in public. They accepted unveiling for us, as if they understood it to be an opening for the new generation. In fact my cousin Fahimeh Azam welcomed the new dress codes and, like thousands, wore a coat and hat, and carried beautiful handbags when she went out. Her new husband could afford these things. You see, the unveiling laws facilitated the coming out of women in Iran, and young children like myself became accustomed to it from an early age. Being seen in public routinely has been part of my life since being carried on my father's shoulders going to the theatre with my mother to see the singer Ghamar-ol Molouk-e Vaziri. Being in the interior or exterior of the house was no longer an issue for me and many of my generation, we did both. Perhaps unwittingly, but certainly, my mother, cousin, and I had become visible in society and part of the women's emancipation movement in Iran.

Education

In two subsequent visits Aki Joon and I continue discussing her development into an adult woman able to make decisions about a future life, and slowly but autonomously to construct that life. Her continuing education within the household and outside it in the developing

public sphere, and her sense of agency and curiosity about life continued to be influenced by the example of her female elders. Ultimately, it
is her grandmother who takes her to the notary public to marry her
chosen man, showing willingness and to some degree openness to new
ideas and possible horizons. Akram continues as follows:

> At the age of seven, like tens of thousands of little girls equipped
> with the mandatory speckled grey school uniform, a separate
> white collar, a white bow carefully placed in my hair by my
> mother, and a metal satchel on my back, I was taken to Vatan
> school to start first grade.[43] I remember I liked the two enormous
> pockets in my roopoosh or school uniform where I hid all sorts
> of things to eat, which incidentally I mostly lost. In fact I often
> got into trouble for losing things both at home and at school, my
> lunch, snacks, pencils, homework, books etc. The memory of the
> teacher putting a conical hat on my head as punishment is very
> vivid. She made me stand in the school yard near the gates for
> everyone to see. I don't remember being upset or crying, but I
> remember the standing and waiting with a hat on my head. Per-
> haps it is because I had seen other children being punished with
> the strike of a ruler on the palm, or a squeeze of two fingers with
> a pencil in between, I did not consider mine too bad by compari-
> son. I don't know, now that I think about the waiting in the
> corner, it seems more of a psychological punishment. Disciplin-
> ing school children was quite routine then; I don't believe it's the
> case now. Apparently, my father who was passing by the school
> gate noticed me in this state, and was outraged. He promptly
> complained to the head and removed me from the school alto-
> gether.

> A new school was found for me eventually after several weeks;
> this was nearer home in Qavamol Saltaneh not far from the Mu-
> seum. The interruption meant that I had to repeat the year. My
> memories of this second school are mostly to do with the envi-
> ronment because I soon became old enough to walk to school
> on my own. I had to cross over at Kakh square where several
> palaces were situated, and I often watched Reza Shah with his
> big cloak walking beyond the gates, accompanied by his son the
> Crown Prince Mohammad Reza and his first wife the Egyptian
> aristocrat Fawzieh carrying a small puppy in her arms. I remem-

ber being fascinated by her hair which was in blond ringlets around her face, and wishing I had a puppy.

I was liked at this new school and the head was kind to me, perhaps because she did not have any children of her own. She would often keep an eye on me after school when my parents were still at work. She lived in a big house with a big garden and my parents had rented two rooms at the end of it behind the greenhouse. I remember observing with wonder that she played a musical instrument, the *taar*.[44] I somehow understood that playing a musical instrument was a grand thing and a sign of distinction. I loved living in that house because of the flowers and the colours which are still so vivid present in my mind. This side of the garden was like a world of my own and I often skipped around and counted and touched the flowers. There was also a dog that followed me up the steps to our rooms and I was allowed to play with it and feed it but not to bring it indoors. Maybe the attraction was because this garden was so different to my Khanoom Bozorg's where I spent many a late evening before my mother returned from the tailor's workshop. There must have been a boom in outdoor clothes, causing her to work and train hard. She was also saving up for the down payment for a pedal Singer sewing machine, which she gave to me when she was old. I keep it in my bedroom and it works perfectly well. I found out much later that my mother did not love my father and that was why they divorced just as soon as my mother became financially independent. This says something about my mother and how she made a choice to go it alone just as soon as she was able to finance herself. But it says something about the character of my father too, his ability to recognize my mother's right to divorce. The new laws were significant in their lives. My father loved my mother very much and respected her and later they both remarried.[45]

School was half daily and it was more about attending and getting through it than making friends for me. You realize this is seventy years ago. Simply, we had to learn reading, writing, and working with numbers, these were done mostly by rote. Learning by rote was like the Qoranic teachings I had witnessed in the household. I found doing multiplication tables in a loud voice in class enjoyable. I remember *mashq* [writing exercises] were always a challenge because we had to use pen and ink, and my inkwell would frequently leak onto my clothes or fall on my notebook. From the fourth grade dictation lessons became really hard and we practiced at home with very short passages from the fables of *Kelileh-o-Demneh*.[46] To get a reasonable mark on the weekly dictation tests was very important. Arithmetic was another difficult subject as we got to the fifth and sixth grades; we had to solve problems which involved multiplication and division as well as long addition or subtraction. We also had one session per week for Arabic, and Qoran recitation. But most of these I had heard being recited in the presence of my great aunts. Sport meant running around and playing games, not really structured at all. In fifth grade however, we had project work in geography which we designed and prepared for at home. In one case this involved creating a map of Iran, which I made on a large tray with wet clay. The map showed the contours in the landscape, the regions marked with a pin, and the boundaries of the country and Iran's neighbours. To show bodies of water such as the Caspian Sea, the Persian Gulf, Lake Urumieh in the northwest, and Hoze Soltan in Qom I used the blue powder, *lajevard*, which was used for rinsing white sheets. I also used pulses to highlight regional produce. But on the day as I was happily carrying my tray to school, I attempted to jump over a water ditch and I fell in. Not only did I lose my beautiful map, but I arrived at school covered in clay and blue dye. I did not cry but I think I was rather dazed for some time.

Having completed the six years of primary education at the age of 13 and a half, because I repeated the first year, my father would not agree to secondary school for another three years. His excuse was that there weren't any schools near enough within walking distance. But I think my father's resistance to my secondary school education was connected to the fact that I had been shocked out of my wits one day walking in the street, when with the speed of light I felt a burning sensation around my neck. I was whiplashed by a carriage driver who must have objected to the seemingly uninhibited presence of girls in the streets. Although I cannot say exactly why this carriage driver had used his horse whip to punish me, I can put two and two together and come up with the fact that at the time there was a lot of pressure by the clerics on the religious classes that veiling should return. It was some time before my neck heeled, and not long before the unveiling laws relaxed. On reflection, I think there were other uncertainties too; many people, including my father, had lost confidence in governmental systems. The country was in turmoil socio-economically, and the British, who had been doing everything in their power to own our entire oil industry, were now the unwanted occupational forces, and there were food shortages.

So there I was, about to become 14, and instead of being at secondary school I was mostly living around my grandmother again. The head of the primary school, our friend the *taar* player, had put me in the first grade to teach the little ones for a couple of hours in the mornings. At the same time my grandmother and mother proceeded to teach me all the skills they had in embroidery, crochet, knitting, and appliqué to help them with their wedding commissions. This, however, meant observing the affairs of the household with a new and almost adult eye. Two of the most striking things I learnt at the household during this period were my elders' knowledge of medicinal remedies which continues to influence me to this day, and their sense of fun. They seemed to have an understanding of the essence and qualities in foods in relation to the four humours. For every condition and constitution they would produce a discussion followed by an ancient recipe or concoction to harmonize or balance the various functions of the body. Bodily liquids, yellow and black bile, phlegm, and blood, and the consequences of their imbalance would be considered in relation to the hot and cold essences in herbs and foods and their purifying qualities. And surprisingly, they would often cure physical ailments and improve mental equilibrium in the people around them. I would listen as I would do the chores they set me; but I never had the presence of mind to ask them to explain these things to me, or write them down; I don't think it occurred to them to explain anything like that at all. It was knowledge taken for granted.

Other than the gatherings they organized to remember the saint and Imams by, and uphold religious rituals, my grandmother and her sisters and friends created occasions to have much laughter and pleasure. They would occasionally have afternoon parties during which they would drink tea and consume quantities of homemade sweetmeats and savoury dishes such as boiled potatoes and pickles. They would speak about intimate and private sexual matters, make fun of sexuality and contraceptive methods they had heard of or experienced when they were younger, and even engage in collective beautifying works such as shaping and colouring eyebrows. There was a tradition of the younger members being invited to the public baths as a group, accompanying a bride or someone expecting a baby, spending hours hennaing hair and smoothing the body. On such occasions they might send trays of foods and sherbets ahead, to be consumed in the dressing area in the intervals between attending to their bodies and keeping up with the gossip.

The best thing I discovered for myself during this period was the bookshop opposite the Military Academy at Kakh Square where you could rent books overnight for a couple of pennies. I would rent volume after volume; I read what was available in Farsi by Iranian authors and sometimes masterpieces from world literature which had been recently translated into Farsi. The pleasure of reading was immense and I was lifted to other worlds. I was very happy because nobody interfered with my reading, and they were such amazing stories. George Orwell's *Animal Farm*, Tennessee Williams' *The Glass Menagerie*, Maksim Gorky's *The Mother*, and *The Call of the Wild* and *The Iron Heel* by Jack London come to my mind immediately; how could I ever forget such books. So while my elders created pleasure in their domestic lives, I found much pleasure discovering a new world through literature.

The next phase of my education started in an extraordinary way. A married friend had asked me to accompany her to the doctor, and when the examination and consultations were over, my friend asked him whether he was in a position to help the two of us find jobs. He suggested we become nurses at the recently opened Ashraf Pahlavi Nursing School, but when he realized neither of us had any secondary education he just put us in his car at the end of the surgery and took us to the specialist obstetric Zanan Hospital and left us with the personnel department to be given jobs to do. I immediately understood how much I needed to go back to school, and whilst working at Zanan Hospital during the day registering the incoming patients, I enrolled at Khazaeli School's evening shift for adults.

Akram in the 1940s

I read seventh, eighth, and ninth grades while working, and I managed to complete these in twelve months. I only told my father after six months when I had settled in really well and mastered the bus routes. I was afraid of his dismissal, but once he was confronted with something that had already happened he could not stop me. Once he knew, he insisted on collecting me from school every night. Maybe this was not so unreasonable because initially there had been some vulgar words said to us young women by the louts hanging around the bus station in Park-e Shahr area. But we had persevered, and eventually either we got used to their behaviour and ignored it, or they stopped. It is possible that it did not bother us simply because we had our own agenda. In any case the bus drivers were kind to us and they themselves watched for us and even sometimes would alter the stops to let us get off nearer our homes. You have to imagine the Tehran of the 1940s with a population of less than a million and very traditional; it was very different from what it is now. There was little public transport or traffic in the evenings, except for some central neighbourhoods which had horse drawn carriages operating 24 hours a day. So there were very few people about at night, let alone young women on their own. We were pioneers in a way.

The fact is that the country needed trained nurses for the several new hospitals that had been opened nationally. Before us there was Shahnaz Pahlavi Nursing School named after the first daughter of Mohammad Reza Shah, where nurses boarded and trained for two years after they secured their ninth grade secondary school certificate. Within a couple of years of that a brand new nursing school was opened offering a four year degree to those who had completed twelfth grade at secondary school. This was named after the Shah's twin sister Ashraf Pahlavi and headed by an English woman. Our group of 17, however, were trained for four years in theory and practice at our teaching hospital where we shared classes with others training to become medical doctors. By the time I qualified, Zanan Hospital had moved to a new location and its premises had been renamed after Professor Amir Alam who had bought and donated it to the nation. It was to become the most important teaching hospital for ear, nose and throat in the country with a team of the best professors in the field and their best students. Plastic surgery under Professor Ossanlu and ophthalmology were added shortly after.

Learning was non-stop and the workload was demanding. I remember vividly in the first chemistry session our professor looked at each one of us in the room and firmly, and in no uncertain terms, told us that we had to distinguish between religion and science and that science alone ruled in that environment. I found this statement profound; you see until then I had understood things, beliefs and ideas, in relation to a mixture of religion and tradition related to me by the elders or primary school teachers. I had been taught prayers, the conditions for fasting, the appropriate ablution rituals at puberty, and routine everyday behaviours and politeness. The books I had read belonged to a part of my head that did not relate to everyday living, or at least I had not yet made the connections. But to practically distinguish science from religion was new to my ears, and very exciting. All through my education I remembered this and worked hard to become noted for my scientific knowledge. I successfully qualified as a medical assistant/senior nurse after four years at the age of 21 and was formally put on the Medical Faculty's payroll for ninety *tomans* per month. Ninety tomans now buys a loaf of bread. Such independence was really remarkable for me at the time, and I have passed it on to my daughters. Financial independence brings with it intellectual independence.

In the first decade and a half I worked with two famous surgeons who insisted on having me in their teams in the operating theatre from 6.00 to 8.00 am most days. They were very particular about dexterity, timing, alertness, and the importance of understanding the mechanical controls in the operating theatre. Sets of sterilized tools being sharp and ready lined up in their appropriate trays was the first rule. Perhaps my few years of training to create exquisite embroidery and needle work was related to my dealing with the fine operating tools and the stitching needles. Anyhow, the operating theatre was another new world, a quiet world of pure concentration. For the rest of the day I worked in the accident and emergency department, accompanying doctors attending to some really horrendous injuries at times. We all worked long hours, on our feet without a moment to think about whom we were and where we had come from. One was overwhelmed and even carried through it by a sense of duty, humility, and awe at what could be done for a patient in need of care. I truly loved my job, all of it, and only very gradually over the course of a decade and half were the length and number of night shifts lessened, and one was allowed to contemplate working fewer hours. Great friendships were made during these years with other nurses and doctors, and when we did have a break for an early lunch or late breakfast we talked and laughed a lot. As we grew old together in the course of 25 years, we witnessed each other's happy and unhappy times in life.

In the last five years, however, I moved to a different position altogether. After an initial period of training in cataloguing and the English language, I collaborated with an eminent medical professor and one other colleague to found the first comprehensive medical library on the site of Amir Alam Hospital. This made it possible for the student body of trainee nurses, interns, and doctors to consult medical materials in their spare time as they worked and trained. As well as documenting and appropriately storing the findings in human organ specimens at the hospital, we subscribed to the most recent and needed medical books, periodicals, specific journals, and research papers from around the world. I recall the latest articles about methods in laryngoscopic surgery were very popular at the time. I had started my career as a nurse with passion and excitement, and I could safely say that the last five years were just as meaningful and rewarding. I have been fortunate to do what I did.

The joy of living as myself

To be a trainee at the hospital with 16 others, and with a little money to enable me to buy books and go places felt like the heavens opened up to me. Although workloads were heavy, when we had one full day free we went out of town in a group. This was even better that renting books and drowning myself in words; it was contact with others, working, talking, experiencing and struggling together. As you know, the Shemiranat, now part of Greater Tehran, was totally rural sixty years ago; this is where our group went hiking and picnicking and even camping overnight in the summer. We did it simply, setting off really early in the morning, just after dawn, on the long bus ride from Darvazeh Shemiran and Darvazeh Dolat, the Tehran gates to Tajrish Square at the foot of the mountains, and then exploring the mountain-side villages and valleys. The bus was slow but we read newspapers and talked; there were great numbers of newspapers during this period and many in our group belonged to political parties. Socialist and communist ideologies were hugely popular amongst medical students and the upper classes, and we joined forces with them. There was a sense of comradeship in the rural areas too, and those who had been our patients at the hospital welcomed us to their orchards and village life with kindness and respect.

Summer camps have existed for hundreds of years, and we felt very safe with the villagers who did not know us at all but trusted our judgement about being the way we were. They did not expect us to behave in a more religious way, or not mingle with the young men in the group. They had great respect for our medical knowledge when we gave them advice, but they knew that we went to the mountains for the solitude and the beauty of the landscape. So we did our gallivanting in north Tehran as we pleased. Places like Golab-Dareh and the shrine of Imam-Zadeh Ghassem, Darband, Pass-Ghal'eh, Manzarieh, and on the other side Fasham, Lavassan etc. became our haunts. The orchards with blossoms in the spring were breathtaking. In the summer and on occasion we would camp overnight and some people would swim but I never felt comfortable about swimming. The fruit farmers or small herders would sell us tea, bread and cheese, their own freshly made yogurt, or fried dates with eggs. Once, the keeper of the Shrine at Imam-Zadeh Ghassem gave us a wonderful hot lamb soup; apparently he had noticed us down below, coming up the mountain and started cooking. It was a carefree existence in the shelter provided by law, even though we were in the minority. Our behaviours were markedly different to what was advocated by the clergy, their specific interpretations of Islam, and their pious followers who would rather women remained in the privacy of the households protected from public view.

I hardly faced any opposition to my conduct from the household, they were open to it even though I had heard that in our neighbourhood a father had scissored off his daughter's hair for going out without permission. I think the Labbaf family, the women especially, respected me without discussing or mentioning it. There was never any discussion of these things those days like there is today; as long as I did not give up my prayers there was no discussion at all about anything. I don't think any of us really understood the power women like me had gained through the protection of the unveiling and education laws, whatever the intricacies of the political circumstances. It is necessary to be protected by laws. I simply did what I did, finding a solution as I went along, somewhere in my head I had set my goals. Naturally I set new precedents in the household for the way I wore my hair, and my dress almost knee short and gathered at the waist, lace-up shoes, and at large in mixed male and female society in pursuit of both education, financial independence, and fun. They certainly understood economic independence because they worked too.

A number of political incidents became significant during my youth because of the continued intervention by the colonial and Imperial forces for Iran's oil and strategic geographical location. The first Pahlavi king, Reza Shah,[47] had been dispatched into exile in Africa in 1941 through a pact between Russia and Britain. This was a punishment for his associations with the Germans who had helped build the trans-national railway in Iran. He was replaced by his son Mohammad Reza under the Allied occupation, and the British practically claimed the country's oil. With the Russians and the Americans they set their goals to steal oil and gain power at every opportunity because of a weak government. There were numerous good newspapers at the time and during our picnics we would read about these, and discuss the consequences and shortcomings of our parliamentary politics, and the clergy's continuous opposition to women's right to vote.

I was introduced to politics more closely during our outings to the mountains by a trainee doctor from the northern provinces. She was a serious activist from the Tudeh Party,[48] working for the wellbeing of the masses, and sympathetic to the Russians who had sought dominance and partly occupied parts of north Iran since the nineteenth century. She was very knowledgeable about the Communist Marxist ideologies and being away from her family in Shahrud, she practically lived with her Tudeh Party friends. We would endlessly discuss the ever increasing interests of the British in the Iranian oil reserves for their own gain, the presence and interference of the Allied forces as a power base for the West, and social insurance for workers. I had not experienced anything like that before, and although I never became an activist like her, I had come to believe that the social and educational reforms by Reza Shah in the 1930s were not enough even though my life had been directly and profoundly affected by them. Through training at the teaching hospital, meeting people like my Tudeh Party friend, and socializing with other trainee medical students I gained a new consciousness. The joy of living as myself, as well as a citizen of my country was part of this consciousness. The struggles for the nationalization of oil which was secured despite the British and their political games in 1951, our insistence on the sovereignty of our country against the British demands for the ownership of that oil, was led by our elected Prime Minister Dr. Mosaddeq.[49] He was our hope for democracy, and this hope was stolen from us by the United States whose CIA organized a speedy coup d'etat overnight to oust him in favour of Mohammad Reza Shah. They simply distributed money amongst the mob and bought the Crown Prince the throne. Literally, when we got up in the morning on 28th of Mordad [19 August] in 1953, the grounds were covered with little white pieces of printed paper announcing this event to the nation. The Americans stole our young democracy, that's all. And all we could do in protest was to tell them to get out by writing slogans on walls. We did this when their president visited. We used buckets and buckets of white paint and with big brushes wrote 'Yankee Go Home'; but the American dollar had more power than our white paint.

Simultaneously, there were new developments in my private life which resulted in my marriage to a relative of mine, Ahmad. There were two or three young men amongst the extended family who had become friendly with me. One used to come to my primary school on his bike and accompany me back home without saying a word. There was nothing to chat about, he would just say hello and get off his bike and walk by my side. I don't remember anything specific about the other two except for Ahmad's blue eyes. Much later when I was 21 Ahmad declared his love to me with great politeness and restraint. He told me in passing that he had been to the shrine of Imam Reza[50] in Mashhad and had said to the Imam, who had been laying there for the last eight hundred years, that he would not return to the shrine ever again unless accompanied by Akram! You see we were all very innocent, and this ultimatum to the Imam combined with his good looks and sensitivity and kindness won my heart and he became the love of my life. I told my divorced parents about his interest in me; they categorically forbade any contact with him because he was a soldier with no prospects or profession and could not give me the life I deserved. My mother was outraged; she had not worked so hard to become the mother-in-law to a practically destitute Ahmad.

Ahmad was the middle son of Mirza Ebrahim Khan a well-to-do land and property owner of an authoritarian nature and a drinking partner of Reza Khan before he became the Shah. Mirza Ebrahim Khan was not a Bazar merchant and rather than giving

his sons an apprenticeship in the Bazar, he had sent them to the
best schools available. So they had no understanding of the value
of money. He died leaving the entire estate to be managed by his
two older boys who much like our government had neither training nor vision for managing the inheritance. One of these sons
had been a playmate of the Crown Prince Mohammad Reza and
gone to school with him and probably knew more about polo
playing than property management. So in the following twelve
years Ahmad's two brothers had proceeded to mis-invest the
family fortune, creating a bus company that did not last, importing fine goods from Europe, buying and selling land which
became enormously valuable only several decades later, as well as
partying with other fashionable Tehranis until the last penny was
gone. Mirza Ebrahim Khan had not taught his sons that if you
are a land owner you do not sell it all up. To put extra salt on the
wound, the Government had set out to construct new buildings
and parks in prime locations in the centre of the city, exactly
where Mirza Ebrahim Khan's house had stood. So the magnifi-
cient house was also demolished, much like the fortune, and the
sons were paid forty thousand tomans in exchange. This was a
great fortune indeed in the late 1930s and to this day nobody
knows exactly what happened to this fortune.

Some months had passed before Ahmad felt it right to approach
my Khanoom Bozorg personally and explain our intentions to
get married. I remember her questioning me about whether I
really wished to be his wife. Once she knew about the strength of
my feelings she made arrangements and took us to the *mahzar*
[notary public] to be married in a civil ceremony. My father, who
had heard of this arrangement changed his mind and managed to
arrive at the civil ceremony in the last few minutes and for the
moment of saying 'YES'. Later I borrowed a beautiful wedding
dress from a friend and we went to the photographers and posed
as bride and groom in immaculate and appropriate attire. From
that day on, Ahmad and I became partners in everything we did
and had. He became the friend, the one who loves you and understands you; he supported me in everything I did including all
aspects of my work, the endless night shifts, and the long hours
of absence from home. He would often turn up at the hospital
midmorning with a take-away breakfast for me and even for my

colleagues. Anything from traditional hot breakfasts cooked in the Bazar to bread and cheese or cakes.

We were fortunate domestically too; we lived with his step-mother who was from the Labbaf household and my grandmother's youngest sister. We called her Aziz, or dear one and she became our saviour, and practically ran our home in my absence during the unusual hours at work and the night shifts. You know we forget the significance of the support system these ladies provided. Could I have sustained my job, with three children without her being there? I don't think so. Aziz was the stepmother to my husband and his eldest brother, she also had a son of her own and we all had a small share in the first house we bought. This sharing was necessary because we all needed a home and none of us could buy one independently. But more importantly for me, Aziz was my co-worker, I went to work because I had chosen to be educated and have a profession. When I was caring for others at the hospital she cared for my three children. Need, tradition and modernity were intertwined and had become the elements of our little network. Certainly there were times that I thought I could do without the two brothers, that the house was too crowded, but I was mistaken and I shall be indebted to her till the day I die for her support and love towards me and my children. I often think about the fact that I more or less live on my pension now, but what did she get for her services? She was a working woman too!

You have asked me whether I might have a specific observation about family life and women in our society. I have said it to my daughters and I say it now: do not bring up your sons as if they are emperors. It is not in their interest, not only will they have a shock because of the realities of life ahead, but also they will fail others through lacking the understanding of the necessity to work in equal partnerships with women.

Meet Naaztaab

Naaztaab is the most agile 78 year-old I have met. Her manner is casual and her conversation is bright and fascinating, bringing the past and present together energetically. Her hair glistens in the light with pure whiteness sporting a very short 'à la garçon' style haircut. She is in functional ankle-length beige pants and a beige hand-knitted jumper. She welcomes me to her sitting room with well worn comfortable and simple furniture, several Art Deco style bookcases, and old photographs of women and men in Qajar dress. This room joins a larger room with classic French style furniture and modern art work by her daughter and other famous painters. There are also two dogs in the house, but it seems that they are not allowed in the sitting rooms. Naaztaab notices my enthusiastic gaze at her footwear, black pumps made of soft rubber lined in red. She laughs and says that her rubber gaalesh are the most comfortable footwear for the house, and that she has worn them all her life. I believe these were the style of the inexpensive imports from the Soviet Union in the early decades of the twentieth century. I recognise them because my grandmother wore similar ones.

Naaztaab is known as Naazi Joon to her family and lives with her sister of similar age in a large old house. Her daughter and granddaughter live in the adjoining ground floor apartments, off the beautiful courtyard with old plane trees and a narrow running stream. Unlike the majority of the houses of its age, this house has not yet been turned into an apartment block and was originally part of a compound built for several families in Art Deco period style. Naaztaab points to the bowls of mixed raisins, roasted chickpeas, and walnuts on the table and says playfully that they were the traditional snacks of her childhood and that I should help myself to some. She picks some up herself and puts them in the palm of her hand and proceeds to say that she has much to tell me, but she understands that I am short of time and leaving Tehran soon. I am then handed a thick bound volume of the collected women's newspaper, *Shokufeh* [blossom]. I am left to spend a few minutes with this volume while tea is being prepared. As I look through its pages I am struck by two things. Firstly, the particular style of the script, and the layout of the columns and headings. These remind me of some of the Qoranic texts I have seen belonging to my grandmother, and I wonder whether this style was adopted for a women's newspaper at the turn of the twentieth century to project status as well as familiarity, charming the reader into accepting secular content with sacred formatting. Secondly, and as I read some of the pages, I am struck by the wit and humour with which serious social issues of the time are confronted and communicated. These are captivating and compelling. In well-executed illustrations, caricature in style, several pages show women as the sharp observers of political events.

In clusters, and mostly present in the margins of events, dressed in their outdoor black voluminous chadors of the time, the women appear doubtful about the current affairs which unravel before them. In a highly satirized manner one of the pages engages in critiquing superstitious beliefs regarding fortune telling, and the acquiring of talismanic scripts and potions for increasing the love of the husband. The women in this narrative are participants rather than just observers. They are shown crowding over a *mullah scribe*,[51] peering into the nonsensical text being written, which one presumes is offering advice. A discussion ensues amongst the women about how much the advice might cost and whether it is worth the effort and the paper it is written on. Everyone in the illustration is labelled by a number in very small print which corresponds to a series of short texts and phrases which tell the reader what is being said and thought. The mullah has a Jewish name and his dog rests at his side.

Along with the critical observations of the Qajar princess, Taj al-Saltaneh in her memoirs, and a series of articles about women's rights signed under a pen name, Tayirah, attributed by some to Ismat Tihrani published in 1909,[52] there emerged a chain of publications by women in the early years of the twentieth century. This started with *Danesh* [knowledge] magazine in 1910, and Shokufeh the first newspaper in 1913.[53] Many more were published subsequently some only lasting a few months. Shokufeh lasted six years till the death of its editor Mrs. Mozayan ol-saltaneh in 1919, publishing articles on literature, education, child marriage, housekeeping, women's morals and superstition.

Naaztaab returns with freshly brewed tea and discusses the newspaper collection, the developments in her education, and her views about young women in contemporary Iran as follows.

> My grandmother, Maryam Amid-Semnani, known as Mozayan-ol Saltaneh,[54] was the founding editor of Shokufeh newspaper the first of its kind published in 1913. She also subsequently founded *Anjoman-e Khavaatin-e Irani* [the Iranian Women's Society]. She had great ambitions for women of her generation, particularly for those outside the aristocratic and notable families. She was keen to create multi-trajectory discussions amongst the women of her time. In her articles she discussed the need for women's education, child hygiene and family health, and the importance of women's creativity. She believed women ought to be informed about the legal and political topics related to themselves and others, and be warned against ignorance and superstition; she

concerned herself about moral issues in society. But she had to do all this it in a very subtle and diplomatic way because she knew very well if she made the political elite and the clerics appear foolish, her newspaper would be shut down immediately. She was very much against the customary early marriages for young girls, and wanted to point to sources other than religious interpretations to question women's wellbeing. She recognised knowledge and learning as key in women securing a moral and social standing in society.[55] As you probably know, women had started to participate in political demonstrations in many big cities well in advance of the Constitutional Revolution in 1906. But it was from 1910 onwards that periodicals and newspapers, such as my grandmother's, written by women for women developed rapidly. My mother too was well educated and founded and managed the Mozayanieh, two private schools for primary and secondary education. Because she was well educated herself she understood how vital it was that more and more women should be encouraged to see education as tools of progress. So for every two fee paying pupils accepted at the Mozayanieh schools she offered one place free of charge.

My sister and I started primary school in the same year and in the same class even though there is one year age difference between us. This was at the newly opened Bagh Ferdows, not far from Tajrish Square in Shemiran. This was the first mixed state school for boys and girls, founded through the efforts of Mr Ali Asghar Hekmat. It became Homayoon secondary school much later. As you can imagine, educating boys and girls equally against the wishes and threats of the clergy, and teaching them in the same classrooms by mostly male teachers, was a great achievement seventy years ago. There were no state schools available in the area at the time, and ours was the only one which allowed for an interesting mixture of pupils brought together from different socio-economic backgrounds. These pupils included the children of the local residents, bakers, greengrocers, shopkeepers, small farmers, as well as those connected to the deposed Qajar royal households such as ourselves. My sister and I went to school with our gardener's daughter wearing the identical uniforms we all had, the speckled grey overalls with white collars, and a white bow in our hair. You see, other than the rural classes and those who had second homes for their summers, not many families lived in Shemiran then.

We loved school, and it seemed that our school loved us; it certainly opened its doors to all youngsters who needed an education. One other factor that made our school very interesting and special in this particular time was the age mixture. Although the age for starting primary school was seven, there were ten and 11 year-olds in our first grade; I started when I was eight. My sister and I also loved school because it gave us an opportunity to make friends with others and many of us have continued to meet once a year and have a newsletter. The school's social life intensified in the summers when the pupils from a girls' orphanage founded by Reza Shah [1878-1944] in South Tehran were invited to join us for summer camp. A cultural programme called *Parvaresh-e Afkaar* was organized for us by Mrs Ardalan to develop our perceptions and intellectual growth. She would organize exciting educational and recreational programmes for us on Thursday evening. There would be theatrical performances, speeches, and much singing of patriotic songs. We would either be taught to perform these on stage, or performers and theatrical groups would be invited to the school to have shows. All of this was of course free of charge and part of the educating of the masses, but it was also to do with the spirit of our heads of school who saw such forms of education as vital to developing and creating the future of the nation. All pupils were encouraged to participate, and whether the baker's daughter or son, or an eight year-old or a 14 year-old, we sat together and learnt together.

Unfortunately our mixed school did not survive the interference and pressures by the clerics. By the time we completed fourth grade the pressures became too pronounced for our head and the teachers, forcing the school to become boys only. However, eight girls from our class including my sister and myself and the daughter of the school head remained, whilst others were moved to another school in Tajrish called Shaapour. I believe my father had something to do with this. Somehow he managed to persuade the authorities to keep my sister and me because of the very bad snow and ice in winter time and the proximity of our house to the school. But winters were bad for everyone living in

Shemiran, and everybody had to walk some distance to get to school! It seemed that my father knew how to get us favours. So we carried on with our education for two more years and sat our sixth grade exams with our male classmates for the first and the last time in the history of our school. As you know later in the 1960s several mixed schools opened and continued until the 1979 Islamic Revolution when they were shut down. I passed with the very average grades, 13 out of 20, but was branded as a top student anyway! How you can be a top student with that sort of a grade is beyond me! Was it out of respect for my father again? My secondary school was completed without much adventure; nothing could be as exciting as our primary school. My sister and I managed to enter Tehran University without much difficulty. But it always seemed that nothing could match my experiences of the summer camp at my primary school.

The university campus became a place for heated political debates for us, as you know, in the latter part of the 1940s and the early 1950s, when there was possibility to read relatively free press in Iran and hold varied political views. Oil nationalization and the democratic elections of the country's prime minister were a huge step towards a dream of independence. I, and my sister too, became aware of our own views and realized that we had turned out to be the sorts of people who demanded a distribution of wealth, social security for workers, transparent and democratic governance, and voting rights for women. We wanted to fight poverty above all. We became political activists after joining the Tudeh Party, and expressed our views on campus about the need for promoting the rights and wellbeing of the masses rather than focusing on capitalism. It did not take long before we were kicked out of the university because of our political views, however.

Being expelled from university however did not mean we were alone. We still had the Tudeh Party friends, and although it took some time we managed to find other means of going forward. I managed to find my vocation in life, and be trained as a teacher and dedicate my professional life to teaching in schools. I chose to serve in the more economically vulnerable areas of south Tehran and I must confess I enjoyed every minute of it. I had a personal mission against illiteracy simply because self-respect and self-reliance are its direct results. There is satisfaction in being with others who want to learn about the world. Learning like that becomes a common goal, and when you are working towards common goals you create common horizons. This is a very special feeling, even though it is always difficult to get the results you have imagined and hoped for.

As you know, the Constitutional Revolution did not succeed in including women in its electoral reforms. The monarchy remained self-serving, and the clergy thought it immoral that women should wish to be visibly active and part of a modern society, and express opinions about the affairs outside the household. Any discussion created either by the women themselves, or by the few intellectuals in the late nineteenth and the early years of the twentieth century, who drew comparisons between women in Iran and their sisters abroad, were ignored by our *Majles* [Parliament].[56] Even the unveiling laws of the mid-1930s were reversed in 1943 through a religious decree by the notable cleric from Qom, Ayatollah Ruhollah Khomeini who ultimately toppled the Shah.[57]

The idea of women acquiring an equal place to men in the socio-political discussions and decisions in the country has always remained the women's vision. The truth is, nobody is going to do it for you if you don't do it for yourself. The history of women's progress in this country has been as oppressively problematic as the interests of the foreign powers in its wealth; it is as if we are swimming against the tide. Just when you think you are going forward, you find yourself against the waves which push you back.

In the 1960s we continued to hold debates about our rights as much as possible while facing the new hierarchies created by those around the monarch. There was much extravagance and little progress however, despite modern urban growth. There was also severe opposition from the religious leaders who believed only in their own ways and interpretations of Islamic law. The debates about women's equal land ownership in 1962, and the Shah's 1963 attempts to introduce electoral rights for women as part of the charter for his White Revolution caused serious clashes with the clerics headed by Ayatollah Khomeini. Ultimately, his sustained opposition to the Shah and forms of secular reform regarding women's status caused his exile to Turkey in 1964.[58] He did not return until 1979 to create the new chapter in Iran's history with the formation of the Islamic Republic.

The recognition of women's legitimate right to vote came late when you consider half a century had lapsed since the idea was first campaigned for as part of the Constitutional revolution! But the right to vote would not have come at all had we given up our relentless pressure and demands; the truth is men work for men's interests. It seems that for every two steps we pushed ourselves forward, we were pushed back a step by them, be it in the name of Islam or other forms of patriarchy. You see, the rules which are given to us as the absolute wishes of the Prophet came from a number of cultural sources and people, including our own, during his life and after his death as Islam developed in the seventh and eighth centuries. That is why these rules are open to interpretations in their essence. Islamic practices in this country are mingled with our old Zoroastrian heritage for example, as it would be the case with other cultural perspectives in other geographical locations within Muslim civilizations. The symbolisms of light and dark, and the wings of Faravahar from our past, implying spiritual transcendence, are present in our day-to-day lives and part of our collective psyche today. That is why we have very specific ritualistic practices mixed with our Islamic heritage.

My generation were fortunate that at least for a few years during our youth we could openly belong to a political party and examine political ideas collectively. But that was before the CIA reestablished the monarch. During the reign of the late Shah there were no political parties other than his. Secular political activism during my youth belonged mostly to the educated classes, those who had the opportunity to cultivate a political mind. The struggle has always been to raise the level and quality of lives through active minds and change. Influenced by our Tudeh party, we saw ourselves at the service of our country and the masses, and we shared a sense of belonging. We had it in our heads to fight poverty, and were influenced by each other. The new generation faces huge economic challenges specific to the contemporary period, and the language of poverty is harsh and violent. This generation know about the world, they want jobs, economic stability, housing, and they are concerned about being successful and happy. The reality however, is that they can only turn to themselves.

The foregoing life histories by the two grandmothers posit multi-layered personal and gendered perspectives which highlight a number of intersections in Iran's social and political histories prior to the 1979 Revolution. There emerges a narrative with simultaneous spaces of transition and continuity, tradition and modernity, mass education and employment, old and new identities, perceptions, beliefs, and social behaviours. The disclosed critical incidents in the country's politics further demonstrate how Iran as a remarkable strategic location, also gifted with extensive natural resources such as oil, remained a covetable concept for the expansionist governments of Britain and the USA. Whilst the former undermined Iran's sovereignty and ownership of its oil in the 1940s, the CIA stopped the course of democracy in Iran by ousting the elected premier Dr Mosaddeq in a coup d'etat in August 1953.

The Islamic Revolution in 1979, supported by the masses, speedily and rigorously revitalized the Islamist forms of patriarchy which clerics believed to be undermined by the Pahlavi dynasty (1925-1979) and its programmes of modernization and secularization. This reversed most of the pre-revolutionary legal reforms at the cost of disillusioning a great many intellectual and secular supporters of the Revolution. It further reinforced the notion that women should be keepers of homes, wives, and mothers. Men thus regained unilateral rights to divorce and polygamy, while women's rights to divorce and child custody became once again limited; women could no longer serve as judges.[59] Ironically however, many of the vast numbers of women from the religious classes with secondary school and university education, and the Muslim feminists, who had visibly supported Ayatollah Khomeini's return from exile, turned their energies to becoming the new workforce in governmental institutions. They thus maintained the infrastructures the Islamic regime crucially needed to sustain itself in daily life, and caused to shape-shift the position of many clerics who had advocated that the place of the woman was in the home. As teachers, administrative clerks, and gate-keepers advocating and monitoring the strict Islamic dress codes, these women replaced the very many thousands of women whose services were terminated by the Islamic regime because of ideology! This concept of women replacing women created political polarities and conflict in identities especially at the outset of the Revolution.

The imposed war with Iraq ensued soon after, and from September 1980 to July 1988 the two countries experienced catastrophic physical, economic, and emotional devastation. Over one million military personnel died, and thousands more were contaminated by the chemical weaponry supplied to Saddam Hossein by the United States. Again, women played a significant part in providing care for the wounded in hospitals and behind the front line. They were mobilized by the state, as volunteers, to cook, sew, and prepare and administer medicines, in hospitals and mosques. Men were neither trained nor available, nor were they ideologically prepared for undertaking such jobs.[60] Consequently, despite the specific gendered interpretations of religious laws by the clerics and the state further shifts in perceptions followed, and women's position as a workforce was consolidated. This however has yet to manifest itself in high ranking positions in government.

During the period of reconstruction in the post-war decade, a women's press re-emerged with new and dynamic trajectories. Women publishers and writers, often with a thorough knowledge of Islam and the Qoran as well as feminist ideology, came together with significant effect and determination to re-conceptualize the position of women within the Islamic Republic as well as the media. The sociologist Shahla Sherkat, a devout Muslim and the editor in chief and founder of *Zanan Magazine* in 1992, and Mahboubeh Abbasgholizadeh, the feminist and women's rights activist at *Meydan.com* and editor in chief of *Farzaneh Women's Studies Journal*, and the director of *Banoo Publishing House*, are amongst many I have met.

The nature and level of debate about women by women escalated through their writings and advocacies. Following the March 1998 women's publishers book exhibition with over 50 female participants, in 1999 the number of women publishers increased to 236.[61] With skill, will and entrepreneurial ambitions, an unprecedented forum for open and critical socio-political debate was initiated through women's press and publications, alerting and informing anyone who could read. Religious, legal, and cultural ground for women was thus reclaimed by women. As sociologists, lawyers, writers, mothers, housewives, and sharp thinkers with secular as well as religious identities, women collaborated. They held interviews in their press discussing and critically addressing variations in Qoranic interpretations, examining the judiciary's practices in relation to the Family Law, creating a collective vision by drawing on shared experience and know-how. These practices not only helped women, but influenced the moment of reform, aspects of which will be discussed in Text Five.

Thus, and despite the continued uneven terrains before them locally, imposed isolation from the West because of the 1979 Revolution, acute economic pressures and frequent interruptions in university education in the 1980s, facing the consequences of the war with Iraq, becoming even more vulnerable economically within the family as a consequence of the sustained sanctions and demonization of Iran by the USA, Iranian women have managed to regroup, reconceptualize, and reaffirm their intellectual presence and as we shall see in the following Texts emerge with vitality.

The Margins

Tehran taxis vary in type, you may hail down an orange taxi on the street, phone for one, become a member in an agency and order one whenever you need it, or patiently queue for the communal route taxis on roadsides at their specific stations. The latter, known as *kerayeh*, or rental, are the cheapest and are shared between four passengers, one next to the driver and three in the back. They follow set routes with as many stops as required by the passengers. One might use two or three route taxis to reach downtown from various corners of the city.

The lady taxi-driver

On the busy uptown Vanak Square I join the queue for a communal taxi heading north of the city. A taxi arrives and it is my turn to share it with three others. I note the driver is a woman, perhaps in her midforties or less. She wears a simple black headscarf and a knitted dark green jumper over a black *roopoosh*, or coat. She has a sun-beaten face and shining light brown eyes watching her passengers. Once everyone is in, and unusually, she makes an announcement.

> Ladies and gents, I intend to miss the horrific traffic ahead of us by taking you round a few back streets till we hit the highway heading for Tajrish Square. I will not be stopping between here and Tajrish. If this does not suit, you may leave now.

To my amazement all the passengers nod in agreement, and we set off for our destination which must now be just one stop: Tajrish Square. On making enquiries about female public transport drivers, I find out there are also those who drive buses and lorries. For taxis, I am told 'it's simple; you have to take the tests and get the licence'. It must be the same for the other types of roads and vehicles.

On another occasion I get into a communal taxi and sit next to two ladies at the back. The front seat is empty, so when the driver sees a man calling out 'straight ahead' he attempts to stop. It is difficult for him however to come to a complete halt because there is a chain of cars behind him. So he is forced to edge forward before the new passenger has opened the door fully to get in.

Taxi driver to man getting in:

I stopped for you, didn't you see me! I was holding up the traffic for you! You must be quick, jump in quickly, life is fast these days!

Passenger:

No, I was not sure whether you were stopping or not. You were edging forward I thought. It's dangerous to just jump in, we have to hang on to these lives or ours despite the traffic! As a matter of fact I have just returned from that eye hospital just up the road. I am due for an operation. I normally drive myself to my factory early morning. But today, at this hour, the roads are that busy I thought it would be quicker to use the kerayeh. The hospital wants to charge me extra for putting me in a private bed, but I have been paying my social insurance contributions for the last thirty years to pay extra now; I am damned if I pay a penny more! It has now come to this – they want to sell you the same hospital bed you are entitled to anyway! They call this a new scheme to upgrade treatment! Now if they had not invented this upgrade business, I would be entitled to the same bed they are going to charge me extra for! Would I not? There is no law, there is nothing left of the law in this country.

The two ladies sitting in the back next to me are in conversation with each other. They are in their black chadors but I can catch their rose-water scent in the air. One says to the other:

No I think you are mistaken mother, she is going to do a degree in tourism now. She was going to do – what did you call it – a degree in 'trade insurance' before, but she has changed her mind. She thinks anything to do with insurance will ultimately be a world of desks and telephones, whereas tourism might actually have some travelling involved. Trade insurance. It does sound interesting, it could be connected to all this talk of globalization. Can you believe it – you can do any degree you wish these days! A degree in trade insurance – it's marvellous!

The front passenger's mobile rings and he proceeds to give a detailed account of the hospital upgrade to someone!

We come up to a junction, where I can get out because it is convenient for my route towards Tehran University campus in west Tehran. I come away fascinated by my encounters, the woman taxi driver makes me smile at her matter-of-fact and urgent modernity even in her absence. The account of the passenger hoping to have an eye operation without paying extra is a familiar debate too. In Britain the National Health Service has intermittently proposed to make certain operations available more quickly if patients were prepared to pay a little extra to enter the semi-private hospital Trusts. And, the ladies in the taxi could not be more contemporary in their reflections about the choice of higher education available to young people. Evidently you do not have to be Western to be modern.

Text Two: Making Meaning, Acquiring Identities

The discussion of the concept of identity, and the analysis of its construction and renewal dominate global discourses of belonging. These relate cultural distinctions and difference, common language, and specificities of geographical location, as well as race, gender, and social class. The Islamic Republic is no exception. The word identity is widely and routinely used by the Iranian government, facing both the nation and the world, to mean primarily the Islamic ideology related to perspectives in Shi'ite Islam.[62] Shi'ism was adopted officially as the country's religion in the Safavid epoch (1501-1722). Its inception is related to a political struggle after the death of Prophet Mohammad (570-632) regarding his successor. Many recognised that Ali ibn Abi Taleb (632-661) was the rightful successor of the Prophet, chosen by him at Ghadir Khum in Saudi Arabia and thus the first of twelve *Imams*. This, the recognition of the twelfth Imam, as *Mahdi* or saviour, and the martyrdom of the third Imam, Hossein ibn Ali in the battle of Karbala alongside his circle of 72 including women and children, are recognised as the centre of Shi'ite thought. The example of the selfless courage and sacrifice displayed by Imam Hossein is perceived to be the essence of spirituality amongst Shi'ites, and in Iran the nation and the youth especially are called upon to uphold and perform moral purity in remembrance and in solidarity with Imam Hossein as part of Shi'ite identity.

If the above could be imagined as one pole, then the other would be the centrality of Iran's historic and cultural heritage from its pre-Islamic civilization. References to this heritage are multidimensional; they might be tangible and in the form of material culture and architecture of which there are multiple examples and remains, both in the country and in museums worldwide. They might be also be abstract in nature, as if etched on the collective psyche of the nation, surviving in layers of memory and socio-cultural consciousness and behaviours. The mythologies of this ancient heritage have been part of the felt collective imagination, and history of the nation through millennia. They have been narrated in song in oral histories as they have been recorded in prose and poetry in the country's classical literature. In fluent Farsi and despite the lapse of time, this literature is read, understood, performed, and re-imagined in the contemporary period. Indeed Persian classical literature has given birth to and safeguarded mysticism in relation to Islam. It has promoted profound understandings of the knowledge, wisdom, abstraction, and, above all, the philosophy implicit in Islamic thought. Thus both *Islamiyyat* and *Iraniyyat* are embraced as sources of belonging and multi-identities by vast numbers of Iranians and Farsi speakers wherever they might be.[63]

Such polarities, however, often overlook what falls in between with regard to the diverse realities of the lived experience of the citizens facing everyday life. Acquiring new layers in identities in order to make meaning of circumstance, time and space, and the variety and richness of the country's ethnicities, languages, and religions, are seldom contemplated when the regime promotes its discourse of identity. While a static one-dimensional address of any of the above elements will prove problematic, the vision of the government remains within an essentialist homogenous framework. This framework predominantly focuses on promoting the excellence of Islamic thought interpreted and put forth by eminent traditional clerics trained in Qom. Though valued by many, it is neglected that these interpretations are indeed interpretations and cannot remain confined to the local perspectives of a few. They often fail to meet with the growing complexity and diversity of contemporary Iranian society and nation, two-thirds of which is under the age of thirty. This category of young citizens particularly, express identities more fluidly and are increasingly engaged with new ways to make meaning and construct lives.

In this Text I shall draw on observations and interviews to project just a few symbolic trajectories young women adopt to express fluid and composite individual and collective identities. While the word identity is rarely mentioned, signifiers of its meaning as a concept are revealed in acts and thoughts. The narratives reveal mindscapes and how layers in identities are constructed anew in response to experience. The Text brings together events from a number of public and private spaces. In Part One, observations of dress codes for women going about their business at Tehran Museum of Contemporary Art are signifiers of imposed, constructed, and contested identities relating complex acts of body management. Thus the acts of covering the body, displaying it, granting it status, and viewing it as a significant medium of expression to display material and cultural competency, are testament to the subtleties in acquiring layers of meaningful identities.

Such observations are extended to include the Tehran metro, an educational environment on a university campus, and a residential street. In Part Two the reader will enter the private and intimate interior of a life drawing class created by a group of art students. This cluster of young women presents a symbolic society where identities are displayed in relation to local perspectives, selves, experience, as well as rich cultural capital and imagination. These however become relevant to both broader disciplines in art and human condition beyond geographical and ideological boundaries. The Text concludes in the interiors of Tehran taxis where drivers' views resonate with the essence of the ideas related by the young women.

Part One: Public spaces
Dress codes as cultural signifiers

Prior to his return to Iran from exile in Paris in February 1979, Ayatollah Khomeini had given assurances that religious laws would not be imposed on Iranians. This was evident in the range of secular intellectuals who surrounded him and acknowledged him as a leading force. Within a few weeks of the victory of the 1979 Revolution however, established clerics prompted a forceful process of Islamization in different pockets of society. In April 1979 a referendum decided that Iran was to become an Islamic Republic. This meant that specific interpretations of Islamic law replaced several civil laws regarding the status and appearance of women. The Family Protection Law was quashed immediately, and women became barred from being judges, the hejab law was reinstated and became part of the everyday realities of women's lives, and beaches became segregated.[64] Such exclusions were seen as particularly ironic and unexpected because women without hejab had maintained high activism in the discourses against the monarchy and dictatorship, and had been important participants in the political processes leading to the Revolution. Notwithstanding numerous demonstrations against the idea and practice of compulsory hejab on and around International Women's Day on 8 March, this became law in June 1980.[65] Nearly three decades later, the hejab dress code has assumed an even more complex face. Many women view it as a minor issue at the interface of economic hardships, persistent housing shortages, and the shortcomings of the revised Family Law. Many on the other hand view the compulsory nature of the hejab contrary to their rights as free thinking citizens; they would like to see a referendum to address this particular issue. They believe conforming to the dress code is a symbol of subordination and see it as sanctioning their independence, preventing the development of a far reaching civil society, and hampering the achievements of equal legal rights activists.

In Tehran Bazar

The most favoured interpretation of the dress code by the Islamic regime has been the black chador, or the outer garment worn in public covering from the head to the ankles. This is usually worn over a roopoosh, trousers, and a *maghna'eh*, or fitted headscarf covering the under chin and neck area. This particular combination was put forth as the *good hejab* by the government representing not only piety but morality observed by the faithful to the regime, implying firm political allegiance. Such a stance made clear the political distinctions the Islamist elite desired, mobilizing a new female workforce. This workforce became the main agent of the political elite to oversee the institutional *cleansing* of women, or ridding the system of them as apparent corrupt elements, particularly in the first decade of the Revolution. Cleansing, or *paak saazi*, took place in all aspects of civic life, civil service, and public workplace, for both men and women. Apart from sacking existing qualified staff who held sensitive and important positions, paak saazi had wider meaning in higher education institutions, which, in

1980, were closed down for a period of three years to make room for a new academic cadre and national curricula. Additionally, women were barred from entry to any governmental institution if their faces showed any trace of makeup, if they wore manicure, and if their hair was showing.[66]

Although the hejab law remains the same today, women have steadily and relentlessly pushed back the boundaries of the dress code, especially during Khatami's presidency (1997-2005). The sporadic attacks on women in the public space, i.e. spring and summer 2007 and 2008, do not alter their position, and they resist the demand by the hardliners to *correct* their hejab. Precisely because of such a sustained process of resistance, built day by day over time, it is impossible to point exactly at the moment of change. For those who dare, the headscarves have gradually become bands of coloured cloth, and the length of the roopoosh is determined to just covering the thighs. The dress code is currently a significant tool to make a collective and symbolic statement, and a means for being a highly visible front in society, declaring identities and social capital.[67] This collective and symbolic expression has no concrete physical centre however, it is read differently by individual women. It is an analysis of situations according to where you are and with whom you are, thus related to space and time.

Signifying status

I visit Tehran Museum of Contemporary Art to meet with its Director, and while waiting I note the interpretations of the dress code and their relationship with the individual's status. This is significant because this office represents the Iranian government at both the national and international levels, and it is thus obliged to adhere to laws, including the dress code, strictly. Visitors and clients from overseas, East and West, view its comprehensive modern art collection kept in the basements under ideal conditions. The Museum was established in 1977 with a design inspired by Iran's vernacular architecture, which offers a centrally open and welcoming plan that facilitates observation from many view points.[68] It has been a significant venue for cultural exchange and interaction since 1997, with a particularly forward looking programme that has been designed to engage specifically and dynamically with the new post-Iran-Iraq war generation. As the major supporter of national and international art events, the Museum is the single most important cultural institution and venue for contemporary art discourses in Iran.[69]

The office of the personal assistant to the Museum Director, and her administrative cadre receive official guests and are situated in a large snail-shaped area which accommodates both reception and distribution point, with several desks, telephones, computers, and cabinets and book cases. This area leads to several large offices and conference rooms which house the senior management team. Although rather exposed because of the nature of the architecture, the low black leather and chrome furniture with clean angular lines allow for a point of focus with different spatial arrangements. On arrival one notes two ladies behind large desks. They are in well tailored but austere roopoosh and scarves, probably mass-produced. Black, brown or dark navy blue are often favoured in governmental offices such as this, cream and other neutral tones might be tolerated during the hot season at private institutions. These ladies wear absolutely no makeup, and their fitted maghna'eh headscarves are in a single colour well secured under the chin, not exposing their hair above their foreheads. Because they represent the senior management team, their status requires strict observation of the dress code, and though courteous and accommodating they do not act in a familiar manner.

The Director's personal assistant in particular seems to have great authority evident in the polite, knowledgeable, and firm manner of her speech. There is a sense of urgency in her actions, and her several phones ring constantly. She manages the Director's national and international diaries and receives his guests prior to their appointments. She is fluent in English and highly articulate in her observations on art and socio-political issues. At a later stage of my visit she tells me she was trained at art school at the time of the Revolution, studying dance. I do not believe she has got used to observing the dress code; rather, she tolerates it with exactitude because of her professionalism and the need to remain employed.

In contrast to this 'front of the house' image and conduct, in one of the side rooms there is a young lady who occasionally comes out with a faxed or emailed message. She seems to know some foreign languages too. She is in a long black roopoosh which is discretely and subtly styled and waisted with well-considered darts and fine buttons and pockets. This outer garment is certainly not mass-produced. One knows immediately that this lady's roopoosh is discreetly fashioned and fitted to her body presenting her as if a beautifully proportioned sculpture, or a well considered symbol of *Self* which is not at all ordinary. The young lady's hair, under a loosely wrapped rather than 'clipped under the chin' black headscarf, is curly and big. It pushes out in ringlets here and there. Her stylish dark blue jeans almost cover her soft flat shoes and one becomes aware of a delicate and well-pampered youthful presence as she steps through the space. There is no urgency in her movements, she might not even need this job.

The tea lady walks in. She is also in a black headscarf, trousers, and well-worn slightly crumpled cotton roopoosh; but this is more like a working uniform which has been washed often. The creases in the tea lady's roopoosh are very different to the creases in the soft linen roopoosh of the previous lady. The tea lady's headscarf is worn with a casual air knotted thinly under her chin, and it does not seem to matter how she wears it. It is highly likely that the tea lady comes to work wearing a chador as an outer and unifying garment, removing it during the tea serving period. It is also possible that she is not at all religious and wears her hejab to demonstrate her socio-cultural allegiances with a residential neighbourhood. The tea lady seems observant, if not curious, and enquires after one's business when there is an opportunity. She carries her tea tray with such deftness and pride you would think she was Cleopatra attending to Anthony with life saving refreshments. She is generous and offers one a second glass of freshly brewed scented tea and white sugar lumps. She seems to be amused by the faces and characters waiting to meet with the Director. Obviously the latter two ladies are not 'front of the house' people who have to uphold the moral identity of the institution, and as a consequence can afford to appear more as themselves rather than signifying institutionalized identities.

Some time passes, and a young woman walks through and heads for the Director's office to ask for more technicians. She is talking into the mouth piece of her cell phone. She is in a very light cinnamon coloured trouser suit fitted at the waist; the jacket falls to about ten inches above the knees. Her headscarf, a wide band of loosely woven soft linen-silk mix, is a radiant apricot cream in colour. It lightly rests at the back of her head with most of her hair and neck visible; each end of the headscarf crossing very loosely well below her chin, falling over her shoulders to the back. Her neck shows off her gold chain. Her eyes and face are fully but carefully and subtly made up, her makeup applied as if a delicate but precise painting; the colours echo the colours of her clothes. She is the curator for the show opening in two days time. She is hanging the show, working with two Iranian modernist painters, one of whom lives in Paris but is here for the opening. She is also an art tutor at Honar University, and a practising painter and installation artist. The colours of her clothes, the way in which she has chosen and wears her headscarf, showing her carefully styled hair, and the length of her jacket-coat, indicate sartorial distinctions as well as a more independent status and identity. She is not an employee of the Museum, but simply invited to work with two distinguished painters. Hence the luminous colours, makeup, and jewellery. Art tutors at Honar University, formerly the University for the Applied Arts, are viewed differently to their colleagues at Tehran University. The latter is and has been much closer to the Revolution's discourses. The new generation female tutors I have met at Tehran University have been the recipients of PhD scholarships in France and wear the chador as a mark of support for the hard-line factions in the government.

About the same time an older lady walks in. She talks and laughs freely and is greeted by everyone warmly. She is a well know Iranian-Armenian art critic who was part of the art establishment in pre-Revolution times. She wears a bright multi-coloured silk headscarf balancing the bright colour of her manicure. A cream coat-jacket over casual trousers, finished with nylons in fine patent shoes. She could be walking on the left bank in Paris. Several male members of the senior management team rush out to greet her, two are artists from the 1970s and with ponytails. They all disappear to the big conference room to discuss the opening of the show, and I hear them critiquing the range of large publicity posters made for the opening night; much laughter and exchanges of pleasantries can also be heard. Such openly chummy interactions are rare in high ranking governmental offices. Here, however, cultural capital and cultural distinction help create the atmosphere comparable to that of an art venue anywhere in the West. It is however a temporary thing and due to the show of the works of the two significant modernist artists from the 1960s and 1970s.

Although the dress code law has not been altered since 1980, and the consequences of resisting it could be grave, the dress codes observed by the new post-Iran-Iraq generation are increasingly expressive in colour and form and fundamentally personalized. Multi-coloured transparent or shiny headscarves of minimal dimensions capable only of minimal coverage, cropped pants, and short jackets instead of 'modest' roopoosh rule the way. Highly made-over faces with eyebrow-shaping, tattooed facial definition, occasional facial piercing, exacting and interesting haircuts and hair arrangement, fashionable accessories such as handbags and glasses, and bejewelled sandals, mules, and other fascinating footwear, display meaning relating difference. They highlight the individual's cultural competencies, economic privilege, resistance and gendered solidarity, claiming ideological distinction. Such presentation of *Self* must be seen as part of a bigger picture which also shows perseverance with education, looking for means to become economically independent, and learning to explore, articulate, and gather pace in the discussion of civil society. All of these are related to the desire to become visible as a social as well as political force, even at the cost of being arrested.

Similar to any modern and aspiring country the fashion industry promotes Iran's capitalist economy and material consumption amongst women. Whether wearing the chador or the fashionable cropped hipster pants and mini roopoosh, women are the much needed allies of the regime and of the market place as consumers. They are powerful initiators of work for others, keeping sections of the economy in business. Numerous boutiques in shopping centres rely on the young generation, women and men, buying fashionable imports with global specifications. Turkish tight fitting roopoosh and hipster pants are readily available and may be further fitted to the body or shortened by male shirt makers. There are fantastic windfall profits in importing the black chador cloth from Japan and Korea, especially in the absence of any such domestic industries. This is estimated at 40 million US dollars annually, making it particularly lucrative for its importers at the *Bonyad-e Mostasafan* or the Foundation for the Oppressed, which is owned and operated by individuals close to the regime.[70] Simultaneously, the love of beautifully designed and woven fabrics have remained part of long-standing heritage and trade which reinforce the tradition and desire for couture of the highest standards in line with the world of contemporary fashion. These however are the sartorial extravagances which remain hidden, and may only be seen in the private interiors of homes regardless of age, religious practices, and political convictions.

The history class

Following arrangements made with an historian from one of the campuses in Tehran, I set off to sit in her third year class in order to join the discussions at the end of the session, and inviting the students to discuss their understanding of the concept of identity. The session starts at 2.00 pm and my colleague has invited me to meet at 1.00 pm and discuss the afternoon over lunch.

On the metro to the city of Rey

I set off on the metro. Moving down the escalator I note the embossed designs on the ceramic tiles, the distinct geometry and colour patterns of which guide the eye and mind along the walls. These provoke sensibilities about abstract art and a visual cultural history. On the platform, the train is about to depart and I jump on. Within a few seconds I realize that in my haste I have got on the carriage for men and am the only woman present. Not a frequent user of the underground and buses in Tehran, I had forgotten that these modes of transport have been officially segregated in cities as a result of the 1979 Islamic Revolution. The coach is full and there are no seats available with many men standing shoulder to shoulder next to me. Although I am obviously noticed I see no alarm in the eyes of the passengers and decide to stay on. I pull my notebook out of my coat pocket and make brief notes of my observations. Four stops pass and at Sa'di Station two students with books, a male and female, jump on. They are in conversation and obviously close friends; I realize that they must be far too engaged in their conversation to choose the appropriate separate coaches. When we arrive at the next stop, 15 Khordad for Tehran Bazar, we hear the muezzin and I note a man pushes his knitted cap to the back of his head and whilst saying a short prayer with closed eyes, he runs his hand over his forehead down to his chin in a familiar gesture of remembrance, humility, and submission; it is prayer time.

At the same time a petite young woman walks onto the carriage without any apparent pause or reservation about it being an all male coach. She illuminates the coach with her presence. I first notice her striking vivid pink lipstick and matching pink eye shadow and highly styled hair, almost all of which is pushing out of her black maghna'eh, the official black head cover students must wear. Her black roopoosh is obviously made to fit her body with exactitude and is cropped to well above the knee around the thighs over black fitted three-quarter length pants. The edge of her black, trainer style, lace-up canvas boots shows her pink socks. In one hand she carries a mobile phone and two books whose covers show drawings of fractional geometry. A dark blue satchel, also full of books, hangs on her other shoulder. I ask her whether she is going to the South Tehran Campus, to which she replies 'No. Sharif University'. The latter is one of the most important universities for the study of sciences, located along this route.

By this time several seats have become available and I take one while I check the number of stops to my destination on the panel above the seats opposite. My mind, however, slides back to the young woman passenger, her body presentation and appropriation of the space allocated to men. If my own act of entering the 'male' carriage was incidental, due to my absent mindedness, hers must be an alert political act which has become routine in nature, modifying imposed regulations. It occurs to me that her personal and colourful reinterpretations of dress codes, much like her books, define her self-perception and identity with little regard for segregation.

On the campus

The last stop on the metro is the city of Rey which has an ancient history from the pre-Islamic Achaemenids (559-330 BC) and Sassanian (224-637 AD) periods to the Muslim era up to the Mongol invasion in the thirteenth century. Rey has a large shrine complex where the religious scholar Shah Abdul Azim (786-865 AD), a descendant of Imam Hossein the third Shi'ite Imam, is buried. It is a popular place for pilgrimage and piety, and the campus I am heading for is a much welcome new addition introducing a new and fresh element to the city through the presence of the student body. This becomes evident in the numerous young couples sitting on the park benches engaged in dialogue, even though such acts could prompt questioning by the police, unless the couples are either married or blood relatives.

A short taxi ride from the metro station brings me to the campus where my entry is registered at the gates by one of the many porters or guards in an office with desks and telephones. The grounds are asphalted with small areas allocated for tree plantation. There are clusters of students and I ask for directions. A male student guides me down some steps to the lecturers' canteen next to a staff room. The staff room is equipped with a large electric samovar which looks more like a boiler. There are chairs and a conference table, and I am greeted by the historian whose session I am sitting in. She is in a black maghna'eh and black chador and as she greets me as she collects her books and files and handbag on one arm and we proceed to the small canteen separated from this room by sliding doors. This is my first time eating with colleagues on campus and I note that there are two waiters in white uniform jackets serving everyone. One comes forward and announces that there are two hot dishes on the menu, one is a lemon flavoured celery and herb lamb casserole served with rice, plus paper thin bread, a yogurt, cucumber, and mint salad, all of which come with water or a cold drink which is a local version of coca cola. All this is offered at a highly subsidized price, less than fifty pence, at all the universities I have visited in Tehran.

By this time two other tutors come in and join our table. Introductions are made, and there proceeds an exchange of pleasantries and enquiry about who I am and what I am doing there. I explain the purpose of the book over the hot and delicious lunch. At this point I allow myself to address one of the tutors, probably in her late 30s, and remark on the aesthetic impact of her turquoise blue maghna'eh under the black chador. I add that I had not observed such bright colour under a chador before, especially amongst the tutors who are often very careful to follow dress codes. Her face lights up and in a passionate reply she tells me that when she started work she simply decided to wear a turquoise blue maghna'eh under her black chador because being a literature tutor and a specialist in Persian classical poetry she felt she needed to express her own poetic leanings through colour. She then added that so far nobody had complained. At this point my historian colleague turns to the third tutor and asks her to tell me the story of her education. Without any reservation, and in complete serenity, this lady explains in detail that she was completely illiterate until the age of 18 at the time of the Revolution, and lived in a village not too far from Tehran where no one had a car, nor had a relative who owned one. She adds that she discovered she could start learning to read and write free of charge with the help of the *Educational Jihad* scheme set up by the government.[71] Within a few years she discovered that she was a quick and talented learner and was encouraged by the Educational Jihad teachers to continue. So she persevered against all economic odds and familial complications and qualified first as a teacher of history and subsequently, after securing a masters degree, started teaching at this university, and now is in the process of applying for a scholarship to do her PhD. At this point, and with great pride and a big smile, she tells everyone that now she is the only person from that village to have owned a car. I find this fascinating wondrous account compelling and make a note of it in my book. I am also taken by the fact that her colleagues who obviously have heard the story be-

fore, perhaps several times, listen carefully with an expression of ex-
hilaration.

Lunch time over, we collectively decide to go about the business
that has brought us together, and disperse to various classes. On the
way my historian colleague comments on the newly founded multi-
story Archive Centre in Tehran housing magnitudes of historic documents, and how research degrees are encouraged by the government
especially in relation to the country's recent histories. She generously
invites me to visit the Archive Centre with her because one is required
to secure a pass. She then tells me that she has to explain two things
before we go to class. The first is related to her chador, in case I am
wondering why she was not wearing one in our previous meeting. She
informs me that it is considered good professional conduct and practice for female tutors to wear the chador if they need to appear as
supporters of the government. She adds that many do it because they
need to keep their jobs, and therefore it is expected of them because it
demonstrates political cohesion even if there is none! With a wry ironic
smile she continues to say that some time ago when she visited her
brother in Europe, he asked her to forgo any form of headscarf because in his neighbourhood people would associate dress codes for
Muslim women with negative political activity. My friend adds that her
brother's concern in this instance was not to lose his credibility, and
that he was forced to safeguard his professional standing in the so perceived developed world by asking his sister to appear in public without
a headscarf. Although this is not funny at all, noting the irony we look
at one another and burst into laughter.

Before we have a chance to discuss this further however, she continues to explain her second point. This is related to what is expected
of me in the session. I am told that students are very bright and have a
great relationship with her and would do well if there was an opportunity for discussing ideas. She explains that in order to be flexible and
open to my plans, she has cancelled her own teaching today and would
like to invite me to run the session. She continues that the students
would appreciate my contributions, whatever they might be, as a visitor from abroad.

Rather taken by surprise and the level of flexibility of my friend, I
struggle to find a response and wonder how to react. There is, of
course, no time to react in any way other than to start the process of
what to say to the students and how to say it. We pause in the corridor
where three young and energetic female students rush over to their

tutor to say hello. I notice their informal manner and rapport with her, and amongst themselves.

The session

The room is large and airy, and eight students are already in their seats. The three young women sit together on the front row. Two are in black maghna'eh, very short tight black roopoosh over dark jeans, and fitted bomber jackets; their backpacks are placed at their feet. The third is in a black headscarf and a black chador over a cream bomber jacket. The tutor guides me to the podium and introduces me before she sits with the students. I find standing behind a lectern on a raised platform disconcerting and reflect on the situation as I prepare my notebook and try to gather my thoughts. I speak about forms of qualitative research compared to quantitative work and give some examples. I explain my own preference for ethnographic observation, as a form of analysis. I explain the importance and relevance of the consideration of the lived experience of individuals in understanding complexities of behaviours and societies. I conclude with the value and contribution of such documented experiences to social history. All except one student listen with interest and engage with the ideas I have proposed and discussed to some degree. The disinterested young women is sitting on the front row and keeps herself busy by looking at her books and sipping at her soft drink. Some thirty minutes pass and I ask the group if they would like to develop this discussion by participating and reflecting on their own experiences.

A young woman in the second row announces that she would like to listen rather than speak. An older pious looking woman at the back introduces herself as Manijeh, a masters student who has joined these sessions for a term because she is required to have an extra history module before she is able to write and submit her dissertation. She speaks about the psychological damages the imposed war with Iraq has brought the nation, and how issues and layers of emotional damage are hardly addressed. She adds that she had to get married to her fiance in 1981 in the middle of the war and bombardment. She elaborates that she was denied the traditional wedding ceremonies and party as 'one of the most beautiful experiences' of her life because of war. She says she 'regrets' the fact that she had to be satisfied with a very simple signing ceremony, before her husband departed for the front. She says that being left like that was too much to endure and a big sacrifice, and how this new generation of women do not know what 'sacrifice' means and have no regard for 'values'.

At this point the young woman in the front of the class who had been reading a book sits up and turns towards Manijeh and asks her exactly what these values she refers to are. Instead of receiving a reply from Manijeh, a young man in the second row joins in the discussion and explains that 'values' must mean the directions and aims set by familial traditions, which are ultimately those values set by religion, and the duties expected by God. He announces he is from a religious family, and although he finds complying difficult, and often feels 'like a prisoner holding all desire and emotion harnessed within', he perseveres with doing what is right and expected of him. All three girls in the front turn around and look at him with outrage. One older man gets up and leaves the session discretely. One of the three women asks the young man if he has ever asked himself where these values originate from, who sets them, and why? The young man has no reply and simply repeats what he has said previously, implying that his family know and that is good enough. The young woman from the front turns back to Manijeh and says:

> What is the point of regretting? And if your criticism is pointed at us because of our free social behaviours, or ways of dressing, laughing aloud in the corridor with the boys, or our freedom in expressing views, then I must tell you it is precisely because we don't want to have the 'regrets' you were talking about that we push the these boundaries.

The third young woman in the front row wearing a chador joins in, she says that she has extremely religious grandparents and she debates with them on a daily basis how religious acts must remain a private matter.

A second young man in the middle row joins in and says he does not understand why women are disturbed when there is a discussion of religious identity and tradition. Agitated grunts, but also firm and decisive replies come from the young women in the front row, and one says:

> You are the beneficiary of these identities, that is why you feel comfortable, that is why you do not wish to question anything, because tradition and religion promote your interests. You have become lazy, you are content with what is given, but I have to think about what such identities mean for me, in relation to my

mind, my thinking … and my life. I do not wish to accept every-thing pushed onto me so easily. That's why we seem agitated.

The young woman in the chador concludes that she is deeply religious but she can also imagine how things could improve.

A latecomer who has joined the session during these discussions seems rather puzzled and looks towards her tutor and me for some explanation. Instead of explaining to him the reasons for my presence on the podium and the context for the debate, I ask the history tutor's permission to conclude the session. I close the session by thanking everyone for their contribution and thought provoking ideas.

Back to central Tehran

Outside in the corridor, the three young women are eager to continue the discussion, and since this was the day's last session they suggest that we, including the tutor who has been very quiet, leave the campus and catch the metro to central Tehran and perhaps go to a coffee shop.

It is a tight squeeze with the five of us in the taxi, the tutor is next to the driver in the front, and in the back I am a little overwhelmed with all the large sunglasses, quilted jackets, and backpacks. The energy and determination of the young women, however, is gripping. They say that although the two young men in the history class spend much time with them, when it comes to debating ideas they often repeat something they have been told by their mothers, or worse by their Ethics tutors. The young women continue their earlier line of argu-ment about how some male students are reluctant to understand that their social interactions with girls on campuses cannot be viewed ex-ternal to the rest of their beliefs and lives.

The student with the chador says specifically that boys tend to trivi-alize social engagement with girls because it is much easier for them to simplify everything down to 'it is our tradition' and revert to the safety of the cliche and formulaic! Her friend stresses, however, that her boy-friend is not like that at all, and that is why they can be such good friends and hold discussions about numerous ideas as well as religious identity and familial tradition. She invites me to follow her to a reli-gious procession in her neighbourhood to see for myself.

When we arrive at the metro station, I note that collectively, we ap-proach the carriage for women. There is a vendor in the carriage selling knitted hats, brimmed berets, with matching scarves. She allows other women to examine the merchandise freely and try the hats on, either over headscarves or directly on their head lifting their headwear. It occurs to me that for those who believe in keeping the hejab, this seclusion offers some freedom of movement. I am also reminded of the concept of the *biruni* and *andaruni* in architecture as well as social life, and discuss the idea of a private interior within the public sphere with the students and the tutor. They say that indeed many women welcome the segregated metro and buses especially during the rush hour when there are simply too many bodies and absolutely no personal space. They say some welcome these carriages as a shelter from the male gaze.

The vendor reaches us at this point, and I realize the knitted hats and scarves are made in China. They are in pale creams, white, and ash-grey tones. The idea that China might influence the colour range in ladies headwear in the Islamic Republic of Iran is globalization of a fascinating nature. The girls laugh at my observation, and when finished with us, the vendor puts on her chador, gathers her goods and prepares to leave the metro.

I ask the group whether in fact religious practices and praying might have been what was meant by 'values' when Manijeh spoke earlier during the session. I am quickly put right and told that 'values' essentially mean young men have to imagine themselves as selfless martyrs and young women as pure virgins. They explain that especially in the context of the session 'values' is behaving modestly and without too much expression. They explain that this is the perception of the pious which differs amongst families, and that it should not be mistaken for the views of all. One reiterates that debating socio-cultural elements in society and having a political voice is normal amongst urban classes and is viewed completely separate to individual's chastity. Another suggests that there ought to be debates about sexuality too, in terms of entitlement and not in terms of upholding morality. At this point I request a fuller explanation, they come up with a collective statement and I take notes as follows:

> Although practiced widely, young people's sexuality is taboo, it is considered immoral and an embarrassment. This is unnatural because sexuality is about love and understanding, it is a question of entitlement too, as humans one needs to experiment and explore bodies. What does it mean to be hot, am I hot? We want to know and understand these things. Just because these things are private and intimate it does not mean they are irrelevant and triv-

ial! There are too many boundaries about our bodies in our society which promote us to develop a profound sense of duality. We practice one thing, and appear to say something else, sometimes we don't even realize this sense of duality in ourselves, but we see it in others.

The student in the chador speaks specifically about sexuality and virginity as an issue more for parents than for the youth. Unexpectedly, she says that she prays and fasts and has a boyfriend too, but they keep their sexual explorations separate from their religious practices of praying and fasting. She adds that if they get married, which they intend to do, then their sexual practices now are merely the prelude to a deeper partnership in the future. But if something happens and they are forced to search for new partners, then that is life, and she would think about finding solutions for not being a virgin when the time comes. She says that her father is a war veteran who was sent to France by the government, and they lived there for one year. Whilst there, she says, she observed how young French people found partners at secondary school and learned about their bodies as well as love. She adds that she tells her grandparents that times have changed and she has different ideas, even if she will never tell them about her boyfriend. The two other students agree with her, and one says 'You must not be fooled by the chador', and the other concludes:

> There is no denying that being strong is attractive. My boyfriend likes me because I am outspoken and playful, and I would not be controlled. We want to reject any control over our bodies and minds. Surely it is about ownership and living a life of our own. If I am old enough to vote at 16, then I am old enough to be curious about my sexuality.

The history tutor leaves us at the following stop. I ask the three girls why she was quiet. They explain that tutors keep their judgement and views to themselves unless they know everyone present very well or if they are specifically asked to give advice, which they would in private. Around this time we come to the end of the metro and say our goodbyes and exchange email addresses. I have to catch a route taxi to take me to my neighbourhood; as I wait in the long queue I reflect on how these young women challenge received perceptions, and how as they do so they locate ideas as if building blocks with which to shape or construct identities. These are meaningful and measured, formed with passion and rationality and according to their time, and place in the world. For them, it is not a question of forgetting who they are as Muslim Iranians but rather remembering who they wish to be.

Innovative public expressions

Welcoming the invitation extended to me to attend the religious gathering, I join Naahid in Nobakht Street in a mid-town residential neighbourhood. She explains that many of the households take the religious rituals of Ramadan and Moharam to heart, and during the months of fast and remembrance, they provide and distribute freshly prepared foods to the needy as well as their neighbours. Before Naahid and her boyfriend leave me to explore, she talks about the kinds of people who live in this neighbourhood, many are middle merchants from the Bazar who are usually considered to be traditional. Some are civil servants in the Oil Company, and some are teachers and small fruit farm owners. I note that we are on a perfectly ordinary street with a few small but well stocked grocery shops, a *sangak*[72] bread shop, a butcher's, and a small mosque. On both sides of the street there are two- or three-storey houses with courtyards, most of which have been converted into apartments. She explains that in the last few years the neighbourhood girls have invited themselves to participate in the Moharam procession and march with the men.

It is the eve of Ashoora, the 10th of the month of Moharam in the Islamic lunar calendar and highly significant date for Shi'ite Muslims.[73] Ashoora commemorates the martyrdom of the third Shi'ite Imam, Hossein the grandson of the Prophet, who was killed in the Battle of Karbala along with 72 of his followers. The belief is that Imam Hossein had not sought violence, and should be remembered for his steadfast principles of honour and courage not giving into the deceit of those who considered themselves the successors of Prophet Mohammad. The month-long period of remembrance has been part of the lives of Muslim Iranians since its adoption by the Safavid Court in early sixteenth century. The Ashoora processions are expressions of public solidarity in mourning the tragedy of Karbala and Hossein's martyrdom with chants, beating of drums, and forms of flagellation. The processions can be very colourful and moving, led by men carrying very large standards, banners and emblems each spanning several metres in width and height. Numerous black and green flags symbolizing mourning and Islam are also carried, and according to the imagination and creativity of those who take part, there might be other artefacts referencing this historic date. Expressions of public grief, Qoranic recitations, and sermons continue at mosques, with the latter assuming more of a political tone in favour of the government in recent decades.

Candle-lit vigil during Ashoora

This evening's procession is elaborate with a front line of banners and emblems carried by several strong neighbourhood men. I am however struck by the participation of the women in the procession itself. Traditionally women keep to an observational position in the margins away from the procession itself, or watch from windows and balconies. The women here, in tens of rows, are mostly young and walk immediately behind the lines of men without a strict barrier or distance kept between them. Being the eve of Ashoora, they carry lit candles and walk in silence and in an orderly solemn manner as if imagining those who lost lives at the end of the battle. On the sidewalks, separated from the street by a ditch of running water, many men and women move forward with the procession. These women are of all generations and although mostly in black clothes worn on such occasions, there are also many wearing colourful expressive scarves. Younger women especially, look bright and cheerful and untraditionally, for such occasions, have fully made-up faces and walk hand in hand with young men. Their often elegant make-up shows off their expressive eyes and styled eyebrows and lips, as if well considered drawings. Their 'high-lighted' hair colour appear more prominent pushing out of their bright and shiny headscarves. I am told that this metallic shiny look is the current fashion and I note how they echo the glistening metallic mobile phones many people carry.

The procession arrives at the mosque a few hundred metres up the road. There are lines and lines of women and children in front of the neighbourhood mosque which is decorated with hundreds of coloured lights and religious flags. Three vast mourning standards several metres wide and high look magnificent against the mosque walls. They are draped in emerald green and black woven cloth and are made of metal alloys with intricate filigree designs adorned with peacock feathers. They are beautiful as they powerfully occupy space.

My eyes move back to the people, standing in large clusters and sitting on the pavements, and I soon realize this is a candle-lit vigil. Women and men together, shoulder to shoulder, almost everybody holds and lights candles. A few very young boys and girls distribute the candles free of charge. I estimate the crowd to be around 1000, and pull my camera out of my pocket and photograph the legs and feet of the women sitting on the ground. I hear a voice saying 'Be careful the *sepaah*[74] [revolutionary guards] are watching'. An older woman says 'Let her take her photographs'. A young one suggests she should deliver a speech in remembrance of Zeynab, Imam Hossein's sister and the Prophet's granddaughter who delivered a political speech on Ashoora when the news of her brother's martyrdom reached her tent. Having taken two photographs I proceed to light my candle, and finally move towards the tent where fresh hot scented tea and pastries are served to the public as alms.

Drinking my tea I reflect on this innovative expression of religion and ritual, and the way the public sphere is claimed for a public display of shared and meaningful identities. The neighbourhood women and men collaborate and interconnect religious historicity and consciousness with their own political perceptions while the sepaah keep watch. I am reminded of an art tutor I have met at Al-Zahra University who explained her private relationship with Islam as follows:

I have been teaching art for the last 18 years at two universities, whilst also practicing and regularly exhibiting my paintings. I am exploring ideas of scale and geometry at present. The famous saying from Madineh Fazeleh *'Do not enter if you do not grasp geometry'* is never too far from my mind when I work in the studio. As you know, this is a reference to the holy shrine/ mosque in the city of Madineh in Saudi Arabia, the place where the Prophet Mohammad was buried. It is a highly regarded and venerated venue for those who attend the Hajj ceremonies in Mecca in Saudi Arabia. This statement has a symbolic meaning as if etched on my psyche. I find most of my Muslim identity just from that statement; its meaning and abstraction offer vast spiritual worlds when contemplated. This concept of geometry becomes literally and intellectually multi-dimensional for me. It provides me with room to be autonomous and imaginative about this heritage of ours. Just think about the significance of geometry in the arts of Muslim civilizations to date. Just think of it as philosophy, and as the structure and formal order of matter. As a tutor I take such ideas forward with my students, these ideas are my tools. This is the meaning of Islam for me, not the headscarf. There are considerable numbers of us you know, women, contributing, and defying restrictions as much as we can. I for one refuse to apply self-censorship and insist on thinking freely, despite the headscarf. You cannot touch my mind.

Reflecting on the vast possibilities in interpreting Islam I move away, past the women sitting on the pavement. I hear myself say there is no 'axis of evil' here, just an axis of intelligence, courage and agency where women play a significant role.[75]

Part Two: Private spaces
The painting studio

Student's nude self-portrait

I am invited to visit the Faculty of Applied Arts and Crafts at Al-Zahra University for Women, the only national university for an all-female student body taught by both male and female tutors. Some of these are clerics who teach Islamic theory and jurisprudence across disciplines. Al-Zahra was founded in 1964 during the Pahlavi regime as The Institute of Higher Education for Girls. It was renamed for a very brief period to 'Mahboobeh Motahedin Institute', a political activist, immediately after the Revolution, and was finally registered as Al-Zahra University for Women in the memory of the Prophet's daughter Fatemeh Zahra. The University is built on the grounds of a small shrine and orchards in rural Vanak in north west Tehran, which was a specific donation by a nineteenth century courtier for the sole purpose of educating women, and not necessarily because of Islamic ideology. However, it has made higher education available to vast numbers of young women whose familial traditions are not in favour of co-education, and those who are sympathetic to the hard-line policies of the regime. The previous Chancellor, Dr Zahra Rahnavard, also a practicing artist and academic, and closely linked to the reform government of Mohammad Khatami, and an advisor to him on women's issues.[76] The Chancellor kept the cafeteria at Al-Zahra campus open to serve hot and cold food to the students during the month of fast when no food or drink is available in other governmental institutions. She further distributed hundreds of coloured scarves to the student body under her care in 2001 to replace the black fitted maghna'eh which has now become mandatory again under the hardliners. Seemingly simple, such radical acts require the sociological imagination to be grasped fully in the context of Iran. Whilst they are also interpreted as political spin on her behalf, they have nevertheless made a difference in expressing identities and are remembered by many students as a collaborative act. Collaboration, and the expression of subtle, personal, and intimate identities are the subject of the following paragraphs

The painting department at Al-Zahra University for Women has large and well-lit studios with big windows. It is bustling with activity and excitement during my visit because the third year painting group are showing their semester's work of self-portraits. The majority of these show fragments of the female body showing posture and flesh; they are painted selves without cover which is considered illegal. Although depicting clothed human figure is widely practiced in the visual arts in Iran, depicting the nude or exposing bare flesh is perceived erotic. Both nudity and erotic arts are categorically banned. The self-portraits here are narratives of meaning, and because they reference the idea of the nude, they will have no wider audience and will not be put on public view. They do bring innovation however when contemplated in the context of the tradition and heritage of figurative art in Iran, particularly prominent in the courts of the Safavid and Qajar dynasties from the sixteenth to the twentieth centuries. The innovation is the fact that these nudes are self-portraits executed by the young women. Instead of the male gaze and imagination, here the women address their bodies themselves. The painting tutor, an elderly eminent scholar in theory and practice and a specialist in colour harmonies has courageously collaborated with her students to create a private and safe interior space to paint identities. One student who has used her large orange headscarf in several of her painting to frame the private parts of her body rather than covering them points out:

Student self-portrait

I like to paint images of my own body, sometimes without any clothes. Well it is only a body isn't it, and we all have it, don't we? My body, your body, it is a common language that's all. I don't know what it means to paint 'beautiful' things, is something beautiful when you can't take your eyes off it?

Another joins in and says:

> We are taught in our Islamic theory class that acknowledging the *nafs*, or bodily Self, is morally damaging, and will deceive the individual into losing her soul and diverting from all that is good. I wanted to imagine and paint my body as an idea and acknowledge the fact that it exists and it functions. I also want to say to our government leave my body to me, fix the economy and poverty, and depression of young people and create jobs. To get something out of my education I need to have a job when I leave university.

Whilst such levels of socio-political awareness are commonplace, I am taken by the clarity of vision amongst these students who have understood art criticism as a radical tool, and have endeavoured to discuss their own location through it.

A private site for learning

Inspired by the above, I accompany an art student to a private home to observe a cluster of 20 year-olds drawing from life and painting identities in a life class. This will illustrate the deeper dimensions of the painting studio visited to view self-portraits. It reveals how a tool for discovering and making meaning is located, and how the life class creates an occasion to construct and relate forms of knowledge, exploring significant ideas relating the real, the intimate, and the imagined. As we shall see the life class presents itself as the autonomous location for reflection beyond the isolations experienced by its participants.

Although the observation and the study of female form and anatomy, or male, is a minority activity, the idea of it containing and reflecting qualities such as emotion, cognition, and intellect is an interesting one. The life class thus offers reflections and experiences beyond the erotic.

As indicated previously, nudity and erotic art are categorically banned in Iran as indeed in many other countries. Contrary to the predominant perceptions in the West that there are no human representations in Muslim art, the observation and depiction of humans alongside other forms in nature have remained a subject of study at art schools in Iran since the early years of the twentieth century, and have been part of the Iranian artistic expression and representation for millennia.[77] As well as seals depicting kings and queens and the nobility in Persian antiquity, amongst the oldest sculptures found are the terra-cotta nude female figurines in Susa in southwest Iran, which are recognised by experts in the field to be the most original popular artistic productions of the period in the third millennia BC.[78] Gold figurine sculptures, perhaps goddesses, as well as carved female figures in architectural panels, are more recent representations of Iran's cultural history from the Parthian era (247 BC to 224 AD).[79] In the last 1000 years, as part of Iran's heritage within Islamic civilizations, there exist exquisite ceramic vessels, plates, bowls, beakers, and other containers, which depict individuals and groups of humans, male and female, in contemplation and in hunting scenes, under a second skin of glazes and enamels.[80] In the tradition of Persian classical drawing and painting, whether in large scale oils or manuscript paintings and illuminations, in colour as well as in ink, there continue to exist extensive bodies of work especially from the Safavid (1501-1722) and Qajar (1785-1925) epochs.[81] The frequency and popularity of such artistic practices however have fluctuated over time according to history and temporal religious and cultural perspectives. Their presence in the imagination of the nation remains vivid.[82]

Meet Nokteh in west Tehran

Saara and I set off at 4.30 pm to Nokteh's house, where Nokteh has initiated a life class. The apartment is located on the third floor in a four storey building with large iron gates opening onto a courtyard which can accommodate a number of cars. We take our shoes off on the landing in front of the entrance door and go in. We take a few steps down into a hall and take off our headscarves and coats. On one side of the grey marble floors there is a large salon and dining room. The large armchairs have light coloured brocaded covers, and the dining chairs, in contrast, have fitted calico covers from top to bottom. There are silk flowers in large china pots, and a few souvenir-type black African sculptures here and there. There is another sitting room visible at the end of the corridor and I imagine there must be a kitchen and utility room beyond my view. Nokteh speaks in a hushed voice and this indicates that there are members of the family about, who must not be disturbed due to siesta time. We are guided up three to four steps where there is another corridor with many doors. I imagine this is where the bedrooms are. One of these rooms is Nokteh's bedroom and we enter. I ask Nokteh's permission to take notes and she agrees. She tells me she is 21 and a painting student at Al-Zahra University for Women and has had one exhibition of her work. The works exhibited were drawings depicting young 'faceless' couples in coffee shops. She explains that she has focused on parts of their bodies like the form of their hands or heads to give them a character. She explains that today's session is part of a three month long experiment which will develop the group's formal and spatial understanding and skills. A painter acquaintance of her own age is the model. Nokteh continues:

I have compiled the history of figure painting since the Renaissance in a hundred images. When we studied the Renaissance, our tutor covered almost every single painter and every single brushstroke placed on a church wall in Italy during that period. We would do project work and often I would be given the job of researching topics in art history to investigate and report to the class. You see I love art history, and it is ridiculous to separate West and East too much. If I am to be an artist, all of art history is my heritage. After all, we wouldn't tell a quantum physicist or a philosopher to skip the parts not related to their own geographical location, would we? Besides, I am a citizen of the globe, a member of the global village, I don't want to see myself as an artist who does not know what world art is all about. I studied the whole history of divinity in Indian culture, and they have so many gods and goddesses. I also studied the Mahabharata, hundreds of pages of it. This was because I wanted to help my boyfriend with his ideas. Can you imagine, I nearly died. He is doing art at Azad University. My work at the moment is about women being sacred! I like to paint prostitutes, women working hard in boring offices behind desks and young couples in coffee shops, I paint them as saints. Well, I give them these bright colourful halos.

I am intrigued and inspired by this young woman. With just a few words she draws a picture of her world; this is a big world where her ideas, mind, and imagination can rise beyond geographical and cultural boundaries. She has determined her artistic identity to be complex and multi-dimensional.

Drawing from life

By this time three other young women have arrived, and Nokteh introduces me as a researcher while rushing around and re-arranging the curtains. I look towards the end of the room and position myself in the corner diagonal to the door, I can observe everything from this point.

Katti is the model, the other two are Bita and Saba. It is interesting to note everyone's personal way of dress in this private house. The media, and the television networks especially, are obliged by law to show Iranian women observing forms of hejab at all times, even in the intimate interiors of their homes. This is not the case of course since even the most pious dress as they wish at home in the company of their blood male relatives, i.e. fathers, sons, brothers, and paternal and maternal uncles. I have observed several young women who wear the fullest hejab as an outer garment in the public space, but wear cropped tops and fashionable 'hipster' jeans at home, occasionally showing off tattooed motifs above a studded belt. Nokteh wears her hair up with a large bright double sided hairclip the colour of crushed strawberries. She wears a blue short-sleeved baggy shirt and light grey cropped three-quarter length trousers with wide fold-ups. The other girls wear tops held up by the lightest ribbon-like straps and shorts, short skirts and jeans with slashed and torn areas, showing the skin underneath. As I write my notes Nokteh says that I should mention the fact that she has done a major tidy-up and pushed everything either against the walls or under the bed to create space. She adds 'Oh yes, tell them that the curtains are well drawn so nobody can see us', and with this she laughs. She is making a reference to creating a sanctuary away from any unwanted gaze, or report to the moral police about young women undressing in front of a window. I immediately realize I am sharing a private world created to conceptualize ideas, and to imagine and put to practice those ideas creatively.

I notice how Katti holds her shoulders, almost up to the top of her ears initially, but as she proceeds with her job of modelling they relax and find their right place. She folds her blue sleeveless t-shirt and brown cotton trousers neatly and places them on the corner of the bed. She stands against the built-in wardrobe, the brass handle and key hole of which are almost parallel with her right breast. There is a slight difference in colour and a faint bikini line around her breasts. Her briefs are folded over slightly so that the change of plain in her anatomy becomes visible. She thus shows a delicate yet sharp curve from her waist to the top of her hips. She has a lean body with soft, almost invisible muscle structure. As others prepare themselves Katti practices a number of poses and a range of positions until she finds the exact formal arrangement she has in mind. Then, she keeps her body firmly in the pose with an air of confidence. She announces that this first pose is thirty minutes long and the only standing one she is planning to do. As if a gentle warning, she establishes her authority and ownership of the situation. Understandably, to keep the body straight and locked in position for any length of time requires discipline and concentration. She puts her watch propped up on the floor in front of her toes to keep time.

Nokteh has been searching for a particular CD, she is very specific about her music. She gives me the details: it is track five of Bach's Messiah-moll Sanctus. The CD player/stereo set is placed at the bottom of the bed against the wall near the door. I note how like the model the five of us have found our positions for observation and work. I have placed myself at the end corner of the room sitting on a stool against a small desk. On my right, Saara and Saba are sitting cross-legged on the bed. Opposite me, the other end of the room, the model is standing cheerful and relaxed. In front of me on the floor Nokteh is wriggling to free and relax her right arm in order to draw better, and Bita is sitting leaning against the wall on the left. These two girls on the floor have one leg stretched in front them while holding the other knee up to rest their clipboards against. Everyone has size A3 paper fastened to clipboards and several types of drawing pencils. Nobody speaks. Everyone works with fast but gentle strokes as if creating a territory for the landscape of the body on paper. Gradually a range of shapes and interlocking forms and perspectives become visible on each drawing paper. Nokteh has located and articulated a likeness of just the model's head and shoulders on a long body resembling a column, as if she is particularly interested in the headness of the head, she draws a halo around it.

Time is up and the model stops. Nokteh gets up and says if she does not fetch the tea from downstairs it will get useless and lose its colour and scent. I expect someone has been instructed to brew the tea for this exact time. On her way out as she pushes her feet into her strappy slippers she looks at Saara's drawing and says 'What's this rubbish' and they laugh. The model puts on her t-shirt. Bita looks at Saara's drawing and Saara says that she is looking for some new 'relationships' in her drawings to help her with her current project. Saba is still drawing, she shades areas of her drawing from memory now.

Tea arrives on a tray with some chocolate, a large bar that has been sliced. It is delicious. I ask the model if she draws and paints. She says she does, and adds that although this is work, she actually enjoys it because it is a kind of interaction and communication with others through the language of the body and form. She says she sometimes makes friends with people through her modelling. It becomes clear that she does this often.

I ask the group if men have models to draw from. Yes, is the response, there are some girls who model for men, or mixed groups, privately. They say they feel more comfortable to have exclusively female groups. They explain that there is a drawing club where men model for a mixed group but you have to be an art student in order to become a member and participate. They stress the fact that it is not legal. I ask the group why it is that they insist on drawing the figure. Nokteh says:

> I am studying the 'sacred', by which I mean the idea of the sacred. I want to show this with the female body, sometimes at rest, or holding a child, a prostitute perhaps, or women at work behind a desk in a boring office. I need to feel the jigsaw in the human anatomy with my mind's eye, and then onto my paper with my hand.

Bita says:

> I am interested in the skin's response to light. I want to understand the variety of textures and luminosity through the skin. I don't go to art school but I paint a lot.

Saba says she is about to graduate from Al-Zahra University, and has a place to do an MA at Honar University already. She says:

> I just love the figure, female figure, because of its formal qualities, it is beautiful. I love to draw it because its parts relate to one another. I know this will feed into my work. Natural organic forms are related, they could be in the body or in other parts of nature. But I actually enjoy drawing the female form for itself.

I am told that Saba has recently got married and her husband is as young as herself and is a Theatre and Performance student at Tehran University. They have known one another for eight years since their early teens, and have come to Tehran from Garmsaar, not a particularly large town near Tehran. They have no intention to go back, they like Tehran. Saara says:

> I don't like figure painting at all. I did it for two years and then a tutor suggested it was my best work and that I could be the painter of families. He put me off with this suggestion. I am interested in abstraction and want to find the relationships between line and form. There is a sense of rhythm in the body; things, I mean parts of the body fit together. These life classes train my mind and hand to coordinate. These feed into my current work which are patches of abstract colour built into large formal structures. I have spent the summer researching the works of the great sixteenth century master of painting Reza Abbasi at his museum.

It is now ten minutes since we started the tea break and Nokteh is changing the music. Katti takes off her t-shirt again and experiments with some poses in a sitting position on a dark brown wooden chair. The music is medieval Spanish/Andalucían with Jewish players, not unlike some old Persian melodies. The model is now settled on the chair at an angle as if about to turn across the seat, with one arm disappearing behind her back and the other at her side, palm pushing onto the seat. Saara asks for a more acute angle and the model Katti adjusts her knees more to the side of the chair. The group proceed with their drawings.

I am sitting behind the group and really wish that I had a video camera. I notice a book near the model's chair, Nokteh placed it there a few moments ago. I leave my post and take a few steps and pick it up. Everyone is drawing. I look at the book, it is *Fra Angelico*, Phaidon 1992, with a stamp from Honar University Library.

It is now 20 minutes since this pose started and the group break for a rest. The atmosphere has become more reflective and there is less chatting. There is a change of music with a new pose, Nokteh plays a CD of the Sufi music of the late Nosrat-Fateh Ali Khan from Pakistan. Katti is sitting on her chair at an angle making a diagonal line with her body, with the left knee up on the chair against the torso, left upper arm almost under her left breast, the right arm over the thigh at an angle. Some time passes, and Bita asks the model to remove her hand from her thigh, qualifying her request by saying 'if that is OK with everyone'. On Saara's paper I see a number of diagonal lines directly

relating Katti's pose but with an abstract structure of many triangles.
There is another break.

Nokteh and I speak about Fra Angelico. I ask her what she will say
to people who believe Western art can only belong to, or be understood in a certain way by Westerners. She laughs and says 'People can
say what they wish. But look at it', she shows me one of the plates
which is 'The Virgin and Child Enthroned with Four Angels'. She says:

> These are familiar to us, we have interiors like these; I look at the
> organization of the space and the whole content, the story, and I
> look at the colour pallet. The subject in painting during these pe-
> riods was usually about some aspect of Christ's life, that is true,
> but many ideas in these paintings are not dissimilar to some Per-
> sian paintings we have discussed in the history of painting in
> Islamic civilization. If you study art history you can see the con-
> nections between early *Bizance* art, and the late Gothic period and
> some Persian illuminated manuscripts. There have been influ-
> ences from East to West. We know that the pre-Islamic tradition
> of the arts of the book in Iran didn't just die. Ideas come back in
> different ways. So, if we know that early and late Byzantine art
> are related to late Gothic, then we can understand Fra Angelico
> on many more levels. In any case in the end artists tell viewers a
> kind of visual story which has something to do with life. Anyway
> we are artists, we imagine. We have studied these things, we
> know who came before who, and who came after. Unfortunately
> most of the best Persian art is in Paris, London and New York,
> so as Iranians we cannot actually see them and handle them, they
> are kept in the best museums in the world. We don't say why do
> those museums want our art? It's art, it belongs to everyone.
> Anyway I respond to art emotionally which is not with words,
> but I hope I shall never be so ignorant as to say that the West
> should not discover understanding and emotion in colour or
> content of the arts of the East.

Saara joins in:

> I never think about what belongs to who in art, maybe I know a
> lot more about Western art than many in the West. I am doing
> what I like, I don't really care, there is no need to make a speech
> about it. I have spent months in Reza Abbasi Museum studying
> his paintings which foreigners call miniatures. I am interested to
> see whether I can recognise the elements in the Isfahan School

of painting from sixteenth to eighteenth centuries. It's a question of understanding.

Saba gets up and looks at everyone's work but does not offer any comment at first. I ask her specifically, and she says:

> I don't know anything. I am not a teacher. We had this professor at Al-Zahra, Dr Mazaheri, she taught us World Civilizations and took us back and forth discussing cultural influences from the East to West and back again. We had three years with her learning about the Persian Empire and its architectural remains, its motifs and the shape of its columns. Then we did Mithraic Persia during the Parthians' rule, then to Christian Rome, and Rome to Ravenna to Constantinople, and to Egypt and Damascus and Andalusia. She showed us slides and I have seen fragments of textiles in our own museums. She made sure we understood that there was no end, and she always stressed on the evolution of ideas.

The others join in with humour, offering catchphrases they remember from Professor Mazaheri's sessions. Nokteh says:

> She would say, 'Now my dear girls, you should see Alhambra palace in order to understand how a ceiling could represent the celestial world, or how water could become sculpture! By the way does anyone know why she pronounced Taj Mahal, Taj *Mohal*?

The life class continues with its work and art-historical reminiscences. Confidence and the ability to be at once Iranian and Eastern as well as open to world art allows drawing from life to be meaningful to the young women. Thus worlds are accessed and imagined in a continuum rather than in conflict. Early scriptoriums in Egypt in the first centuries of Christianity are mentioned by the students where monks and nuns lived a life of prayer and toil together, and made copies of the Bible. Charlemagne is remembered to have developed a passion for illuminated manuscripts having exchanged gifts and ambassadors with the Muslim world under the Caliphate of Harun al-Rashid in Baghdad (789-809 AD). And then Katti announces the length of the last pose.

Nokteh tells me about the art class she teaches in a primary school once a week. She explains how she once encouraged the children, ten year-olds, to imagine what would happen if sheep could fly! She explains how this was a great exercise to get the children to imagine extraordinary things outside the reality of life. She says they did some wonderful drawings/paintings, and gets up quickly to get their work from a pile of papers next to the DVD player. These are notebooks as well as loose papers. Katti, who has been listening makes a statement:

> You should get the pupils to draw and paint on suitable A4 and A3 paper, rather than in their lined notebooks or loose pieces of paper. The children need to imagine their work as paintings or 'creative' work rather than some kind of homework. After all it is presenting art!

At 7.30 pm the session ends. I notice again how Katti holds her body when not posing and not needing to present her body.

Downstairs while putting on our headscarves and coats each person pays their share of the costs and Nokteh puts the money in an envelope and hands it to Katti. They do not accept my share, as I am their guest. I thank them for allowing me to sit in their session, and to have insights to this very creative private world. They announce the next session at Saba's house. We all pour into Nokteh's car, borrowed from her mother, and she drives us to central Tehran to an exhibition. There is some negotiation as to which roads to take, and we feel our way through the traffic and the various one-way systems before we get there. Nokteh's headscarf falls to her shoulders twice, but she ignores it for a while. I sense she wishes to exercise power for a few moments resisting the law; and then I note she puts it back on again with just one hand, whilst driving with the other. I can see she has been practicing and is quite quick. Others are talking noisily in the back about the qualities of a perfect lipstick.

This is when I ask Nokteh why she is interested in the idea of the sacred. She tells me that just over a year ago, when she was not yet 20, she was arrested because she was talking casually to three of her male friends in the street. She says she has got over it because this sort of thing happened to many young women because for a while there were disagreement between factions in the government. She says that she has many male friends as she does female, and on this particular occasion she was taken to the police station for questioning, on the possibility that she might be a prostitute. She adds that her parents were informed and came to the police station to bear witness that she was not a prostitute. She says it took 72 hours before she was proved innocent and released. She says that she met a lot of different women in the prison where she was kept for most of that 72 hour period.

Some had stolen money and were involved in drug trafficking and some were poor prostitutes. She explains that rich prostitutes have a list for their clients and use mobile phones rather than hang around on roads and be arrested. She concludes that in her eyes all of these women were in a way innocent, so she would paint them as sacred.

Dumbfounded at the straight forwardness of Nokteh's account and analysis of her experience, and compelled by her profound sense of integrity and self-worth, I stop myself from enquiring any further. I choose to make absent her specific memories of prison in words and reflect on the pertinence of her critical intelligence, and making emotional repair through art in a dialogue of colour and paint and reality and imagination.

The exhibition

'Drawing from life', engaging with experience at one level, and with perception and imagination on another is precisely what is in store for us when we arrive at Tehran Museum of Contemporary Art. For a period of time, and to a notable extent it overcame the complexities of power politics in relation to artistic expression and artistic freedom, other than nudity. Under the banner of 'New Art', the Museum has held three extended exhibitions of 'conceptual' art where numerous male and female artists have imagined, explored, experimented, and created installations, performance art, happenings, video art, and web art engaging with the digital technologies.

On this occasion the exhibits are numerous, and many demonstrate highly sensitive and original visual vocabulary succinctly locked into the grammar of current trends in art globally while also relating poignant local narratives. One exhibit is particularly haunting and exciting. The work starts as a sound piece. This is an intermittent and penetrating female voice, a soundscape which rings through the museum space calling out 'help ... help ... help me ... help me out of here ... I must get out ... I need to get out ... help me'. The quality of the sound is alarming and compels me to look towards its direction to locate its source. I make the journey across the museum space passing many installations depicting Iranian contemporary art. I arrive at the installation. It is reachable by a narrow set of constructed stairs, at the top of which two black and white video projections of the same face become visible. One face is deep in the ground as if at the base of a constructed cylindrical water well. Looking up the face calls for help. The other projection of the face is fixed to the ceiling several metres up, and placed precisely opposite the opening of the well looking into it. The image in the ceiling is silent but animate. I am gripped by the juxtapositioning of the sound and the site of the installation on the one hand, and the two images of 'Self' face to face, on the other. I reflect on the idea of 'inaudibility', being and feeling ultimately alone in life in a singular existence. The piece is relevant to the life of many in Iran perhaps, rising from the lived experience of individuals, male as well as female, in contemporary Iran. But also evidence of a state of mind anywhere in the world, reflecting on the notion of isolation, alienation, and entrapment. Despite the complexity and specificity of its locale, the piece travels beyond boundaries and reflects on human condition globally. Such visual and aural deconstruction or dialogue cannot be confined to a specific geography at the beginning of the twenty-first century.

I move through the gallery to find the art students. I come across a large scale photography installation. It shows urban spaces in the streets of Tehran. As if wallpaper, the installation wraps itself around the walls of the long and curved corridors of the spiral architecture of the museum, creating illusions of distance and perspective. The forms, colours, and atmosphere are familiar yet surprising. One is confronted by a chain of visual metaphors depicting vitality and life, and decay. Skilfully captured through the strength of the photographer's lens, the images show Tehranis, including girls with their own sartorial brand of resistance. In colourful and expressive summer roopoosh, scarves, and makeup, the latter mingle amongst the congested traffic jams of old battered cars. The old and battered machinery remain static, devoid of hope, while the young women are on the move, weaving a path forward.

The Margins

The brief narratives that follow are reflections by taxi drivers who's views, directly or indirectly, express their concerns about who they are, defining and redefining themselves through a critique of others. In the orange taxi the driver sends a message to the West just as soon as he realizes his passenger lives there. The 'private car' taxi driver speaks of having started a dialogue with his daughters as a result of having been culturally isolated in Holland as an immigrant. Such cultural interface has pained him but has also facilitated a better understanding of the needs of his young daughters. The subsequent agency taxi driver is concerned about his persona as a retired man, whilst also being mindful of how to protect the nation from the chaos and disorder Western values might introduce to the society he belongs to.

Tehran orange taxi

I see you are carrying a tape-recorder. Are you actually recording? Are you a journalist? Are you recording me now? Is your machine on?

Oh a researcher! Who for, the British? Are you sure that is wise? Imagine that, an Iranian woman researching her book to be published in Britain. Imagine that!

Be careful, the British have a history of colonialism, don't add to their bank of information. Of course, of course, knowledge is important. I suppose what I mean is that they know what to do with knowledge there. They allocate budgets to collecting knowledge, but what do they do with it? They make knowledge which others have to buy from them.

But tell me this: what good is recording the sounds of taxis and motorbikes in the middle of the Bazar to research? How does that work?

Oh I see, just experimenting with the new tape-recorder. You should record sounds up-town, at least there is less pollution up-town. Imagine it, recording the sounds of the Bazar!

Can I ask you something? Can I send a message to the West through you? Will you tell them this from me? Will you tell them about the poet who says:

I am the eagle…

I am the eagle sitting on the barn wall

I am the eagle sitting on the barn wall because my wing is injured today

My wing is injured today and I am sitting on the barn wall

Oh you beautiful owl, you have your barn

Oh you beautiful owl, you are safe in your barn

But I am the eagle, I fly the greatest of heights
I am the eagle, and this barn is not my place of flight
It is just today that I am sitting on the barn wall, oh you
beautiful owl
Because my wing is injured today

Will you tell them about the poet?'

The private car taxi

I have to supplement my income by driving a taxi, I am a junior
clerk in the government and the only member of my family with
secondary school education, it was really something when I got
my high school diploma. Like many, I lost everything to the war
when Saddam Hossein attacked Iran. I left my wife behind and
fled to Europe in search of work and safety. I was in an immigra-
tion camp in Holland for one year hoping to bring my family
over once I got the right papers, but it did not suit me. I did not
think I could sustain a whole existence there, even if I had my
family with me. Something to do with the soul I think. To be so-
cially isolated indefinitely is difficult I thought. It is one's identity,
it becomes meaningless under such circumstances, or perhaps
you could say it intensifies. In the end I returned.

I have two daughters, they are 18 and 16 year-olds. One is beginning to prepare for university and I am not sure how I am going
to pay for it all when they are both at university but I want them
to develop their ideas and dreams. I have learnt from my experiences in Holland and listen to them and try to see things from
their point of view, try to understand their desires. They talk to
me about what it takes in our society to be independently
minded. I used to think independence for girls was vulgar for
families such as ours, god fearing I mean, but I have changed my
mind. They are teaching me, and I remember what it was like in
Holland, where I did not feel I belonged. My wife and I have always had a traditional existence, and it was not right for her to
dress like our daughters because we were a different generation.
But my girls, they teach us about life today

Taxi driver from the agency

I see you are heading for the Museum again. Are you some kind of artist? I am asking because I am interested in the arts. I have never had an opportunity to study it, but, well, I make models of aeroplanes – well I used to make them. In fact you might say I was good at it because a research institution got wind of it and bought the whole lot. I believe they have made a permanent show of the collection in their company. They were taken by my ideas. They asked me if I was an inventor! You see I would look at lots of pictures of planes in technical periodicals and based on what I saw I would make them from pieces of carved and polished wood in 3D. Sometimes I would juxtapose parts according to my own intuition to see what the new finished piece might look like according to my imagination. I really enjoyed crafting them – making them smooth and beautiful. I feel I could have done something more concrete with my ideas, but when you do not have the right qualifications it is very difficult to get a decent job in aerodynamics in the manufacturing industry. I was good at drawing as a child you see, so it stayed with me. I still make things because I am retired now, well I say I am retired, this taxi job helps me supplement my income. I have two children at university. In fact you might know one of them; he does music at Tehran University in the Faculty of Fine Arts.

This business of retirement is a joke, the cost of living is so high that no retirement benefit could stretch enough to cover costs! At any rate my lady wife would not like me around the house all the time! What do retired people do over there where you live?

Incidentally, what do you think about the – excuse me – the nudity and immoral programmes on television in the West? Now that we have satellite television our children will be influenced. What do parents think about these unsuitable programmes there? Do they have any means of protecting their children, they must have traditions, values, fears.

Text Three: Presences

This Text will draw on a chain of narrative testaments of women's strong presence in the private and public realms. The selection will take us through the heart of the their experiences in interpersonal and societal spaces. We shall see how they adapt and employ tools, minds and bodies, to examine and analyse and posit alternative trajectories relevant to their lives. We will meet Saanaaz, Esmat, Marjan, and Maryam who will demonstrate how they have created solid and autonomous structures in their personal lives to specifically change the mindsets of their male relatives. Their narratives demonstrate their sense of agency, ambition for self-development and self-reliance whether through higher education or economic independence. Other participants, Pariya, Soraya, Morsaleh, Maaha, Roya, and Shiva reflect on forms of participation, registering presence. Whether through playing football, riding a bicycle, going to a coffee shop, making art, writing, or having an intimate sensual encounter, the young women address social issues and thus demystify perceptions.

Meet Saanaaz

I meet Saanaaz in late afternoon at her desk in the gallery space which is currently showing the work of three young female painters. She is the curator and gallery keeper working with an entirely female management team at a cultural centre with a reputable school for teaching art history. Saanaaz appears thoughtful and reflective and explains to me how she believes that 100 such interviews, as hers with me, ought to be made and published for other women to read, describing the complexities, triumphs, and uncertainties of young women in Iran. She explains that at times people like her need sustenance, others a sense of solidarity to keep going because it is not easy yet it has to be done. She continues with the following:

> The single most important factor in my life, I would say, is economic independence. I have been working continuously since I was 18 and all through my university education. Now after five years I feel I am doing something relevant to my education and character. But finding jobs and staying employed is extremely dif-

ficult. As you know youth unemployment is one of the biggest
problems for us and for the government here. It is practically
impossible for many of us to be employed in relation to what we
have studied at university. Imagine if you have studied 'forestry'.
How many forests are there in Iran that need keeping, and therefore keeping all the graduates in forestry employed. This is
especially true if you have spent four years studying art. People
say 'What are you, a painter? That's not a job, what do you do for
work?' People still really do not make the connection that painting could or should have a commercial identity as a job, or a job
is not just sitting in an office or a factory, but it could be in a
studio. My first job was as an assistant in a nursery school looking after toddlers for working mothers; I was preparing for my
national university entrance examination at the same time. It was
just so important to earn some money, and I owe this to my
mother always telling me as I was growing up not to end up staying at home, and not to depend on a husband for finances. I
suppose these became my goal.

When you have a job you create another identity for yourself, at
least within your own family where you were brought up. I have
noticed this with my brothers and father. Becoming visible in society at large and gaining status is no longer related to taking on a
husband. At least not for a while in my case. It is not so simple
anyway; it is vastly different to when my father and mother did it.
Don't get me wrong. I would love to find someone that I could
love and talk to and ultimately share my life with when I am a little older, but, without any exaggeration, since becoming 18 I
have imagined myself only as me: Ms Saanaaz Lotfi in the workplace. Being addressed by people first and foremost as myself
rather than someone's wife or even someone's daughter is crucial
for me. If it works differently for some girls, and they feel they
must be married in order to change their circumstances, then I
am sure in their hearts they too would wish to change those particular sets of circumstances which put them in a position to
want to be married. The point is, you have to demonstrate, with
all the tools you can find, that you have and are capable of an independent mind and pocket. It becomes a goal. If this is
different for rich girls, then I would not know. I am not rich and
my parents live in rented accommodation. So perhaps it is not

just my mother who taught me about not sitting at home and becoming financially independent, perhaps it was necessity too.

My father came to Tehran for work when he was young, and he has the general view that women must be modest and simple in appearance in order not to attract men, that they should not wear makeup, at least until they get married, never be home late after school, never smoke, especially in front of him, and use the telephone only to call known friends and family rather than strangers. But I have changed all that because change was and is mandatory for a number of personal and social reasons. I remember it started with my treatment of my face and plucking and re-shaping my eyebrows when I was leaving high school. As far as my father was concerned 'a girl does not disturb the beauty of her face so long as she remains a girl and unmarried'. I remember I simply asked him whether we were talking about my face or his, and that if I was able to vote to elect the president of the country and to decide to go to university, filling in the forms for the national entrance examinations, then surely I was able to decide how to deal with my own face. You see the older generation and my father fail to see the relationships between all of these three acts: voting to be politically involved, educating yourself to have power in society, and making decisions about your own body to show your power in the family. It was some time before my father smiled at me again, but he realized that it was he who had to change his thinking, because I was going to decide for myself.

Once I completed my first year at university I realized that I wanted my work to be related to my field of study, so I started looking for a new job. Eventually I was lucky enough to find a job in publishing, working for a magazine and image composition and editing in the graphic design department. I was barely making any more money than at the nursery looking after babies, but I was pleased even though I had to wear the governmental form of hejab. I worked there for a year but became seriously short of money, especially because art materials became so much more expensive in the latter years of the course, so I had to find a fulltime job. It took one whole year before I managed to find a job in a bookshop. By this time I was not required to be on campus very much because in the fourth year all work is project-based and you are expected to start writing your dissertation and executing the practice-based finals project.

Tehran street

The new job did not finish till nine at night and I often did not get home till ten. It was particularly unpleasant in the winter in the dark because near the bookshop there is an area where prostitutes work, and even if you are not one, men would stop their cars and either shout abuse or make offers. Well that is men for you, would it occur to them at least not to shout abuse? The answer is no, it would not. It's really very difficult to sustain yourself and your job under such conditions. I am embarrassed to say that I carried a knife on my person at night when I left work in case I needed to defend myself. The interesting thing was that by this time the family, my father and two brothers particularly, viewed me as a solid element in the household because of holding down a job despite the difficulties. Being men they don't really know the subtleties of such difficulties for women, it is not their experience, and if you talk about it too much they simply say don't work, don't go to university, don't have a boy-friend. So we have to prepare them psychologically. OK, if I have to I will prepare them psychologically. I would never give up the space I have created for myself. How shall I say it, I like this more official status I have created for myself in the life of our family. It is important for me to see I have changed their opinions about young women by becoming financially independ-ent. My brothers have started talking about how important it is for them to have girlfriends or wives who are working women, not just for the sake of the economy, but for the air of confi-dence and recognition it has brought for me.

Around this time I had become close friends with a boy on my course, and it really bothered me that I could not bring him home as my boyfriend. But it was simply unheard of in our fam-ily to bring a boy home, and perhaps even an impossibility for my family to accept that I was seeing someone. My younger brothers had not ever mentioned girls in front of my parents. I thought highly of myself however and did not wish to limit my-self to seeing him outside the house only. After all, I was not one of those prostitutes who had to hide in the dark when meeting men. After thinking for some time about finding a solution I de-cided that the only way forward was to discuss this with my father, so I approached him again. This time I was much more worried about his reaction. Eyebrow shaping and wearing makeup seemed so much simpler by comparison. I sat down next to him one Thursday evening when my brothers were out, my mother was in the kitchen preparing the ingredients for Fri-day lunch, and said to him that I wanted to explain something very important about myself. He of course looked alarmed but listened. I explained that I did not want him to see me in the street with a man and be shocked, and that I had met this young man at university and wanted to invite him to our house and this was not because we had intended to be engaged or get married but simply to be friends.

He was livid, he shouted at the top of his voice saying 'Now I have to be the pimp for my own daughter, I thought you went to university to study, but this is what it has come to?' I thought he was either going to kill himself or me, that is how devastated and angry he looked. I just got up and as I was leaving the room I said that he had to change his views about relationships between men and women before marriage otherwise he would end up with his children telling him lies and doing it despite him. Then I left the room. I believe my mother came to his rescue at that point, saving him from himself. But it was very difficult for a few weeks, and he would not speak with anyone without shouting. I just had to explain to him again that I would go and live on my own if I had a job which would pay for my rent, and that if he could not think independently outside tradition, I could. I explained that I did not want to be ruled by his generation's values and the values of my aunts and uncles because he was worried about them, what they thought, rather than me. He never said yes, but I gave it a couple of months and then asked my boyfriend to come over one Friday afternoon when my brothers were at home and there was a family atmosphere with everyone watching something on television together. He tolerated it, and that is what I wanted; I cannot know or perhaps will never fully understand how he feels, whether he is changing in his heart, or whether he thinks it is right or wrong for his daughter to have a boyfriend. My mother thinks that his tolerance is in itself an unbelievable change as well as understanding.

Since you are interested in my experiences, I feel I am obliged to discuss them also within the wider context of our society. Although resistance and demand for change is becoming part of our existences as the new generation, we face severe difficulties catching up with our own liberated or intellectual selves, because we love being with our families and we want to be approved of by society. I believe our age, our generation, and our society, is a paradoxical one. We want to be free, but we also love our families and want to please them. We want to have boyfriends and be open about bringing them home to our parents, but the idea of marriage, and all that goes with it, is still at the back of our minds, we are conditioned to think about it, it is a big social issue.

Virginity is important, and at the same time it is not. The question of virginity is increasingly becoming a personal issue, contrary to our parents' generation or even people just a few years older than us. It is really related to the individual's private and social circumstances. That is why we continue to view it as an enigmatic concept; in any case where are we suppose to lose it when we suffer from a lack of privacy. For those who have got over the question of virginity there remain other serious social issues of how easy it is to change partners, and how frequently you can introduce someone new to your family. You see, it's very difficult to handle all this single-handedly and individually, we have to change the society. At the moment I am contemplating travelling with my boyfriend to look at the remaining ancient mud-brick architecture in Kerman in south-eastern Iran, but how to travel with someone you are not married to is a serious social and legal issue in our country. It will no longer be between my father and me, it will be a national scandal to end up in the same hotel room without the required documents. We could be arrested. Although many people including my friends do it, as far as the government is concerned it is illegal. To be truthful I myself doubt whether it is wise considering the circumstances. I wonder about how far I can push these restrictions. The complexities of our existences are quite exhausting. But let me also tell you this, the struggle for improving the condition of Self is ultimately the struggle for improving the condition of society. Perhaps I will find a way to travel to Kerman to look at the thousand year-old architecture, or perhaps I will have to abandon this particular one, I don't know. I could always ask my friend to marry me, but that would not work either since he is not someone I want to marry!

Clearly despite the courage, insightfulness and clarity of Saanaaz's acts, there are uncertainties alongside triumphs. This became evident to me when during our interview she dropped her voice when reflecting on the difficulties that could occur if one changed boyfriends frequently. It is clearly extremely difficult for girls to sustain the social change they create. While I was struck by the depth of Saanaaz's thoughts, and how she has obviously thought her ideas through to clarify what they might mean in the long run, I could see that wherever change occurs, in any social setting, there would follow a period of adjustment. Saanaaz's desire for being actively present in her own life as well as the life of society, and not wishing to hide that life from view is most poignant. She will no doubt continue to assert ideas, sustain considerable independence, financially and bodily, and explore paths to take her life forward. As we shall see she is not an isolated case, and the narrative continues when Esmat, Marjan, and Marzi provide us with glimpses into the ways in which they shape their lives, and while doing so they take their male relatives with them. Saanaaz's motto that 'the struggle for improving the condition of Self is ultimately the struggle for improving the condition of society' thus becomes more meaningful.

Meet Esmat

Although Esmat has not been able to undergo the processes and spaces higher education offer, as she will relate below, she too has the determination to persuade her male relatives to take up new ideas, see alternative possibilities, and change their mindsets. Her clarity in expressing her ideas however echoes that of Saanaaz's. On the day of our interview I find Esmat in her workplace, she is in a pale blue fitted shirt, long faded jeans and trainers. She wears her highlighted hair in a pony tail, and explains that she comes to work wearing a chador over her headscarf and roopoosh because most young women in her neighbourhood dress like this. She says that she does not follow this dress code because she is religious, but because her focus for self-development lies elsewhere and she does not wish to create unnecessary fuss in her neighbourhood in the outskirts of Tehran. She adds that as soon as she reaches her workplace, she removes her headscarf, roopoosh, and chador regardless of men being present or not. She gives her consent for a photograph but requests that I use it only in conferences abroad to show her as a successful young woman. She says that she does not wish to be seen in the press in Iran because she does not like fuss and has to get on with her work in order to finish paying for her flat. Esmat continues with the following:

> I am 23 years old. I work as a caretaker in a foreign company, I work in their guesthouse. I look after this floor which has a large kitchen and six large bedrooms off this corridor, and several bathrooms and lavatories. This is a cleaning job really, but I also keep an eye on the facilities in the kitchen and bathrooms and report any breakdown. I have keys to all the rooms. Although I am happy with my job, nobody in my family and amongst my acquaintances knows what I actually do. Even my husband doesn't know, I have chosen not to tell him, in fact I have kept it a secret from everybody including my parents and two brothers. My husband knows I come to this location to work, I have told him that I am a helper in the library; it sounds so much better

and respectful and fits my education. I have a secondary school diploma which I am proud of. I neither had the money nor the head for continuing my education. I knew I had to find work somehow and quickly. It was very difficult and I asked everyone I knew to let me know if they heard of even the possibility of work.

My family could not really help me. We are originally from Hamedan but my parents came to Tehran after the Revolution and settled in one of the shanty towns in south Tehran. They did not have proper water and electricity for years because of the location, it did not fall under the municipality. My father did odd jobs for people; he queued with the line of casual construction labourers on the road side and got something like carrying bricks, digging, etc. most days. I think that's why I had understood that sooner or later I had to stand on my own feet. But the nice thing was that I made friends with a boy one year younger than me when I was at primary school. For years we used to come across one another in the little dirt road on the way to school and eventually we said hello and talked. Things like where do you live, who is your mother, what grade are you in. In fact we continued this till we married when I finished high school; he did not finish his studies. He was not like me, I have had to tell him to have a system in life. He is an electrician's labourer in a mechanic's workshop, he understands wires.

I have never asked my father for help even though he is my 'primary' relative and supposed to be responsible for me; neither my two brothers. Well they are incapable of helping me. The memory of my mother stretching her hand to ask my father for money day in day out kills me. All those years she had to ask. I thought then that I had to be financially independent, because even though my father had no education he could rule my mother; we call this patriarchy don't we? It's not right. Now, neither my father nor my brothers can tell me what to do; I guide them instead, I tell them to try and buy two rooms for themselves before it is too late and prices have rocketed. I tell them instead of smoking they should feel responsible. In fact my brothers are jealous of me because I have put down a deposit with all my savings from the last three years, and have bought a tiny apartment consisting of a bedroom, kitchen and bathroom in a new development 10 kilometres past the airport. I have insisted that the deeds are in my name. I told my husband it was my idea to marry you, it was my idea to save, it was my idea to buy a place, and it is my savings. I said if you accept come with me if you don't I will do it on my own. My husband and I pay the monthly instalments together now and should finish in ten years. So I must work for at least another ten years before we discuss children. It is not easy to work, I catch three buses to get to work in the morning and it takes two hours. I work for seven hours and then catch another three to get home. But I love having a place of my own, it's worth the effort, I am happy working. I feel I deserve this and I owe it to myself to work hard. On Fridays we go out to a park and have fun. I don't mix with too many people because I work most of the time, in any case people tend to want to put their nose in your business; I know that no good comes out of people around me. They are not going to pay my bus fares are they?

As a young woman I like to take care of myself, I consider myself important. The truth is that no one will respect me unless I respect myself, presenting myself clean and fresh, with highlighted hair and makeup and ready. I have learnt how to do my hair myself so it isn't that expensive, you buy the kit and it tells you exactly how to lighten and darken strands of hair.

In answer to your question about religion, I know that we are Shi'ite, that's all. I don't have a lot of knowledge about these things, they are not my concerns. I think people in the provinces or rural villages might be much more religious, we have relatives in Hamedan who are. I would not want to live in a village, they are more patriarchal. To be a peasant or small farmer you have to work on the land for six months and be out of work six months. I cannot imagine living like that, what kind of work would I do in the second six months? Besides you cannot have an apartment with your own bathroom, you will have to use the public baths. No, I like to live in the city. I want to say something else, can I? I have never talked to anyone like this, I feel relieved, I feel lighter all of a sudden. I think I need to talk about these things with other people, but it didn't occur to me.

Words such as agency, by which I mean having the presence of mind to participate in authoring one's own fate as much as realistically possible, and autonomy, empowerment, social capital, and self-esteem find real meaning in Esmat's creative management of her life. The statistics presented in the Introduction and the suggestion that the gender gap is closing in education, and the fact that girls are overtaking boys in secondary school education assumes further meaning here.

Meet Marjan and Marzi

Presence and altering the mindset of male relatives continues to find resonance in the lived experiences of Marjan, and Marzi in the following paragraphs. Although both come from highly religious families, neither see religious beliefs and practices contrary to being fully present and participating members of society. Indeed they carve out their desired paths forward through their choice of higher education.

University students on campus

I interview Marjan in the open air public space at Tehran University sitting on the concrete benches in front of the Visual Arts Department. Interestingly the combined sounds of the muezzin and the roar of the traffic bring new and relevant textures to the recording of the interviews. The following is Marjan's experience:

I am from a political-religious family, and I am a supporter of the Iranian government and its stance on theology. The Revolution is after all the Revolution of the minorities. I would like to ask you to make it clear in your writing that I observe the dress code of the chador and maghna'eh because it is my desire to do so. When I joined the department many people here viewed me as a fundamentalist because of my chador, it was difficult and it can be very isolating at times. Very few students in the Faculty of Art and Architecture wear the chador. Well let's say this has been my experience at least. If you stand in front of the Faculty of Political Science it is quite ordinary to wear a chador like mine. But gradually and despite the initial prejudices I have made friends and in fact I mix mostly with the top student in the country in our year who got the highest mark in her national entrance examination. She read science at secondary school but wanted to do fine art at university, and here we are together. I am mentioning this because of what I feel I have achieved to be here.

My father did not think studying was suitable for me, let alone studying art. This is because sadly one or two cousins lost all sense of their roots when they went to university, smoking and drinking was the least of it. I have had to go in a roundabout way in order to arrive here. I got married when I was 15, to someone I approved of, and immediately had a child. But despite the exhausting responsibilities of being a young mother, I persuaded my husband that I should go back to studying to pursue my interests in art. The adult education courses and the Educational Jihad helped me to make up for the lost years. All this was made available to me free of charge. I also attended some drawing classes run by a well known artist tutor who taught at Tehran University before the Iranian Revolution, but I soon realized that I did not like his style because he insisted on everybody following his way of drawing and was in my view rather single minded. I was subsequently assisted by the Educational Jihad to complete a foundation course, and was taught art history to help me prepare for the university entrance examination. Mind you I could not have achieved all this without my husband's support. We discussed my ideas and he learned that I needed to be out in the evenings going to my various classes. Now, I get home when I get home, sometimes after nine o'clock. Whoever gets there first, cooks dinner. But don't get me wrong, raising our son is taken seriously by both my husband and myself. I see that raising my son holds me back even with all the support I have, so my work suffers at times. It is naive of women to want it all and have it all, terms such as 'liberated' and 'free' are difficult statements. They become meaningless when you translate them into the reality of life. I am trying to work out what I have to do to succeed, once I have goals I try to reach them. I have persuaded everyone that my goals are important. I investigated a number of universities including Al-Zahra University for Women which I found unappealing due to the student body being all female. It became clear to me that I wanted to study at Tehran University in male and female company. There is more opportunity for learning in mixed company, we have to grow together, to learn how to have a dialogue, how to understand one another and see each other's perspectives. My chador does not stand in my way, I don't let it.

I have a set of aims you see, I hope to go abroad to Germany where I have relatives, to familiarize myself with other ways of looking at art. I believe they are much more scientific and progressive in their approach. As the Prophet has said, learning is a duty even if it is to be sought in far away China. I think travelling would feed into my work, and perhaps, I might be able to pass what I learn in Germany to others.

Incidentally, I only mentioned what I said earlier, about my dress code I mean, because we had some French television crew here and they sent us a copy of what they had recorded in the painting studios. Without consulting me, they had added that my clothes were preventing me from my work. That was stupid of them, if I am stopped by anything at all, it is the weakness of my mind not my clothes.

To collaborate with one's husband or partner in order to expand one's horizons and bring ideas into reality are intelligent acts wherever they occur. Marjan has first imagined and determined a future for herself and has subsequently set out to construct that future. She has succeeded in bringing her husband and her father into her team of supporters and helpers, initiating rethinking and re-addressing social issues from perspectives other that the traditional. We imagine that because of her piety Marjan might have preferred an all women University and student body. Not so however, she will not be stereotyped because of her religious beliefs and practices, she is far more interested in the inclusiveness of Tehran University working with male colleagues as well as female.

Meet Marzi

Marzi's perspectives in the following paragraphs consolidate Marjan's; they provide yet another layer in forms of being, and presence amongst Muslim women. The following is how Marzi demonstrates this:

> I am my parents' first child to go to university; my parents themselves have completed primary school, but my mother has continued with Qoranic learning. My father is a lorry driver and quite pious, he is very protective of our mother's body, that is why she will only wear thick opaque stockings under her chador. My sisters completed their twelfth grade and married within a couple of years. My mother's friends from her weekly recitation classes introduced their sons to our family and my sisters accepted the ones they liked as husbands, and are very happily married women. I am not against marriage at all but I have a feeling that my eldest sister would have liked to experience university education before getting married, but she did not demand it like I have. You can see it in her eyes and the way she asks me about what the lectures are like. Her husband is a historian and teaches history at secondary school. I think she could have become a teacher too, you can see it in the way she teaches her little boy every evening, and the way she checks his homework.
>
> I think my big achievement is to change things in the family. I insisted on going to university, and I had to work very hard on my father because he was very reluctant, saying 'aren't your sisters happy?' But I am neither my mother nor any of my sisters, he cannot take my ideas so lightly. I have made my father sit down and listen and understand that I have a different idea for my future. Firstly I don't wear the chador even though I pray every day. I wear white or cream in the summer and colourful patterned coats and cropped pants in winter. Initially I stood out a bit, but gradually people got used to the idea. It is always very difficult at first, but I simply don't tolerate black as my mother does. I wear bright and shiny scarves, bright things suit me. Maybe it seems easy just saying it, but you have to work very

hard to change things. One of my cousins with two kids has started going back to adult education because she is influenced by me. She took all her jewellery to her husband and said I am going to sell these things to finance myself at night school, and this is exactly what she is doing. The thing is her husband will take her to Mecca for the Haj ceremonies any day if she wanted it, but to put her through proper education is not forthcoming it seems. But no worries, my cousin has started it herself. It's not too late for my sister either, her time will come soon when her little boy does not need her anymore, she will have to learn how to teach other children by going to university herself.

The observations and critique Saanaaz, Esmat and Marzi offer of the location and circumstances of their mothers are of significance here; these circumstances are not what these young women imagine for themselves and would wish to emulate. Their demands for change thus arise from the knowledge of their immediate and intimate environment.

The following narrative is an incident which does not routinely happen in Iran, and yet it demonstrates the perceived dimensions for change amongst the new generation.

Meet Pariya
The day we played football on campus

I meet and interview Pariya at the home of her grandmother. I am very pleased to see that both her grandmother and her aunt are present and listen. I note from their eyes and calm conduct that they simply want to show Pariya their unflinching mental support whilst she speaks of her recent experiences on the university campus. Pariya speaks with a quiet but determined voice. Her green eyes project her moments of emotion, anger and joy when mentioning the triumph of playing football in public.

Most days at this time between lectures the boys kick the ball around and have a game and if the girls are free too, they sit around the field on benches and watch. It was around 2.30 in the afternoon and there were seven or eight of us girls who hang out together. We came out of a session and noted that one of the boys had fallen over during play and broken a finger and was being taken away in an ambulance. Most of his friends had

dispersed. The ball, however, was sitting on the pitch as if waiting for us, so we looked at one another and just went for the ball
passing it to one another and playing. Some of the boys who like
us had a free period joined us and we became two teams, boys
against girls – segregated in a very 'Islamic' way [laughter]. This
was great fun and we played for around 15 to 20 minutes, then
we thought we should mix it up a little because even with three
of us as goal keepers we had a lot of balls in the net. So we
changed the shape of the two teams so that both teams could
have boys and girls passing and dribbling the ball. We fixed it.
You see the boys were much better football players with a lot of
play experience and mixing the teams up worked very well releasing the three girl goal keepers to run around and join in more
and enjoy play. It was just great.

By this time we had quite an audience, we had created an atmosphere because the pitch is in fact in the parking area where there
is also a cafeteria and a place for students to hang out. The
groups of students who hang out there have a reputation, constructed by the religious zealots, as lacking in moral fibre and
being on the loose. But that is another story because if you do
not agree with the fist of authority, then you are labelled as lacking in moral fibre. Anyway our football match did not last as
long as we wanted it to because the news reached the *Heraasat*, or
Ethics Office, who consider themselves as moral guardians and
are present on all campuses to prevent so called immoral and un-
Islamic conduct. So suddenly in the middle of our game we
heard a few unfit men in grey suits holding 'walky-talkies' calling
out 'Stop the ball, stop the ball, don't move, don't move, present
your ID cards'. If this was on television it would make a hilarious
cops and robbers scene, especially because of the way these men
looked, heavy and greasy in grey suits. But the reality of it was
that it was far from being a joke. These zealots were really treat-
ing us as if we were criminals.

Of course us girls have strategies to deal with situations like this,
we know how to protect ourselves. So exchanging a glance we
communicated to one another to keep calm and not to hand out
our ID cards. They said we had to go to the Heraasat Office in
the administration block for questioning by even heavier men in
greyer suits. On the way there we cleaned off our lipsticks and

pulled our maghna'eh headscarves forward pushing our fringes well under, just as the boys pulled up their low-cut hipster jeans as far up as they could. We also decided not to be argumentative in this instance especially because some of us were graduating before long and did not wish to jeopardize our final marks by becoming registered as trouble-makers or anti-regime. We really do need to get our degrees. I have begun to look into doing an MA already, so securing my first degree is very important for my life to come.

At the Heraasat Office, the men in grey suits were sitting behind their desks, one addressed us, adopting a fatherly tone and avoiding eye contact with the girls, implying piety. He obviously knew every single one of us, our subjects and background, and whether any of us drove cars. He basically said that as students who have been around for a while we should know better, and should set a good example for the freshers by refraining from ungainly public conduct and playing football with the boys. We just listened, and were dismissed after a little while having handed in our parking passes; you can imagine the difficulty because our campus is in the middle of nowhere about 100 kilometres from Tehran and we need cars.

Eventually the parking passes were returned, but after a few weeks I received a letter summoning me for questioning handed to me by the department secretary. When I presented myself, there was just one man who proceeded to tell me that a file was set up for me because of my immodest acts contrary to the standards of public behaviour. I explained that as we had explained before, the group had not been aware of the irregularity of our behaviour at the time and that we had in fact apologised as a group and thought the matter was closed. He said that I should write all this down in a letter in my defence, sign it, and hand it in with my phone number and marital status put on the back of the letter. Although I found this rather odd I did it by putting down my home number. He noted this however, and asked me for my mobile number and proceeded to say in a hushed, shaky, and horribly aroused voice that he was there on Sundays and Wednesdays if I wanted to visit. He had the audacity to continue in his meek and cowardly voice and manner to suggest that if I visit him he will erase my record. This simply violated my sense of integrity and dignity, I found his unprofessional and hypocritical behaviour totally hateful and was utterly disgusted at his vulgarity and obscene suggestion that I might wish to visit him privately with a request. The problem is that if you report such things it might become even worse for you.

After a week I had a phone call from an unknown number on my mobile, and as soon as replied I realized who it was. He said that I should go to his office. What choice did I have but to go? In his office he simply said that the outcome might not be so good for me as the case has gone to the *Comité*, or the local revolutionary council, for a final decision, which could mean either discharge from the university or one term's ban from attendance. He finished by asking me why I had not been to see him on the days he suggested, because he could solve my problem easily. I felt sick as I listened to him and I wanted to shout: my problem? I was looking down, observing his prayer rings on his fingers supposedly symbolizing his piety, or link to purity and goodness. I reflected on his small and deceitful mind. I wondered how our Supreme Leader can sit there and tell us we cannot go to footballs matches and football stadiums because it might be lustful, when there are these desperate characters sitting in the Heraasat Offices behind desks creating files, and posing as keepers of moral order and piety!

I know all about real Islam because I have watched my elders. My paternal grandfather was a prayer leader in his village and my maternal grandmother is an educated retired professional who has taught us fine things about Islam from the Qoran. The behaviour of the Heraasat is not the Islam I know. The first rule is not to deceive others. I am clear in my mind about these things, I don't need this superficial piety.

Anyway, we might even continue to play football, perhaps in the parking spaces in our apartment blocks, who knows what will happen tomorrow, we might change laws after all.

Although playing football, or any other sport, with boys in the public space is not tolerated by the government, women in Iran currently participate widely in sports. Riding bicycles and motorcycles are not illegal for women but are rarely practised perhaps due to cultural perceptions. The lack of clarity and transparency about what is

permissible or impermissible causes confusion. During a conversation
with a first year student at Tehran University I was told the following
by a confident and reflective young woman called Morsaleh:

> We don't feel helpless. I was born at a time in Iran when war
> devastated the country, at the end of the war our parents cele-
> brated the very fact that we survived the war. But it is not just
> survival, we have survived very well, I am now 19 and a first year
> student at Tehran University. My mother tells me that there were
> times she did not know whether she could find the milk powder
> she needed to feed me with. Our parents have spent their pre-
> cious youth raising us. And besides having to witness losses in
> the eight years of war, standing in queues with their coupons for
> fuel to keep us warm, and collecting food rations to feed the
> family, have taught them much about life. They have passed this
> on to us, they have talked about these things to us, giving us an
> understanding of their struggles. So struggling for us has become
> routine. Now I am able to do something for my young sister, I
> am teaching her how to ride a bike. I take her out in the evenings
> to the derelict land around our neighbourhood and let her ride
> where there is no traffic. I learnt to ride a bike from my mother
> when I was ten when we went to the Caspian Sea. It seemed
> quite routine there, but in Tehran it is not clear whether we can
> or not. Someday we will know for sure, and then my sister will be
> ready to show exactly what to do with her bike on the streets of
> Tehran.

Morsaleh's optimism and planning for the future will not be wasted
and must be seen as symbolic of many desired social behaviours yet to
be transferred to the public sphere. Many sports now routinely practiced were not permitted by the government in the first decade after
the Revolution. There is indeed much enthusiasm and hard work put
into sports by women, and young Iranian women's participation in
sports internationally has brought the country outstanding recognition
and top medals in the last decade. The sole female athlete from Iran to
participate in the 2004 Olympics was 19 year-old Nassim Hassanpour,
a teenage markswoman in the ten metre air pistol event.[83] The first
Iranian women's sports magazine *Shirzanaan*, or lionesses, reports
regularly and extensively on the national and international participation
of the country's all-female teams and individuals. Mountain climbing,
car racing, skiing, polo, soft ball and volleyball, pistol shooting, tai chi

and tae kwon do in martial arts are just a few amongst many. The latter is explained to me by Master Shokooh Divani, the leading practitioner and tutor in women's tai chi chuan in Iran, who has published articles and books on the subject. As she has explained to me, after a period of not having the appropriate clothing which could combine the approval of the Islamic regime and ease of movement, special clothing has now been designed to perform this sport in the public sphere nationally and in championships around the world. Further, the Iranian women's football team participated in the Asian games in Jordan in August 2007, and there have been attempts to allocate and develop a grass pitch for women's football, though not without opposition.

Notwithstanding the restrictions, in parks in big cities one can witness the activities of young and old women engaged in tai chi, aerobics, jogging, fast walking, etc. Thousands of female hikers use the mountains around the capital to enjoy and to keep fit. The women's sporting federation is actively promoting sport and creating conditions unparalleled in the region and amongst Muslim nations, all of which were once just a desire waiting to become reality.

The coffee shops: dialogue and public engagement

The public presence of many young women is further articulated in recreational activities in the coffee shops. This is understood as a new concept different to the traditional tea houses for men which have been part of the culture for centuries, and to the cake shops serving hot drinks. The idea of coffee drinking as a daily refreshment remains an alien concept for the great majority of Iranians, this is except for Iranian Armenians who drink the short thick coffee much like the Turks, Greeks and Arabs. Amongst urban Muslim Iranians drinking bitter coffee is a symbolic act when visiting those mourning the loss of a loved one. The coffee shop in its contemporary sense has developed in parallel with the opening of the internet cafes in the 1990s. As an entrepreneurial idea and mild capitalist enterprise, a venue for consuming commodities and a source of income by the young, the coffee shop has found its place in most shopping centres. As a marker of socio-political change and a site for holding a dialogue with the opposite sex. The coffee shop is thus claimed as a young idea viewed with enthusiasm and excitement by the secular youth; it is nevertheless a subject of disdain and verbal attack by the clergy and sporadic harassment by the Heraasat.

In the processes of my enquiries I have visited many different types of coffee shops; the following however was a particularly valuable experience because I was guided by a young student and her boyfriend.

When I set off to meet Soraya at Gandhi Shopping Centre I had some idea about the area of town being an expensive one, but I was surprised to find this small commercial community unaffordable by the majority, and outrageously exclusive because of the the luxury clothing on sale. Fine quality leather boots, delicate sequined tops amounting to just a backless-frontless band, designer low-cut jeans and belts, large and buckled and studded handbags, perfumes, etc. were on display as if great works of art. Though inviting in colour and allure I became curious about Soraya's choice.

I enter the small open plan shopping centre on three floors and climb the staircase to the third floor towards the coffee shops. I find Soraya and her boyfriend waiting for me. She is in a long jacket and instead of a headscarf she wears a pulled-up knitted hood from a jersey worn under her jacket. The young man appears awkward rather than shy; he has pulled down his contemporary style wool hat as far as his eyebrows, and his thick knitted scarf and thick woolly pullover have similar stripes to his fingerless woollen gloves. We are introduced and I find his name, Daarang, unfamiliar, he explains that his parents found it in old Avesta texts from Iran's pre-Islamic tradition of Zoroastrianism. Soraya explains as we enter the coffee shop:

> I have chosen this area and these particular coffee shops because they are supposed to be ostentatious and are amongst the trendiest in town. You come to this one dressed up and with someone special, it's a place to have a date, so it is not a place to be noisy and be with your friends from the campus. Here everybody is supposed to be 'in love'. In any case it is far too expensive because you have to get here in the first place, it is neither on a communal taxi route near any of the university campuses, nor is it reachable by a straight forward bus line. But once in a while with your boyfriend it's great.

With his arms folded as if he feels the cold, Daarang looks uninterested and explains that this area is not for a Marxist like him. I ask him whether he is studying or working. He says he is doing neither, and that he is thinking at present. I stop myself from asking him who pays for his trendy clothes. Soraya is interested to know whether coffee shops in England are similar and I explain what I know about the chain of coffee shops which have become popular because of similar entrepreneurial endeavours since the late 1990s. Daarang watches my notebook and pen placed in front of me on the table, he appears a little uneasy.

Coffee shop in uptown Tehran

We consult the board on the wall, there are soft cold drinks, milk-shakes, hot drinks, and lemon and coffee cakes. We order three hot chocolates which arrive quickly in tall glasses placed on white saucers with a fine tall spoon. The coffee shop is just a large room with 12 tables for two with square wooden tops and two chairs in wood and woven raffia. There is a smart wooden counter at one end with facilities for preparing refreshments. Two young attendants with sculpted hair styles await orders. Young men and women are sitting at most of the tables drinking milky looking drinks in tall glasses and in dialogue with one another. Some smoke. Soft light is let through the windows, half covered with finely woven netting material. The simplicity and minimalism here contrasts with the commercial allure of the boutiques on the street, the colour and atmosphere is provided by the young women's bright and shiny headscarves, fitted short coats, cropped trousers over different designs of boots, and makeup.

We finish our drinks, and pay just under two dollars for each drink, and leave to walk around the shopping centre. One floor down there is another coffee shop which appears not dissimilar to the one we have just visited. At least this is the impression I have from the outside. Soraya explains:

> This one is more for shoppers and every shopping centre has one, some with high chairs and some with low, good places for groups of friends and mixed company rather than tucked away on upper floors for a special meeting. The half curtains on the windows of the one we went to were to create privacy even though it is quite possible the owners are related to, or are sons of people in positions of power in the government and therefore safe from intrusion. The big ones, like the one on Vali Assr Avenue, are often raided but never closed! The ones in the big book shops are completely closed down now. So we don't know how it works. But let's miss this one and go to my favourite little place in this area, they serve excellent hot soup at lunchtime. The owner knows everyone, and it's a place where some artists or writers go to occasionally. But because it is small you have to share tables and you either join the conversation or hear other's. If the owner does not like you, he will remember you the next time you are around and might put the 'FULL' sign on the door.

Daarang adds that the big one on Vali Assr Avenue is where boys and girls go to be seen and exchange phone numbers, with one or two special corners and evenings for gays. We enter, and the place is indeed very small. There is a counter and stools where five people are sitting and chatting. There are only three large tables each with as many chairs squeezed around. We join a table with room at one end and cannot help but hear people's conversation. I am noticed for writing in my notebook. Soraya explains that there are many coffee shops like this but her parents sometimes go to a wonderful historic place called Cafe Naderi which has a restaurant with the same menu as before the Revolution. We discuss the ideas in my book and I ask both what their experiences are about the idea of a civil society. Daarang says he needs to think about it because he is not very good at discussing things verbally, and if I agree he will write a page for me according to Marxist theory and pass it on via Soraya. Soraya, however, says 'well doing this, talking and having opinions and participating could be part of the idea of a civil society, the freedom to be here and say what we think'.

Owning bodies

In the course of my enquiries I approached a number of institutions and individuals whose students would be willing to be interviewed. As a result of one such visit I hear from, and meet, two architecture students who study art history and English in their spare time twice weekly in the evenings. As we shall see in the following paragraphs, they are interested in discussing topics related to their bodies. They indicate a conceptual understanding of the body as a site to claim, possess, have knowledge of, and adopt or use as a social tool and material for presentation. However explicit, or subtle the expressions and meanings, such body autonomy and body economy signify consciousnesses and being physically and visibly present in daily life. One of the students, Maaha, maintains regular contact with me by email and continues a dialogue with me. I will include one of her emails later in this Text to reference presences through cyberspace. The subject of the particular email I have selected is exploring sexuality as well as body presentation and ownership. I am interested in the email also because it references millions of weblogs where ideas are exchanged amongst Farsi speakers globally, Farsi is the fourth most frequently used language for keeping on-line journals worldwide.[84]

At the site of the interview, the door opens and two energetic and very young looking and petite women walk in. They have medium sized backpacks which they place on the table once they say hello and give me their names and age. They are 21 years old and have just started their third year at university. Both have large dark piercing eyes which are at once serious, interested and sharply focused on me and my notebook; both have thick black hair combed over one eye in an asymmetric fringe, both wear short to the waist and very tight waterproof quilted jackets with frontal zips over short roopoosh and tight three-quarter length jeans, and both wear chunky trainers with colourful laces tied around their ankles. I am fascinated by the structure of their hairstyles which hold their headscarves well away from their foreheads somewhere in space behind the crowns of their heads. As the interview progresses, I understand what this interesting presentation of Selves means.

Meet Roya and Maaha

Roya starts without any introduction:

I was rather sceptical when you asked for an interview. The truth is that this idea of yours, coming to Tehran to look at us from above in a patronizing way, and gathering data, bothered me. It reminded me of nineteenth century anthropologists from the West who took themselves to some undiscovered, underdeveloped community in remote places away from the so-called civilized world. I would hate to do that, why do you wish to do this?

Rather taken by surprise, I explain two points at length. Firstly, that a request was put to the students to engage with their opinions, and that if none of them did volunteer to take part in an interview, then there would be no pressure to do so. People were free to decide. Secondly, I explained, there are misperceptions about women in Iran, and making aspects of their lives known to the wider world is crucial and relevant, especially at a time when there exists deep ignorance, and imperialist politics of disinformation and aggression towards the country, portraying Iranian women, amongst other things, as subjects in need of the West's liberation. Roya continues:

It never occurred to me that people around the world might imagine us differently to what we are. This is ironic because we are not simply these creatures who don't leave their homes, are forbidden to go to university, or simply move around under the demand of men. I am shocked to hear that in this day and age we could be imagined as undeveloped Muslim women. I would hate that. We do so much more than being educated. I want you and everyone else to know that I am a very critical person, I am critical of our political system, I am critical of our legal system, and I am worried about my work and economic independence in the future. I give myself the right to be critical of everything because it helps me find a way forward, think things through, and by saying the worst, then I push myself to start considering the positive things in my life. I sometimes get very angry and wonder about this country of ours, I am saying this because in my head I feel I am 100 years ahead with my aspirations and imagination. But which one counts, I don't know. My mind or my circumstances? Well perhaps my circumstances are something that I will continue and continue to put right. I will certainly try.

Maaha joins in:

We are the type that people gossip about, calling us wilful, so we should be able to put some things right with our wilfulness, change something in society. The point is that at the moment we like to live, we like to dance and go to parties. Don't get me wrong, see where you have found us, we are studying the Renaissance outside the university campus, I have learnt English in order to be in communication with the world, and I am one of the best students in the department, already thinking about a project for my finals next year which could be continued into a Masters degree. But at the same time my appearance and my acts are provocative for others [the clerics]. You see we can vote at 16, and that suits both the government and us, so if we are old enough to vote, we are old enough to live as we choose!

I ask Maaha to explain:

What, you mean parties? We mix with a lot of boys, and girls, and we like to dance. We persuaded our parents to send us to Dubai last term in a mixed tour group of boys and girls, and we all slept in mixed beds. Why do we have to go to Dubai to go to a mixed beach! The idea of beaches has become so special that we are thinking of taking contraceptive pills before we go, if we go again that is, so that we can enjoy the beach. Did you know that contraceptive pills stop your period and you won't have your period when you are stretching your body on the sand in the sun?

The other thing about us is that we set trends for headscarves, roopoosh, and hairstyles. I design them and we take them to a dressmaker and have my designs done in suitable fabrics. At the moment we are wearing a slightly gathered under the breasts style, like a fitted short pregnancy dress. But even when we buy readymade roopoosh we have them tightened and shortened to fit our individual bodies. I have a maghna'eh and longer roopoosh in my backpack for the campus, if I am stopped at the university gates and if necessary I change my clothes when I leave the campus. I don't know, I think these things are ordinary for us, we like to be completely different to what is expected, and we like to laugh and have fun with the boys.

Roya joins in:

I don't think you understand, we have to cover ourselves and our bodies in public but when we go to parties we make up for it. When we wear our headgear, our face is the first thing that makes others notice us, especially boys, so we work with this. Nose plastic surgery is very common and very important, both of us have done our noses. You have to have a good surgeon which means a more expensive one who does not ruin your nose and face, and can operate from inside without too much damage or a big line on the outside, as if your nose was broken first and then fixed [laughter]. This is serious for us, you have surgeons who charge a million, and surgeons who charge five million. It's true to say that the rates also reflect class issues. Well I wanted a good nose, wouldn't you?

Maaha:

We want to attract the best boys, we want to stand out and so we work with our faces to do this; To have a well-defined nose is important, with eyebrows which work with the shape of the nose. But we are very particular about being ourselves, having your nose and eyebrows shaped is one thing, and having badly done hair colour, too much makeup, and vulgar tattoos is another. In fact we make distinctions between being well attended to, looking good is different to looking as if you have been watching too many bad makeover programmes on satellite television from Turkey and Los Angeles. We don't wear more than just a lip gloss.

But it is more than just having an outstanding face, I think it is about wanting to be an individual demonstrating freedom. I am the eldest child of my parents, brought up by what we call an 'intellectual' family with a nationalist sensibility.[85] Neither of my parents are from Tehran, they met here when they were students just before the Iraq war. My father studied mechanical engineering at university and makes and invents pieces for small industries. He always has rough and blackened finger tips because he works with metals. My mother runs a small gift shop and gallery. She is going to show the work of the children I have been working with as a volunteer in South Tehran. Dad was jailed as a young man because of his political ideas. This was during the previous regime before the Revolution. So you can imagine the sorts of things discussed at home, if it is not related to socio-politics then it is not discussed very much. All of my family hold Iran very dear to their hearts, they don't just call it Iran, they call it *vatan* [motherland]. The most upsetting thing for them is when we critique life here and say that we should leave the country. They tell us that with all the difficulties that exist, we are still moving towards democracy. We cannot persuade them otherwise.

My point is that their aim, I mean my parents' and their friends' and millions of Iranians of their generation, circles around a collective goal which is to develop Iran. At least this is the way they talk about things. This is unlike mine which is at the moment a personal and individual one. I insist on arguing that I have to see, and experience what things really mean for myself, not solely relying on the words and views of others. I have to rely on my personal existence, before I can think about the nation and the country, after all would I understand anything if I did not understand myself! I have to hold myself upright, firm, and stable in my head. Making my face and body presentable, the way I figure it out, is my way of showing something of my own ideas first. My body is my own, isn't yours? Maybe their ideas about the country and nation are too big for me just at the moment, don't you think? Well I think I am entitled to experience everything for myself.

This is not because I am selfish, if I were selfish I would not be teaching the children in Shush in South Tehran. As you know parts of Shush are very poor. I help in the camp for Afghan children that our government has rejected, I teach them painting. These children can no longer have schooling because their parents' documents have expired and they have to return home to Afghanistan. There are also some Iranian children there who have come from other cities with their families in search of work and better life. These children are street sellers, flowers, chewing gum, and matches; they do it on crossroads, you know the ones who hold a single rose and come to the car window. Some of them are really talented and I have become attached to them, but I feel depressed when I think about the dark and unpleasant future ahead of them. I am teaching them very simple ideas about art and architecture inspired by their immediate environment. Just to show them that there is always something to think about, look at and play with in terms of colours and structures, and emotions. I feel powerless…we are all in search of better futures.

Roya joins in:

Our families also debate disempowerment, and our mums especially get depressed still dreaming about their own unfulfilled fantasies from their youth. They faced a Revolution and an eight year war. Segregation in schools and how their children have to wait till they are at university before they can mix with the opposite sex bothers them. They believe that it is the youth who will ultimately develop the country. Our fathers get depressed too, but they are good at hiding their feelings and worry about earning the money that is required to give us reasonable lives.

I must critique my own generation. We are not a studious enough generation, we could be more political. I mean to say that we do not go to university just for the sake of books and learning. One major attraction for the student body here is meeting other young people who might think alike; meeting the opposite sex is an incentive too. We are not there just to contemplate the archaeology of knowledge accumulated in the space and walls of the lecture rooms, the history of philosophical thought, or the new and innovative architecture the new blocks on our campuses offer [with laughter]! We are there because it is one place where the distance between the library and the lecture room might become more interesting through exchanging big ideas, a comment, a glance, a telephone number, possibly a date [laughter]. We don't meet each other on the beach, our beaches are segregated.

Maaha:

In our lives we are trying to regain the confidence many of our parents lost because of the hard realities of their youth, the outcomes of the Revolution and war. Last term my father approached me one night and pointing his finger at me shouted: 'What are you doing with your life, what are you up to, who are you out with till late?' Of course both of us knew exactly what he was referring to: my boyfriend. But he did not ask who he is, what he does, where I met him etc. He just attacked. Suddenly I found myself shouting back with my arm stretched out, pointing my finger at him. I said: 'You are shouting at me, you want to condemn me, you don't want to know me as an adult. When I was a child you turned me round and round till I was dizzy and had to hold on to your knees, you taught me to think, you read poetry to me, you taught me to read poetry. Now I want to experience life, I want to see what it's all about, and you should not condemn it'.

I was shaking. It was the first time I was behaving like that to my father, but I meant it. It is not as though I am a lazy layabout, I am 21 and reading architecture at the best university in Tehran, and I know what I am doing. I have got this far haven't I?

Anyway my mother told me to go to my room and calmed him down. After a few days of silence, my father came to my room one evening and asked me whether he had ever read the short stories of Sadeq Hedayat to me.[86] He said he lived on them when he was my age and he wanted to read them again and he did not want to become an old and shrivelled up recluse who had forgotten his own youth and young mind. I think my father wanted to tell me that although it is hard for him to see me independent, he is determined to not become reactionary. It's hard for all of us. There are paradoxes in our lives that overlook the bigger ideas. The authorities are watching young women's dress and behaviour, and our parents get scared and forget they had similar aspirations when they were our age. Both fail to see the bigger picture, they forget that we are worried about our economic future and place in the world. Instead of guarding us, they should guard the future of the youth in the country.

Observed presence

In their critiques above, Maaha and Roya have revealed the range of ideas which engage with both minds and bodies in order to create socio-cultural perspectives, consciousness, and sense of belonging. These are relevant and part of both the local youth culture, and discourses of difference in global existences. In the following paragraphs we shall see how in addition to engaging with ideas physically in bodily representations, the participants register presences through abstraction, whether through creating art installations or writing.

Meet Shiva

Shiva is a fine art student at Tehran University. In an interview at the vegetarian cafeteria at the Iranian Artists Forum, 'Khaaneh-ye Honar-mandaan', she takes me through her visual sensibilities in her portfolio. The following however is how she summarizes her most successful art projects. She says:

> At the moment I am following a few strands in environmental art; 'site' specificity, the idea of the ephemeral, and forms of per-formance art are occupying my thoughts. I am designing a vertical sculpture made up of large hard, but not dry, adobe mud bricks. These will have hollow centres. I intend to construct the adobe blocks from the earth/mud dug up at the site of the sculp-ture and use the hay I have gathered in its vicinity. This economy is crucial to the message of environmental art, there will be little displacement if any. The origins of the work will be in the work. The hollow centres of the stacked adobe blocks will be filled with crushed ice chipped off the ice blocks acquired from the last remaining traditional *yakh-chaal* icehouses. So we will have a col-umn whose centre is made of melting ice. As the process of melting develops, the stacked mud bricks will absorb the water, change form, and start to disintegrate, collapsing on themselves. The sculpture will be just a temporary presence on the horizon, limited in its existence. Environmental calculations of scale, time, and weather conditions and temperatures are important parts of the processes; and the whole process will be documented with a hand held video camera by an assistant.

> The idea of art is new in our family because my father thought studying art was problematic, neither here nor there. I don't think he considered it as proper education. But I persevered and managed to secure a place at Tehran University. In my second year I entered for a national biennale on 'New Art' at Tehran Museum of Contemporary Art. For this project I created a nar-row path in human scale to barely hold one person, articulated by two parallel walls in thick white polystyrene six feet high. I pierced and embedded these pure white walls with over a thou-sand very large shiny quilting needles, the largest you could find. My father is a tailor and I asked him to find the longest and sharpest. At the end of the path I placed a thousand soft new

green leaves inviting the feet but perhaps also deceiving the eye's mind. Just like life, and its pleasures and pains. I won a prize for this, a gold coin, and now even my father thinks studying art is OK. Creating art has meant registering my thoughts and presence.

Shiva's works are expressions of her own felt physical presence. projecting the transience of an imagined Self in the form of a column against the horizon. Crossing a needled passage in anticipation of soft leaves beneath the feet too posit philosophical reflection. The function of a needle becomes a metaphor, a conceptual tool to communicate experiences. Her 'New Art' trajectories are simultaneously related to a global language and vocabulary in art as well as intervening in the iconography of Iranian art. In 'registering her presence' Shiva introduces familiar elements such as quilting needles, adobe mud bricks, and ice from the nearly forgotten traditional yakh-chaal icehouses, to discourses of art in her locale.

Maaha and the moments of innocence

Observing one's own presence through the imagined and the felt has been an interconnecting element in the narratives and Texts presented. Maaha has expressed enthusiasm in being further represented in this Text through her fiction. This is an intriguing short story of approximately ten thousand words indicative of her desire to imagine, to create, and own autonomous intellectual space. I respect and admire Maaha for being effective in creating such dynamics. However, since Maaha is also in touch with me electronically and sends me pages from her diary, I have chosen to make room for just one of her many emails below, and will give just a brief summary of her fiction.

The story is the accounts of the roaming around of an infant in and out of a typical neighbourhood in Tehran complete with a small park. The infant, however, possesses certain characteristics of the mind, perceptual ability, and emotions of a young female adult. The story may thus be perceived as a psychoanalytic self-portrait, returning to the moments of innocence when life might be experienced stripped of rules created by adults. In the story the infant is silenced by a *red* pacifier bought by the author from the chemist. This repressive and perhaps symbolic act is soon forgotten and it is compensated for by the ability of the infant to break social taboos and behave as she pleases. The joy of such experiences as rolling down the grass slopes, sleeping on the park bench, and staying out till early hours just watching the cats fight in the streets are narrated. The infant notes everything as she plays, she hears as she sings, and she reflects on the actions of others as she observes the lives and rituals of the neighbourhood alley. Slowly, the reader becomes familiar with this sensory existence where the body as well as the mind become sites of exploration relating textures, imagination, reason, and fantasy. Details of conversations with the neighbourhood boys' mothers, as well as interactions with numerous boys, including the infant's brother, are related. The language used in the piece is surreal, at once disturbing and tender, challenging, and pushes the reader into a position of having to distinguish between the toddler and the adult female. The boundaries of child-adult expression are blurred.

The following is Maaha's email:

My mother's uncle died four days ago, he joined my grandfather, I knew them well. They gave us toys.

Yesterday evening I was home alone so I invited Mohsen to visit. He is a talented illustrator and works with paints, we have known each other for some time. We turned all the lights off, and lit all the candles we have in the house. I made rice to eat with a yogurt and cucumber sauce, I put them in beautiful bright orange dishes. My father makes wine at home so I opened one of the bottles and poured some into a tall pink cup. Pink, orange, red – the dishes are from my mother's collection of ceramics. Her father made little clay whistles for us when we were children, he painted them red, my grandmother misses him.

I put on a movie. Our movie trader visits homes in our neighbourhood every two weeks, we look at his long lists and choose four DVDs or VCRs. We rent them for one or two weeks until he returns to collect them.

I wore my beautiful orange dress and black shoes with heels, I looked nice.

We sat on the dark blue armchairs, ate some food and drank some wine and talked about everything. I discuss everything with Mohsen: my younger brother who is a mathematical genius, my friend Borzoo, my grandmother, all those who have died, my passion for Zen philosophy, love, and all other nonsense in my head.

Nothing seemed more important than the moment. I told him about all the books I am going to read when my exams are over as soon as my exams are over I am going to just read and sleep.

Then I became dizzy from the wine. It was horrible, I had to rush to the bathroom and bring up the party, the party I had designed for the two of us. I thought I would die but I didn't. Then I thought I am young I must live, experience, and taste life, live each word.

All the time I knew that Mohsen really understood. You could see from his eyes that he understood, just like the way he understands colours like orange, he understood the orange dishes. I could see in his eyes that he senses colour inside him and it is not just outside on the dishes. He has eyes that understand and that's what I need.

But I know we should understand each other's physicality, find out about our concrete reality as physical beings who also have minds and can think.

Mohsen was hurt, he said that I was talking to him about everything because I just wanted something new and fun. He said I used him, I was in love with the idea of a male friend rather than Mohsen the person. I told him that he was 21 like me, so how did he know; did he have any experience in these matters? He said no. Then we got very close

When I was better we went out for some fresh air, and we had hot chocolate. Then, Mohsen hailed down a motorbike in front of the book shop Shahr-e Ketab just before they closed for the night. He looked at me and I said 'brave enough?'. He sat behind the rider holding on to him on the shoulders, I sat behind Mohsen holding on to his body tight. He told the rider to go as fast as he could, and the rider went very, very fast, and we screamed, we screamed as loud as we could.

We were really lucky we did not come across the night police, we would have been taken for 'question and answer' to the police station without a doubt.

Maaha's email is not an isolated case. As the following email to me indicates, living lives and expressing curiosity about how to do so are not only ongoing but generate their own nuanced structures, solutions, and dynamics:

> Tehran is very hot and my father has taken my brother away to the North for a week to help him recover faster after his anxiety attacks.

> The moral policewomen were standing in front of the shopping mall today arresting the girls in tight and short roopoosh. We think these young trainees who stop us these days must have a quota and are obliged to make one or two arrests per day. But I believe it's part of a girl's beauty to have a good body, we can't just hide our bodies. My grandmother says it is in the Qoran that *God is beautiful and loves beauty*. In any case we are young and need the company of male friends. We create our own codes of communication with the boys in public places. If we are in a car for example, we manoeuvre by driving round and round, circling, or up and down the street, using the indicators and windscreen wipers to let the boys know we are interested in going out and will take their contact numbers. If we are on foot we just exchange numbers on paper. It's easy.

> You remember I told you one of our friends who was 17 committed suicide? Well he hasn't. Actually he feels he is a *she* and has fallen in love with a guy and wants to do a couple of operations to become a real *she*. Do you have such cases over there? Is this simply accepted by people over there or is it an issue?

> I finally made up my mind and finished being virgin in my life!! My boyfriend is really lovely and a real friend, I am really glad that I broke this stupid taboo in my own mind. Now I am a woman.

The Margins

I include the accounts of the views of two taxi drivers of similar age, which provide interesting perspectives on society. The second is an agency taxi driver. Many households have an account with a taxi agency who takes their name and address and provides them with a membership number, making it possible for each journey to be recorded and traced back if necessary. The agency might thus be called any time of day or night for a taxi. The following is part of a conversation I had with a war veteran taxi driver from the agency near my residence. He had benefited from the government's scheme making education available to the war-damaged free of charge and with an allowance. Although not the case with my driver, many war veterans are chemically damaged in Iran and some return to education to study art. I knew two at Tehran University, and one called himself *chemical* Hossein and carried a briefcase full of medicine at all times to ease the physical and psychological pain he felt constantly. So meeting Mr Mass'oud the taxi driver and getting to know him was a great joy to me. He said the following on one journey:

> Driving a taxi is my second job, I am a technician. I am a war veteran from the Iraq war. I was the radio operator for one of the top generals in the army at the age of 19. I could have stayed in the army if I wanted to, but I don't like guns and wars. I went to the army initially because we have compulsory military service in this country. When the war finished I worked part-time, I was exhausted all the time, I worked two years here, three there. But I felt I was wasting time after a while, not thinking straight. Then I found out I had a chance to go to university for four years with a small salary. I met my wife there, we became friends. It was the best thing that happened to me. I have a little girl now, I love her, I carry her on my shoulders when we go to the park or up the mountain; she'll be four soon. But I don't know what it will be like when she starts school. I will find it difficult. She will have to cover her head, wear a white maghna'eh, but she is still a child, she will be just six. I don't know how I will cope with that; don't get me wrong I can conform to tradition too, but to cover the head of my little girl at the age of six is difficult for me. You know, ultimately the more you tell them to cover up their bodies the more they would want to reveal. That is the nature of things. Now that girls are wearing these cropped trousers and colourful things the government is making more arrests. This is disturbing. It is not necessary to make arrests, it lacks integrity, it's disrespectful to our women, we should change this attitude towards women. I saw one young lady the other day being interrogated by a female colonel with a chador on. I wanted to get out and ask her if she had any children. You could see her uniform with all the brass, and the line of badges on her breast pocket. It's not right, we are playing with human rights, we are playing with fire. I wonder what the colonel would do with her own daughters!

Lock them up? I met my own wife at university and we became friends, nothing wrong with that.

Tehran Orange Taxi

Yes, certainly I will wait for you to get your ticket confirmed and return back here; look for me just outside on the opposite side of the road because this street is one-way now.

So, do you travel to Iran often? What do you think about the direction of our country, you are lucky living abroad, life has become very expensive here, you would think we never had a Revolution. The clergy have got so rich now it's unbelievable. They don't even wear the thick camel-hair *ghabaa* [cloak] any more. Instead of moving from village to village deep in snow in cold weather looking to see who was dying, who needed a verse of the Qoran recited on a gravestone, they are now in offices. You don't need a thick camel-hair ghabaa in centrally-heated offices, behind desks with your lunches subsidized. Poor people like me still have to work 18 hours a day in the heat and in the cold to feed the family. But have you noticed our girls, have you noticed how free they have become? They seem to have lost their way, they have become over-affected, purely materialistic. Have you seen them in the streets, their hair, their lips. They don't even seem to want husbands anymore, who can afford them? Just the other day two sat in the back, and from the moment they got in till they arrived at their destination, they laughed. They just joked and laughed with one another. I think they were sales people in that big luxury store. I said to them when they paid their fare, I said what's so funny, let us know what it is that you are laughing at for 20 minutes. But they just slammed the door. I think our girls have lost their way, don't you!

Text Four: Visions of a Civil Society

This Text concerns the body of ideas and structures which are necessary to develop any realm in which women's social and legal status is considered equal to men. It questions the judiciary relating the triple axis of women's rights, human rights, and civil laws. It puts forth young women's civic vision and their significant political contributions in the context of a collective and egalitarian struggle for change through individual participation, private institutions, and non-governmental organizations. The narratives presented are testimony to the leading role of women in the battle of ideas regarding the condition of women in society, and developing a grassroots non-violent civil society and civil rights movement in Iran. Despite restrictions on public gatherings and public debate, and media censorship, women activists have created an arena where citizens might collectively and effectively participate in the struggle for democracy. They resist and challenge static religious interpretations of Islam in favour of fluid ones. They introduce new trajectories and interpretations which possess a deeper understanding of the excellence and possibilities of Islamic thought. Women's autonomous strategies and political campaigns for change have been significant also through their social groupings in developing societies and syndicates as well as non-governmental organizations.[87] The number of women's non-governmental organizations reached 500 during the reform period.[88]

In this Text we shall witness the forming and evolving of a number of these organizations with national profiles, and with specific perspectives in civic vision. Amongst the participants are nineteen year-old students at Tehran University campus who create a forum to highlight gendered behaviours and invite their male colleagues to be intellectual and work partners in a future student organization. A freshly qualified lawyer who joins forces with colleagues in a recently established legal campaign to prevent the stoning of women because of adultery at national and transnational levels in the Muslim world. A young journalist creates an organization which operates in real space and cyberspace to claim and own sections of public space by advocating the right to entry to sports stadiums. And a young activist joins a rapidly growing organization and dedicates her time and intellectual capital to penetrate the judiciary and the current family laws in order to change lives and society.

These non-governmental organizations argue for the recognition of women's equal and rightful ownership of the public sphere, whether legal, political, or social. They perceive women's contributions to this public sphere, not only as mothers and wives, but as legal and professional agents and advocates whose participation are elemental in the creation of a more comprehensively developed democratic country. As they reach out for a strong collective voice for change, they aim to inform and empower members of the public, engaging them in a widespread public debate about women's rights and legal entitlement. They recognise that informed collective activism is the only way forward in this competition of ideas, reaching for pragmatic tools to achieve their goals. They adopt cyberspace as their far-reaching technological tool, facilitating a national and transnational digital arena for information distribution and dialogue. Despite the variety of restrictions and harassments, they fearlessly campaign for change, face-to-face in the workplace, in educational institutions, on public transport, and in parks, to mobilize, train, engage and work with ordinary people at grassroots level in different pockets of society.

Meet Narggess and the One Million Signatures Campaign for Change

I meet Narggess at a small park in central Tehran in mid morning in late Spring on the grounds of The Artists Forum Cultural Centre. Although there is a wonderful cafe inside the compound, we sit outside on one of the benches near the flower beds. The gardens are refreshing and pleasant and there are numerous green benches occupied by young couples in conversation. Narggess is an energetic third year law student who also dedicates much of her time to the *One Million Signatures for Change and Equality Campaign* which is a mobilizing force demanding equal rights for women. Her shining brown eyes, solid leather lace-up shoes, and bulging colourful backpack exude a sense of mission, and she discusses the history and ethos of the campaign as follows:

The Campaign searches for justice in practice, and engages with the citizens regardless of gender and class wherever possible, in different private and public environments, to collect one million signatures of support. This has become a massive national petition with branches in all major cities and towns, Kermanshah, Rasht, Shiraz, Sanandaj, and many more. It is intended to raise consciousness about our shared legal status, whether as mothers, wives, or simply citizens. The right to divorce, custody of both male and female children without age limits, equal status in death with regard to blood money or compensation for loss of life, revision of marriage age for girls, and the disbanding of polygamy are amongst the proposed changes. We have just published a Women's Calendar which discusses these issues in a straight forward and brief language on every page. We have included tens of photographs of women protesting and debating such issues, as well as of Iranian women pioneers in the legal system as judges, surgeons, writers, ministers, and good mothers. We need to raise consciousness and get support and change the law, and our photographs demonstrate we have a history of activism.

Our Campaign was founded in the Spring of 2006 by leading women activists, lawyers, publishers, and writers in response to the sustained and legalized patriarchal antagonism we face. It is sometimes difficult to accept that the law is against us because in our culture women are truly loved and valued and even the religious elite discuss women as the essence of society in their capacity as mothers and wives. But there are two fundamental problems with this view. Firstly, what if not all women wanted to be wives and mothers, would we then take this notion of 'the essence of society' away from them? What if I wanted to dedicate my life entirely to public service and law, and did not wish to be legally married or a mother? Would I not have any rights as a citizen, does the Qoran really say I have to be a wife and mother to be valued? I don't think so. Women scholars are now translating the Qoran anew for clarification. Secondly, these laws are based on specific interpretations of Islamic laws by men, and presumably applicable only to Muslims. So what about those Iranians who are not Muslims? Besides, if we look at the Muslim world today from the Far East to Africa and beyond, we see huge complexity and diversity which indicates the possibility of different interpretations.

Just as an example, when my aunt returned from the Haj pilgrimage in the house of God in Mecca, she told us many Muslim women from different races and cultural backgrounds and coun-

tries attended to the Haj rituals without the full hejab we know in
Iran and nobody stopped them when their legs were showing .
This tells us that the dress codes for women are flexible, and are
interpreted differently according to local cultures. The excellence
of Islam allows for diversity, but the interpreters of Islamic law
fail to see such diversity and neglect its capabilities. Unfortunately our country's Family Law neither shows the love and
respect for women which we pride ourselves in, nor does it practice depth and complexity. Much like the rest of the world
including the 'Christian' countries and laws, they project severe
patriarchy. As a student studying law I have become sceptical
about any law based on religion and therefore I turn to secular
laws, civil laws, and our equal rights as humans and citizens.
These have become my ideals. We are currently debating how
women can become presidential candidates, we are re-reading
certain phrases used in the Constitution to clarify this. For example the term *Rejaal* is taken to mean men, as in Arabic, yet it
has a wider meaning referring to 'distinguished humans' and
therefore includes female citizens, so we can legitimately be a
candidate for presidency according to the Constitution.

The Change for Equality Campaign is meaningful to me and millions of others because of these reasons. With the help of legal
experts and advisors, both men and women, we are able to reveal
injustices and discrepancies in the law. We are able to learn from
real situations within the family and the social system by high-
lighting real cases in courts. The Campaign has legal articles
online, and a number of other 'women's websites' regularly publish relevant material for the ongoing discussion of these issues
through weblogs.[89] All this is a teaching system for me as a lawyer. But the Campaign also understands that there are those men
and women with work and children who cannot access the internet. This is where activists like me can help. We are all trained in
workshops and have learnt and practiced how to communicate
the aims of the Campaign face-to-face with individuals. As activists, we might work individually or in small groups, male and
female, and go to different parks and cultural centres and bus
stations, and even engage with people we meet in taxis. We want
to increase understanding and rectify the legal system through legal and peaceful means. With your permission, I will demonstrate
this to you through a brief discussion of the kind of things we

are concerned with in the Campaign, and I will then invite you to sign our petition

In your case for example I would discuss the legal right of your children to Iranian citizenship as an Iranian mother, and how mothers like you who are married to non-Iranians, unlike the men, are not able to pass on their nationality to their children. We question this law which allows fathers to pass on their nationality but does not allow mothers. This has caused serious and life damaging problems for thousands of children born of Afghan fathers and Iranian mothers. They are not recognised as Iranian citizens and have no IDs. Their rights to free education and health are seriously undermined.[90]

When I sign Narggess's petition I reflect on her rational argument and clarity of vision, courage, and determination symbolic of the collective efforts of women's movement in contemporary Iran. Whether as Muslim feminists or secular human rights advocates the majority of women like Narggess have overcome differences in their particular political location, and cultural and ideological trajectories, to face the contradictions of the Islamic State and institutions.[91] In a series of gatherings since 2006, individuals and groups of leading women have come together in person proposing a Women's Charter or *manshoor*. They have engaged in debates about their common experiences seeking new trajectories and solutions. They have taken their proposed ideas to wider audiences using digital technologies aiming to reach women in Iran as well as those in the diaspora; they invite comments through their website at Meydaan.org. The Charter thus aims to draw on the knowledge and professional aptitude of hundreds of leading activists, not only to consider the fate of the marginalized and vulnerable, but to create an empowered force to influence political decisions.[92]

Meet Shokooh from the Anti-Stoning Campaign

In a fourth floor one-bedroom apartment in West Tehran, I visit Shokooh a young lawyer activist. We sit in the sitting room, which is part of the open area of the entrance hall joining a kitchen, bathroom, and bedroom. Her one year-old is cared for by an older woman who is also preparing lunch in the kitchen. Shokooh explains that this lady and her mother share looking after her son when she is at work. They all come from Shooshtar, one of the oldest cities in southwest Iran whose cultural and artistic heritage date back to the third millennia BC.[93] Shokooh explains that her family fled to Tehran during the air raids and bombing during the Iran-Iraq war before she was born. Slender and petite, Shokooh has short black hair and is in black pants and a sleeveless top fitted to her body like a second skin. The room is minimally furnished, and, other than the cream carpet, three comfortable armchairs in dark blue, a glass fronted cabinet in one corner against the wall, and two bright green glass vases on a coffee table; there is a large exercising machine with a shiny label which reads 'Universal Abdominal Exerciser'. She smiles and says 'have to keep fit'. She enquires about the book and the method of data presentation, and listens with interest. She expresses her enthusiasm for the narrative structure of the book saying that *naghl-e ghoal*, or *ravaayat*, or direct quotations, often reveal more than just an answer to a question, they disclose layers and qualities in 'being'. She proceeds with the following:

> I am 25, and an activist lawyer aiming to eradicate the stoning of women. I work with the Volunteer Lawyers Network two days a week, and we have just published our first bulletin. I would like to tell you a little bit about myself, and my educational and political orientation. I come from a very religious background and I consider myself a practising Muslim. When I leave the house I wear a maghna'eh and over it I wear a black chador. But I don't believe this form of outdoor dress should be the law for all Muslim women, it is a question of interpretation. In fact it is much more complex than that. I wear the chador as a familial habit, a combination of my own familial expectations and circumstances, and my environment, the neighbourhood I was raised in. I would like people to know that this outdoor dress code is not a moral statement for me. As you probably know, wearing the chador has steadily attracted social stigma in recent years, which I experience routinely. Both sides, the ones who wear it and the ones who don't, view one another with some prejudice if no longer with hostility. If it was once the symbol of political polarity for some, in the first decade of the Revolution, it is now a kind of factionist political stance which I dislike.

> Increasingly I reflect on the usefulness of the chador, how useful it is to me, how useful it is for me to carry my briefcase, my files, and hold my chador in place. I am not concerned with the pres-

tige of wearing a trouser suit with a long jacket-coat. But I am concerned about my father's feelings, how to tell him that the chador is becoming superfluous, how he would receive this idea – but perhaps it is me who has not been ready yet, perhaps it is not my father at all, he will be proud of me no matter what I do. As I am discussing this with you it is clear that it can only be my decision, my father would trust my judgement without a doubt.

The other thing about me is that I married at the age of 19, right in the middle of my undergraduate studies; I fell in love, we fell in love. My husband was 23 then. In fact, at the age of 25, I have been studying non-stop to be a licensed lawyer. I don't think it would have been possible if my husband did not love me and respect my ambitions. I think he loves the fact that I am able to study, train as an associate lawyer, be married, give birth, etc. He loves to be part of it all, I see it in his eyes, so he helps me unconditionally.

I became conscious of the concept of advocacy as a child through television programmes. I was captivated by stories of people's lives, their troubles, and their clashes with law. This was mostly through foreign serials and films, the majority of which were American actually. Education around our family meant technical ability, and had always been tied up with becoming an engineer. That is why I majored in maths and physics at secondary school. As you know, entering higher education, and going through the processes of the national university entrance examination and selection, are interdisciplinary in our country. I discovered that in my year the Women's College at Imam Sadegh University was accepting maths majors to read law. Imam Sadegh University is an Islamist University bringing Islamic seminary and academia together and it was established in the early 1980s.

Our campus, also known as 'Sisters' Campus', is run entirely by women. As well as an able academic cadre trained in Iran, in France at the Sorbonne, and in the United States; the administration and all other services are run by women. It was always wonderful to see the campus gardens being kept by women gardeners. From the feminist point of view this was a huge achievement, but a number of us felt let down by our tutors and professors whose sole focus was to transfer their knowledge to us, but refrained from discussing politics. They simply did not engage in any political discussion or the examination of political ideologies. A number of us objected openly to this and caused disruptions, but in our second year because after that I was too anxious to be marked down as problematic. I, especially, had to give an undertaking not to be disruptive and argumentative. I faced this rationally, distinguishing between my ultimate goal of becoming a lawyer, and my secondary concerns regarding having open discussions in politics on campus. So just as I was sitting my finals exams in my first degree, I managed to secure a place at Shahid Beheshti University to do my Masters in law. I wrote my dissertation on 'The effectiveness of territorial disputes' in international law. Simultaneously, I took up a training position, as an associate, for 18 months with a double final written and oral examination to become a licensed lawyer. I believe the process of training is referred to as 'being at the bar' in Britain. I know this because we have had excellent tutors teaching us English.

My activism is connected to my political interests through which I have met likeminded lawyers at the Network of Volunteer Lawyers, and visionaries like Shadi Sadr at Raahi Nongovernmental Organization. We campaign for an anti-stoning law, with an ultimate goal to abolish stoning as a legal solution altogether and forever both nationally and internationally. Raahi was founded in September 2004 and has established the Women's Centre for Legal Counselling. I guess its founders have come to the conclusion that the existing laws prevent the realization of women's rights and offer legal services to women.

The Network of Volunteer Lawyers defend women accused of severe and critical crimes with long-term sentencing and capital punishment, including extra-marital relations and adultery. Stoning can only be passed as the sentence if there are four separate confessions given at the courts by the married individuals accused of having engaged in the full act of intercourse. Or, if there are four different witnesses who have observed the act taking place in its entirety, and when the judge has full knowledge of the act having taken place. In real terms it is impossible to prove such a crime to have taken place at all; the conditions for passing a judgement are hardly ever in place. The articles in the law relating the crime are numerous depending on the circumstances of confession and witnesses (articles 68, 70, 71, 73, 75, 77, 86), or related to passing sentence (articles 103 and 105, and article 37) for annulment. We also have numerous sources in religious texts which indicate the conditions under which holy Imams and holy personalities at the outset of Islam, directly or indirectly, declined from passing a judgement and stoning. It is always the case that such a sentence was not deemed appropriate, either as a result of doubt in the accuracy of the witnesses' accounts, or by requiring repeated confessions. Although sentencing should be the same for men and women, we never hear of it being considered for men because they are allowed to take more than one wife and sexual partner!

There is cooperation from the judiciary in principle. Their position is that no such verdict will be carried out even if passed. Our concern, however, is to establish whether or not a sentence for long-term imprisonment, death, or stoning, have been passed at all as a result of committing adultery. Even if such a verdict was reached initially and abandoned subsequently because of impracticalities, we would wish to know. We would want to know the exact numbers and circumstances of such cases nationally. We would want to know whether the conditions of the trial itself implied discrepancies. It is crucial to know whether stoning had been mentioned, contemplated, or demanded by the claimant at the various stages and processes of the trials in any of the cases. I personally am very particular about the context, the lives of the individuals who are accused of these crimes, and why were they driven to such acts. Time and again we find that the records are incomplete. This is worrying because there are very occasionally rumours that in rural areas a form of such practices was conducted in secret by families, and the victim ran away. As a lawyer, and a member of my volunteer network, at present I allocate my time to researching the archives in two prisons in Tehran. I have been studying specific cases of women's criminal records connected to adultery, and have visited two in prison. They could not believe that we were looking into their cases free of charge. I ask them many specific questions about the circumstances of their trials, but I also told them that we are concerned with their wellbeing in the prison as well as when they come out. I explained that they should have full knowledge of their legal rights with the hope that we can find any legal discrepancies which have worked against them.

I am confident that we will eradicate the stoning of women, whether in its religious capacity or in the legal system. So it is vital to gather intelligence to understand the dimension of current cases and current laws even if they are not practiced. We have colleagues in many parts of the country who share their insights and experiences with us and help us. I very much hope that we build a body of knowledge which will help us present papers in international conference to open up the discussion in North Africa and the Middle East in conjunction with human rights.

I leave Shokooh in her home in West Tehran with all its cultural and intellectual particularities, and reflect on her immense political determination and conviction to improve human condition within the world she knows and understands as well as aspiring to reach for making improvements beyond geographical borders.

Meet Parastoo and her campaign for a share of Freedom

I meet Parastoo in the sixth floor apartment of a mutual activist friend. I am conscious of the fact that this young lady has to be careful who she meets because she remains on bail along with a number of her fellow campaigners. She arrives self-possessed, cheerful and enthusiastic with a subtle air of celebrity about her. She is in pale colours, light greys and blues, which are refreshing in early summer. She removes her scarf and roopoosh and we sit at one end of the huge wooden dining table in the wide open plan of the apartment. I invite Parastoo to choose a name she might like to be referred to in my work, and she proceeds as follows:

Oh, thanks for explaining to me about anonymity, but please use my own name in your writings. I don't believe in anonymity, I believe in being myself and be completely transparent about what I say and do. My name is Parastoo and speaking as myself is a form of keeping myself in check with a commitment to consider events and ideas in a more balanced and fair way. I respect the law and the legality of things. I take full responsibility for what I say.

I think my journalism started in my early teens when I started collecting newspaper cuttings. This makes sense because I have always been keen on reading, and I think I am a pluralist in my actions. I would make collages of these cuttings and put captions and commentaries around news and current affairs. I don't know how, but somehow Mrs Shahla Sherkat the Editor in Chief of *Zanan* [Women's] magazine, got hold of these and showed them to one of her editors. Before I finished my final year at school they offered me a job. But my mother advised me against this. She said I should focus on completing this pre-university last year, sit for your National University Entrance Examinations, and then go to work at the magazine. This is exactly what I did, and the day after the national exam I presented myself at the magazine and they gave me a job in the news archives office. But you must know about the worrying processes of entering university. They are interdisciplinary. The quota for reading journalism from a maths background was only ten places that year, and through sheer luck I got a place. It seemed that good things were just lined up for me, so while working in journalism I also studied it. After *Zanan* magazine I worked at several other important dailies with high circulation figures. I believe there was something about my approach they liked. I write simply in the everyday language of young people so the story might make accessible reading.

As it turned out, we were not paid our salaries at one of the papers, so we went on a strike demanding pay. I would report all this in detail in my columns, but especially in my weblog starting by saying 'I have been sacked but I must write'. The newspaper itself was shut down by the government, as were many for voicing views deemed unacceptable. This kept happening but as one would be shut another would open with more or less the same team within a short period of time. It was a trend to secure a licence for a new daily with a new name just in case you were shut down. We have all experienced some form of socio-political isolation or alienation, loss of livelihoods, a brother in prison, harassment etc. These are our collective experiences. The socio-political circumstances in our country makes people find themselves in solidarity with you. So gradually I also learnt that journalism is not just a job, it goes beyond that; for me, it manages me, it examines and registers my questions. Through which means do I demonstrate my citizenship, or how do I show my intellectual and emotional commitment to the society I live in? These thoughts became part of my journalism.

I think moving from journalism onto activism was inevitable, I started my work at *Zanan* magazine so I became increasingly aware of the incoherence and the subtleties of women's issues in Iran. In any case women's issues are society's issues too, personal, economic, cultural, political – all such issues relate to the health of a civil society. You see, I became interested in the development of a civil society through experiencing these issues. If supporting myself financially is one of my issues, it must be an issue for others too, the youth and women anywhere. Besides these personal perspectives, I also became interested in non-government organizations by covering and converting their news to the promotion of the idea of a civil society. It was clear to me that I was an activist, so I expanded that activism into my project about sport stadiums in Iran.

Demonstrating for the right to enter sports stadiums

In the summer of 2004 it was announced that Germany's national football team were coming to Tehran. They were bringing their wives-partners-women with them. As activists we were at once happy and outraged about this. This was a direct insult to

Iranian women who wanted to go to football stadiums to watch football but were prevented by laws put in place after the 1979 Revolution. What's more, the insult was two-fold in this case, a double segregation. Not only were we viewed as separate from men in the simple act of watching a game of football, but now that the German team were bringing their women, we were being viewed as separate from other women too, as if we were two different species. This unacceptable state of affairs drove me mad and others mad. I had to do something about it. I and other activists decided to go to the match no matter what, so the first thing we had to do was to buy our tickets. Buying tickets is not gendered we thought, anyone can buy a ticket.

On the day, we were confronted in front of the first gates at the stadium by the most aggressive heraasat security guards who had never in their lives imagined that women too might want to watch a game in the actual space of a sports stadium. That is why they used that most vulgar language towards us as if their very manhood was severed from them. We asked for their supervisor, who came and said the other women in the stadium were German and therefore different to us, and that not knowing Farsi they would not understand the vulgar language males use during the match. We were so angry at this feeble statement that we shouted and screamed back saying they were not different, we were not different to other women, we were all the same, we were all women. This idea that stadiums are a place for vulgar and obscene language is an attitude which has emerged after the Revolution. Many women went to sports stadiums before 1979.

However, because of our demands and the noise, they said they would let us in if we gave them our IDs. Once they collected our IDs, they proceeded to tell us to disperse quickly if we wanted to have our IDs back. At this point we started running towards one of the back gates to find a way to enter, but in a few minutes we were surrounded by the security police on motorbikes with funny police walkie-talkies the size of a brick! Some were carrying batons and pushed us against the gates. We were not there to tolerate aggression, we were not there to be physically assaulted, we were there to watch a football match, and if we were barred we would leave. We did have the number of one of the chiefs of police in Tehran and we called him. He said if we had press

cards, which some of us did, we could go in. But this was not
what we had intended; we wanted to watch the match because
we were entitled to it as citizens, not as an exceptional case just
for reporting it. Going in as a special case meant we would leave
behind those who are not members of the press but want to see
matches, it would be betraying them. We left only to see how we
could come back, and each of us wrote reports and letters of our
experience in front of the stadium and published them in the few
newspapers which had not yet been shut down. We made a lot of
noise with our letters.

In front of Azadi stadium

The following spring, when the Bahraini football team were due
in Tehran, we wrote to the office of Tehran's Governor General
to apply for a written permission to watch the game. A hundred
and fifty women signed the letter. We were told that we would be
supported at the gate of the stadium. 32 of us congregated at the
main gates of Azadi stadium, which, incidentally, means freedom.
We carried placards, we tied red ribbons around our calves as a
symbol of having been stopped before, and in solidarity. We also

wore matching white headscarves which we had block printed on
one corner in bright read. The great big letters read *sahm-e zan
nimi az aazaadi* or 'half of Azadi belongs to women'. We wanted
to be seen, we wanted the message on our headscarves to communicate a clear and symbolic message.

We waited in front of the VIP gate which was also the area allocated to the press for both Iranian and foreign media. We told
the security we wanted to stay together, that we would not disperse or be separated from our friends, and that we would only
keep quiet if they let us in. But they didn't. After an hour and
half the Bahrainis arrived and we pushed through with them.
One of us fell over and broke her leg in the crush and confusion.
Remember, we were a group of over 30 women trying to get in
by running. We called out together, 'broken leg, broken leg, ambulance, ambulance'. It took some time for the ambulance to
arrive, and meanwhile we were told to be quiet, polite, to put our
placards down, and undo our red ribbons if we wanted to enter
the stadium proper and watch the match. We knew that President Khatami was there watching the game, so we screamed
louder. Finally, a short time before half-time we were let in
through the VIP entrance onto the press stands. We took advantage of every moment we had, and with our unified white
headscarves on our heads shouted out our slogans at the top of
our voices, and added to our normal themes the fact that Mahboobeh Abbass Gholi Zaadeh, one of our forefront activists,
had broken her leg and had been taken to hospital in an ambulance. We narrated the whole thing in song. But, we were truly
elated! What a feeling to be there and watch the game! The first
women in 29 years to attend a football match. And, Iran won,
and qualified for the World Cup. Everybody celebrated with
great emotion, and a great feeling for the place – that we were
watching our football team proudly in our country, that we had
got into the stadium as citizens, as is our right.

Perhaps it's hard for others to understand how important all this
was to us. You have to imagine it to understand it. The stadium,
wow, what an atmosphere! It was wonderful to actually feel our
own sense of belonging. Apparently our *female* voices were
transmitted all around the world. Many people around the country in Iran were apparently puzzled, not knowing how it was

possible that they could hear female voices calling out in Farsi, coming through their radios with the voice of the commentator. This was unprecedented in the Islamic Republic. We are not supposed to be heard in the stadiums, we were not supposed to be there! The impact was great, our pictures were shown round the world. But, more importantly, many young women, and men, who were neither activists nor feminists wanted to support us after that. Well, by supporting us they were supporting themselves. Surely many men would wish to go to matches with their wives, sisters, and female friends.

In March 2005 many young teenagers joined us at the gates of Azadi for the match between Iran and Costa Rica. Some had wrapped the Iranian flag around their bodies. But we were deceived this time; we were put in lines, and were told to get into the minibuses they had lined up for us so that we could be taken to the right stands inside the stadium as a group. We believed them. But instead, we were driven to Azadi *Square*, miles away from the stadium. About 30 of us felt more determined than before and hired another minibus to take us back to the stadium directly. On this journey back we called out to the passers-by from the windows and got a lot of attention. When we arrived back at the gates again, we sat on the grass in front of the stadium in protest, and hung our yellow tickets on the trees. The security guards surrounded us this time, and some colonel told us that we were loose women and had neither faith nor morals. We told him the contrary was true, that it was he who had no clout and no moral values, it was he who was a liar, it was he who had to cheat us by putting us into minibuses to get rid of us. We told him he was misguided, and that we were the ones who had stood up to the Western media's misperceptions and objected to their publication of the cartoons and the portrayal of Prophet Mohammad.[94] We told him it was us who had condemned the cartoons. But we could not get in.

We wrote letters of complaint to the courts in the following weeks supported by our photographic documentation at every stage. In the spring of 2006 President Ahmadinezhad lifted the ban and announced on television that women's entry to sport stadiums was legal.[95] Although we knew this was for his own political gain, we were pleased and saw this as great progress. *But,* this was annulled by the Supreme Leader who issued a decree to the contrary effect on the grounds of it being an arousing act for women to see the bodies of the footballers!!

We were not going to give up however. A year ago, in June 2006, 30 of us took a television and erected it on the grass in front of the stadium in protest, and proceeded to sing songs, shout out slogans. But they were expecting us this time, and shamelessly attacked and physically assaulted us and confiscated our cameras. They had understood that our campaign had become a bigger idea. We were fearlessly occupying the public space, we were staging a street sit in. This time they had policewomen in chadors circling us as well as a second line of policemen. This meant of course that we were viewed as a threat to national security!

We now approach a new season, so we intend to print pamphlets to distribute in girls schools to raise awareness there and to extend the debate. Surely some of them would take these pamphlets to their homes and the debate will reach a wider audience. We request individual letters to be written to the President who supported us but quietly and without a debate gave in to the clerics. We want young men to join us in greater numbers than before. We want to argue for the essence of football itself as the 'nation's sport' in our pamphlets, discussing its techniques, analysing and understanding its rules at the national level, and promote the love for it as a game for all to enjoy. We want to be heard by the men, the boys in the streets when they kick a ball around.

I think, as the youth of this country, we could do more; if many thousands, many hundreds of thousands of us protested, women and men, it would make a much bigger impact. They wouldn't be able to arrest and assault every single one, there won't be the prison capacity. It would be sad if men just took up their comfortable seats in the stadiums without any consciousness of our struggles.

My weblog is *zannevesht* which literally means woman-written; it is the natural progression of my work and ideas. I also had the weblog.parastood.ir site which became heavily filtered.[96] I receive as many as 700 hits in one day sometimes. The biggest hit was after the arrests in March 2007 when I had 7000 hits. 33 of us were arrested, as you know, while assembling in front of the Revolutionary Courts. I think to talk about the details of our imprisonment would take too long, and I do not wish to trivialize it. It was a terrible experience, but a great lesson. To be in the company of 30 or so outstanding women in prison was a great privilege. I watched and learned from them. We had techniques for protesting, and protecting ourselves, and we demanded things, from cell-phones to soap and blankets, and we did not do it quietly. We had strategies, even though the experience was unbearable. I was released on the third day. Bizarrely, I had just had a shower, so I came out of prison all clean and shiny with wet hair! The point is we were imprisoned illegally. According to Article 57 in the Constitution of the Islamic Republic, we have the right of peaceful assembly. As long as we are not armed or do not protest against Islam, our assembly would be legitimate and legal. So we were not disrespecting the law in anyway, just fighting for every bit and every fragment of our rights, our identity as Iranian women. I also learnt about life outside prison, about endurance, and about my parents, their integrity and patience with me, and how they have put up with me over the years never attempting to stop my activities.

I am a war baby, like millions of other children who were born in the middle of Iraqi bombs. Did you know that we attended television school? We had very little, a bunker-like two metre square room, a television screen to see the teachers, and a lot of love and tenderness from the people around us. We laughed so much. If only our television teachers knew how much we laughed during their lessons. I have been fortunate to be of the generation and the time when the presidential candidate spoke of *mardom saalaary* [people's rule]! At 16, those were exactly the words I needed to hear to be inspired. With those few words, Mohammad Khatami opened up a way for our collective reflection on the concept of democracy, introducing the possibility of a civil society to us as a collective body. Maybe this had been discussed before, but it was my first time to become conscious of it. So two years after his presidency ended, even though I was not in agreement with him in his manner of running the country, I am still inspired by the *possibility* of contemplating the idea of people's rule, democracy, and civil society.

Now that we are talking about all this, I think I should also tell you one other thing. I played basketball at school and at 17 I was invited to join the national team, which had been my goal since the age of 11 when I started to play. But having a national team was meaningless then simply because we had to play in an *Islamic* environment with no men present! You see, the facilities for these things were not in place yet even though it was only six years ago. Having a national team could not go beyond an idea. But younger girls in recent years have been so steadfast and determined to realize their goal that now they have appropriate clothing for play. Although these are not very attractive they do the job, suitably covering the body. And now they have the kind of uniforms which enable them to play internationally. To see this quality of development in just a few years is owed to the huge effort by my generation and tells us something of the direction of the future, does it not?

Parastoo and I part but we keep in touch through her weblog with the possibility that there will be an opportunity to meet in London in the near future. She is undertaking a Masters degree in Journalism in the UK.

Meet Reihan from the Women of Peace Campaign

To talk to Reihan I have to come to Niyavaran Park in late evening to escape the heat of early summer in Tehran. The park is filled with people enjoying themselves: families, young couples, older couples out to keep fit by power-walking, noisy and buoyant children, the youth who congregate in clusters talking on mobile phones and sporting the latest fashion in hair styles, long fringes covering just one eye regardless of gender, and those people who play games, eat supper, and sit on the grass or benches near the fountains. Petite and without a trace of any adornment in her appearance, Reihan greets me and guides me through the park to a relatively quieter corner where we find a white stone bench. Next to us several young women and men sporadically tell each other jokes and laugh at the top of their voices. Reihan is sombre and deep in thought. She explains that she is worried about Iran being attacked by America or Israel, and how this would be the worst thing that could ever happen to her country, the region, and the world in this century of scientific progress. She continues as follows:

I have only recently joined *Zanan-e Solh* [Women of Peace] Campaign, and I am very much trying to learn how to develop this
commitment amongst my peers and raise consciousness. My
background is student activism, this is what I have been most interested in and done and I am without a job. For the post-Iran-
Iraq war generation there existed an atmosphere of relative
openness and debate, to the point that we dared to publish our
ideas as teenagers. I published my first article in *Jame'eh-ye madani*
[Civil Society] Newspaper, when I was 18. My motto is that you
cannot take the individual out of society, and the society out of
the individual. I see the world, no I imagine the world as a mega
civil society, and the idea of war is painful to me. We say in our
poetry that 'humans are members of one body, because they are
created from the same gem': *bani aadam a'azaay-e yek peykarand,
keh dar aafarinesh zeh yek goharand.* This is something we have been
taught at primary school but did not have the intellectual capacity
to reflect on. I wonder how the youth in America feel about this!
I see the threats of the USA to our country as a direct attack on
my body, my existence, my freedom, my society, my peace, and
my stability. I protest against unacceptable political aggression
both internally in Iran and internationally and I believe in non-
violent resistance to power. It is no longer a question of just local
democracies on their own, and the rest of the world on its own.
This also means that America cannot call itself a democracy if it
is prepared to attack different countries at will.

Our peace website has many contributors and releases news and
analytical statements regularly from both local and global media,
and we keep an eye on other peace-seeking institutions and developments globally. We are in touch with Sweden, for example,
and have attended peace workshops and conferences there, and
in Jordan. But there is much room for developing and gaining
strength. We see ourselves as a pressure group. We promote
consciousness amongst Iranians, we hold meetings, and discuss
global politics, we invite people to reflect on torture, human
rights, and hanging in public. Alongside these our website projects the call for a referendum by Shirin Ebadi, lawyer and 2003
Nobel Peace Prize winner, who urges us to examine the implications and dimensions of our nuclear development in a national
debate, simply because of its inevitable socio-economic effects
on the life of every Iranian. We have articles and news analysis

on the importance of peace in Afghanistan and Iraq. We raise consciousness about the condition and the fate of Afghan children in Iran no longer having access to education because of their parents having remained in Iran without legal status. They refuse to go back to their home country because they have no prospects there and because the United Nations is not active in clarifying their situation under partial occupation. A peace activist links these issues and sees the complexity of peace as a concept which must be safeguarded by all collectively.

Naturally, many of these topics are also linked to my personal sensibilities as a student activist, but the recent clamp-down on the student body has prevented us from exchanging ideas with our peers openly in society. I have a passion about democratic processes and became involved with the Society For Art and Architecture at my university. Eventually, I became part of the central committee bringing together cultural programmes for our student members. Although this was in the last year of Mr Khatami's presidency when he was under great political pressure by the hardliners, we were left alone by the government agents who are present on all campuses.[97] The elections were near and the hardliners were busy campaigning for a new president I guess. Maybe the fact that we were like a very small non-governmental organization and self-financing helped us through without hassle. Our aim was to create a culture of intellectual assimilation and participation through regular meetings and outings for any student who cared join us. Discussions of philosophy, hiking, and presentations by members of our society about Iranian architecture, or any other architecture, were the essence of our gatherings.

The most interesting thing about our Society was the diversity of our group, many students from different disciplines and religious background had joined us. I myself had some experience of religious intellectuals' gatherings from my childhood and early teenage years at home. As a result I have developed a passion and some knowledge of Qoranic interpretation which became very useful in the month of fasting and prayer. I suggested that during the lunch hour we read one page from different religion's texts, whatever people could prepare and contribute, and then we would discuss them. Personally, I have this view that the Qoran might be read metaphorically as if it is art, with meanings which are unlimited and even abstract. The majority of our members had never read the Qoran at all, and this was a completely new thing for them. We had one Armenian Iranian member who brought a parable from the Bible. At each session we endeavoured to select one text at random from the pool of texts people had brought, and we would try to understand how these religious texts might be viewed and compared. You see, political perceptions and other ideologies are the same, you need to reflect on each without isolating others, this is for the sake of understanding. We think we need to understand more and more so that we think less about war and more about peace. We are not like our parents or the generation of the Revolution who considered our own religion as the only way of discrediting others or see the 'left' and the 'right' as the only possibilities of real politics. We want to live in a society which welcomes such an exchange of ideas, citizenship, participation, peace, and dialogue. This is how politics becomes meaningful to us and not by exerting power; in a way, by speaking for peace we have risen from our own nationalism, we want to engage with the world, the civil world, in peace.

Reihan looks at me at this point and reiterates the point she has made earlier about how she is in the very early stages of her peace activism. I on the other hand am struck, as have been so often during conversations and interviews in Tehran, by the depth of perception and verbal and emotional eloquence of my interviewee. Quite how one marks the power of such an encounter with one so young remains an area of reflection for me as the researcher and translator.

In the park, we become aware that there are fewer people around us. The air is pleasantly cool now and the breeze brings the fountains' spray to our faces. It is late and we leave the park behind reluctantly. I hail down a taxi and attempt to say goodbye to Reihan when she announces with a big smile:

Oh, I want to come with you to your residence, it is fun to ride in the streets late at night when there is less traffic. The same taxi can bring me back home again.

We jump into our taxi talking and laughing about our own behaviour, and perhaps in celebration of being here and being alive and not

ing. You know, I have had an opportunity to think, and to re-imagine a world for myself. I am learning how to understand my life.

My private thoughts are about my anger, my rage directed to-wards positions of power, and my helplessness as a child raising the family. And laws, little laws and big laws which affect women's lives. I have been training for the last two months to bungee jump; but I haven't been given the permission to do it by the authorities because I am a girl. I don't understand why there should be this discrimination against girls. It is part of my charac-ter to be ambitious and take up challenges, expressing the difference in my perceptions, so I find training to jump challeng-ing and satisfying. But in our society you're expected to accept the norms and if you want to divert from those norms somebody somewhere will find little laws to stop you. You know, you have to experience these things to understand them, perhaps the peo-ple who run Omid-e Mehr have themselves experienced something similar, they won't dictate ideas they talk to you about your ideas and imagination. It is about being creative.

My positive thoughts are about imagining myself as somebody who can make a difference – who can examine systems of power and comment on them for change, or make a contribution by re-sisting them. Customarily when we ask for someone's promise we say 'give me a man's word that you will do so and so'. But in my home even my little five year-old sister has learnt to say 'I give you a woman's word of promise'. I have done that, I have made a change. I have taught her that a woman's word is just as worthy as a man's. And my younger brothers know that I have a boyfriend and they are OK with it. I have taught them that and I think that is great progress.

I am also a rapper, I write lyrics and one day I will stand on a stage and rap my heart out. You can imagine the double impact of being a girl rapper here! My songs are little stories, sometimes very angry little stories. When I write my lyrics I wish to be the best and I feel the best. Rapping is practically an underground ac-tivity here, it's not recognised as a legitimate form of expression or art. But I have discovered this for myself, it belongs to me. I belong to a global community of rappers, we meet and chat on line and they are very taken by the idea that I rap in the Islamic

Republic. The perception that rapping is for Westerners and a girl from a Muslim country cannot or should not rap does not make sense to me. It's about creativity, the art of expression. I was on a bus one day, and I was watching the people, and noticed many young people listening to their MP3s and moving their heads in rhythms which seemed closer to the sounds of the buses, than some kind of classical musical. You must understand we have an urban life here, an urban life with a violent beat. When you're required to work nine hours a day, and catch three or four buses back and forth to your home, you require a different kind of beat and rhythm, music of a different character. You need something to keep you moving with the urban beat on your journey, especially in our society where there are so many young people.

Naazila recording her song

Anyone, in man's history, who has wished to separate themselves from the mainstream, to show individual creativity in life, has created a tool to express that particular feeling. The beat in rap music is a counterpoint for me, it's a step outside the immediate society, with a different note, a different verse, a different brush. Rapping is like having a conversation with myself, but also beyond myself. When I rap I feel I perform my anger out of me, it's exciting. I think rapping in Tehran shows a particular kind of courage and resistance, and this suits me. No more, no more, ever, will I be sacrificed for the will of others, as I was when I was a child.

Naazila's accounts of her experiences and her solutions to her problems demonstrate characteristics consistent with the narratives presented in this book – courage, the need for a personal mental space to reflect, and the longing to be recognised as part of the bigger world beyond boundaries and restrictions. The desire to make meaningful yet personal contributions, and to reach for new horizons relevant to both the individuals' sense of wellbeing in her locale, and more widely to youth cultures of the new century is poignant. While globalization might mean exploiting the vulnerable for cheaper labour costs in many instances, the participants here speak of the form of globalization which provides membership of the wider world.[98] The Omid-e Mehr Foundation has facilitated the stability and space Naazila needs to reflect on her young life, to realize and re-define her self-worth. She has been shown that the world is not an exclusive entity. Her critical and emotional intelligence can flourish in this new space allowing her to reach for a different brush with which to paint herself into the bigger picture. As I write her narrative I hear Naazila's lyrics, ringing and rapping in my head as if they were my own; I sense the universal essence of her argument:

> you stand on your own
> alone naazila
> it is your tomorrow
> in the mirror naazila
> it's your future
> i am talking about
> it is your awakening
> your voice naazila

At Tehran University

To be a student at Tehran University is a source of pride for the great majority of the student body, and to contemplate art theory and practice in the studio at the Faculty of Art and Architecture is considered a great privilege and opportunity to work with a number of imminent masters of art and culture. Although university art education was first established in 1939, it was housed initially at The Marvi Khan School in the Bazar before it moved to its vast and numerous studio spaces, designed and built to high standards and specifications, at the present location on Tehran University campus. As the first degree-awarding institution in art and architecture, the Faculty has been the site for the development, continuity and innovation in perceptions in visual culture over the past decades. Whether in the graphic arts, schools of calligraphy, photography, painting, or 3D sculptural works, the Department of Visual Arts which became a Faculty in its own right in 2006 has set the cannon of excellence in practice and theory nationally.

Theory session at Tehran University sculpture studio

The student body too, from all 28 faculties at Tehran University, has played a major historic role in political activism, critically analysing, debating, and objecting to the actions of the previous and the current political regimes. The 1979 Revolution mobilized great numbers of student activists and marked Tehran University campus as a major landmark and venue for demonstrations and ideological debates. The central site for congregation and debate leading to the Revolution, just inside the main gates facing *Enghelaab*, or Revolution Street, is now converted into a large mosque where hard-line religious rallies, sermons, and mass prayer take place every Friday led by the religious elite.

Whilst on this campus during a particularly challenging time during Khatami's presidency, I am approached by four students from the Department of Visual Arts to lead a seminar on feminism. Conscious of the implications of such an event, I explain the reasons for my reluctance to the 19 year-old first year students. They listen carefully to my concerns, and particularly note the fact that my ethical commitments and responsibilities demand that I remain faithful to my agreement with Tehran University's International Relations Office, and maintain a strictly researcher/observer position. I can see in their eyes, and the concentration of their brows, that though puzzled and disappointed they will not take 'no' for an answer. As they look at each other searching for solutions, one announces that they will simply have to take their proposal to the Head of Visual Arts. They explain to me that when he received them as first year students earlier in the academic year, he gave his word that he would do everything in his power to help them advance on their educational journey.

When I return to the campus the following week I meet three of the students in the department lobby, they inform me with great pride and enthusiasm that they have secured the Head's permission to hold a seminar. They explain that they simply made an appointment through his personal assistant and visited him in his office requesting a written permission bearing his signature for such an event. His signature, they add, would be sufficient to persuade me that it is ethical to participate, and to show to the right people to book rooms and equipment. Thus the four young women, Aazita, Naazanin, Golnessa, and Parniya, set out to create a seminar in the gallery just off the lobby, opposite the tutors conference room, at the very centre of the department. They further design, have printed, and distribute strips of coloured paper across the nine departments in the Faculty, advertising the event. As if trained for this occasion all their young lives, the four collaborate and proceed with plans with a great sense of agency, transforming their idea into reality, and encouraging their peers to join in.

In admiration of the students' determination and courage I become mindful of how to proceed with such a task myself, especially because the Head's reputation is one of a staunch political hardliner, and perhaps disapproving of the students quest for 'feminist' ideas. However, he proves to be first and foremost a supporter of the student body under his care, allowing them to engage in practicing democracy regardless of his politics and ideologies. This is significant particularly because of the unrests inside and outside the campus, with 'sittings in protest', opposing the religious elite and in solidarity with many Members of Parliament. As a consequence every student's ID card is checked on entering the campus, and visitors such as myself, are only allowed in by appointment, and after depositing their IDs at the Security Room on arrival.

On the day of the seminar, over 30 students gather together in the gallery at 12.30, where seats are brought in from the large adjoining alcove, and arranged roughly in a semi circle by the organizers. One-third of the participants are young men, and one student is in a black chador. I note that the Head of Department peers through the door twice, briefly observing the processes of the seminar for a few moments before disappearing again.

Aazita opens the session:

> We have taken this opportunity to discuss some issues. For me personally, it relates to a project I submitted to my group in the Islamic theory class about the health of the family unit in society.
>
> I elected to discuss some of the points in the situation of women historically. But just after half an hour into my presentation I could see that everyone was bored [laughter from the audience]. And in the discussion we had afterwards I was told that my analysis were too lengthy and irrelevant because I had started too far back in the history of primitive man [laughter from the audience]. Some people said that it was better if we were more socially realistic, and had a discussion about our own history now. As we say 'whenever you catch the fish, it is fresh'. So we want to invite opinions from a group from my year, and create a debate about our own situation.

At this point Aazita turns to me and invites me to share my thoughts with the group. By way of an introduction, I explain that feminism is an ideology, and a huge evolving subject area. I highlight the different phases. I clarify my position by stating that at present I am most interested in discussions which discuss aspects of gender and identity globally, rather than specifically focusing on the Western history of feminist thought. I also explain that although in the Farsi language we refer to feminine and masculine with one and the same word, I have become interested in the meaning of gender through experience, and like them I need to learn much more about the dimensions of the subject. I suggest, however, that since I live in England it might be interesting for the group to reflect on a few different perspectives from there. I submit a prepared list of interconnected topics to the group, which one student volunteers to translate from English to Farsi, and make photocopies for everyone.

I proceed with an example of a discussion, a paper given at the yearly British Education Research Association conference, where a well-known professor in education examines and scrutinizes progress made in overcoming the continued patriarchy and gender hierarchies in her society. The professor revisits the stages in her own development as someone from the low income and underprivileged classes in society. She fights poverty with difficulty in the 1960s and 1970s in the industrial towns of the north of England, overcoming circumstances through education and hard work, and subsequently towards economic independence, becoming a scholar in higher education teaching, writing and publishing from the 1980s forward. I explain how the professor told her audience that she felt she had succeeded in altering her position in society by becoming a recognised and respected academic, who exercised choice, dressed in well-designed clothes, travelled widely, and acquired other identities too, learning about and becoming a connoisseur in certain types of music and good wines and foods, etc. But, she felt that women's battle for recognition, equal pay, and equality in domestic responsibilities was a never-ending one. This was because even at the age of retirement, with all her achievements, the professor felt she was not taken seriously by many of her male colleagues and believed men in Britain needed to change their perceptions about women more radically.

I conclude by mentioning areas of research in gender studies I know about, regarding child pregnancies, the plight of exceptionally young and economically vulnerable teenage single mothers, the new and 'chic' forms of prostitution amongst very young women, arranged and forced marriages in some of the British Asian communities, and the circumstances of foreign domestic workers from countries such as Mexico and the Philippines, who have no legal protection and are treated as if the new slaves of the twenty-first century.

Several young women make comments about how awful it is when they are not taken seriously by boys, and how this is something they experience in direct and indirect ways routinely. One student says that mostly when boys speak to them they want to tell them how to do things starting their sentences with 'what you should do is this ', failing to understand that girls are perfectly able to decide for themselves. One student says that in her view boys know only too well that the girls are able, but they think they will appear more authoritative and strong if they deny this by their actions. Aazita invites the young men in the group to make comments, they all decline and one says he is there simply as a listener. Aazita introduces Naazanin as the next speaker, she says:

> I am interested in issues of women profoundly, this is because I have watched my mother's life! I really do not want to end up like her. She is a nurse, in her forties, and exhausted all the time. Her health has suffered because of long hours of difficult work, and bringing up four children. She has to work to support us financially, sending me to Tehran, to university, and looking after the affairs of the house. Now that I live away from home in the dormitories, I can see things better. I think it is unjust for people like my mother to sacrifice their lives like that. It is too much to expect of women I think. Laws should change about paying women with many children, they should be able to retire earlier, or get paid more. I want to enjoy my life, I do not want to suffer like my mother. I would like to find out whether there are any systems for protecting women in the work place. There should be debates about these issues, we should learn to prepare ourselves for smaller families because we have to work too.

One student contributes by stating that women should understand that they cannot do everything they wish to, that they should understand they have physical limits. Naazanin who has just spoken asks the questioner which direction she would choose, would she have a family and not work, or would she work and have no family? Aazita, who is keeping time, asks Parniya to speak next:

> My problem with our society is the double standards for women and men, especially when we are participants in such double standards. Because I am a girl, there are far more restrictions on my behaviour. Women are expected to consider 'good behaviour' at all times, why is that? Are we the guardians of the family honour! My brother however can get away with anything under the sun! He has a licence to do as he wishes! My parents have practi-

cally given him a private flat with a key just downstairs. My mother protects him, she tells me things which she would never tell him. She says he cannot handle it! So, if we are these strong beings who can take anything, if we are expected to be thick-skinned at all times, then let us announce it loud and clear and get recognition for it. I think we should debate these things and act together now that we are at university with boys. The problem is that even my own generation, my own friends, and I, compromise when it comes to boys. I cannot stand it.

There is some shuffling, and the boys especially appear surprised about what they have just heard. Aazita waits for a few moments, and when there are no comments made, she invites the last speaker Golnessa to address the group. She says:

This is my first year at this university, when I come through the gates I feel a sense of pride. I often think about all those who walked through those gates and made something great out of being here. I want to say that this is our moment. One thing I am concerned with is the relationship between the sexes in this department. We want to work with the boys at every stage, but we don't want to be told what to do. We are here for co-education, and co-education is what we want, and hope that this is what they want too. I find the fact that the boys hang out together separately irritating. It seems that they are mostly interested in girls as girlfriend material. I want to reject this position. This is self-segregation. I think we should have a strategy to mix and work together with boys; I am here to learn from others, hope that others learn from me. At the moment the only time we hear others' views is at the art 'crits' when we show our work for discussion, and that is probed by our tutors. Well if we worked together outside the sessions, we would know about others' views earlier and we might consider something new. I didn't come to university to just keep to female company or become someone's special girl!

Aazita invites comments; but many keep quiet though some nod in approval. She has to close the meeting because there are people waiting to come into the gallery to put up a student show. But finally, and poignantly, one young male voice comes through, his comment is brief. He says:

> Girls have it easy because they are not expected by their families
> to work as well as study, and this gives them time to want to dis-
> cuss issues all the time.

The speakers look at one another shaking their heads, and Golnessa
responds to this by saying that girls want to mix with boys and exchange ideas when on campus, during the sessions and in between
sessions, or during the lunch break. She suggests that girls are often
responsible for many things within the family, and that is why they
wish to break the mould. Aazita suggests they start by having a once
weekly meeting or get together and see if it would be interesting for all
to create a 'work together society'.

It must be acknowledged that there is no opposition to, or restric-
tion on, collaborative work between male and female students by the
department. Though infrequent, students at Tehran University do collaborate in executing art projects. I was told by a group in their final
year how they submitted a bid and succeeded in winning a project to
paint a large mural for Tehran Municipality. They explained that their
tutor had helped locating the bid, and they organized meetings
amongst themselves to prepare a smart portfolio to present their ideas.
The project involved painting several ten-metre long concrete walls for
which they had to make and submit extensive drawings. Allocating a
specific period of time for this, they had first divided the group into
those responsible for time-keeping, visual documentation, report writing, and purchase of materials. Girls participated at every stage. They
had organized site viewings to understand the social context of the site
and how best to gather ideas suitable to an urban residential
neighbourhood which overlapped with the site of a helicopter landing
pad. They had then discussed the iconography of classical Persian motifs, and become interested in a number of different interpretations of
the 'winged sun' from the heritage of Persian antiquity. They incorpo-
rated these with hard edged formal arrangements related the form and
function of a helicopter. The project was graded on site by both the
tutors as well as a number of residents. The students provided me with
photographs of girls while at work on the scaffolding.

The Margins

Sitting on a bench in the grounds of Tehran University opposite the
sculpture studios I go over my notes and highlight the parts of special

interest to me. A tall well-built young man in fine clothes in soft leathers and suedes approaches me. Cell phone in hand, he says:

> Hello I have seen you around, you are some kind of a researcher yes? I hope you don't mind but I have noticed that the people you have chosen to talk to are from the lower classes. But many of us meet outside the campus and come in just to attend lectures. You should go to *Tochal* mountain resort, or the skiing slopes to see the advance of our society. I can give you some mobile numbers if you like, you can contact those students for interviews.

This data becomes more interesting when I present a paper about the student body I have encountered in Tehran at my University in Canterbury. An eminent professor in the audience comments that the research seems to have focused only on the middle classes in Iran!

These comments reference the particular perceptions and perhaps hidden ideologies of the two individuals. The young man in Tehran and the professor in Canterbury search for clues which confirm their personal anxieties and presupposed convictions relating Self and Other. Perhaps the professor expected the photographs from Iran to depict a bombarded and devastated site. It is often the case that the Middle East is imagined to be nothing but a ruin, much like the war-torn Iraq, Afghanistan, and Beirut in 2006, robbed of infrastructure and hope. Or, it may be the case that the professor expected Iranian students to not be wearing the kinds of contemporary footwear or hairstyles most young people access in universities globally. I wonder if the young man in Tehran really imagined that instead of working with the student body present on campuses, I would seek those on ski slopes, or playing other fine sports like polo and golf in private clubs!

However, I do understand that the present work has its limitations and take this opportunity to mark absences, whether of existences, ideas or visual material.

Text Five: Arrivals and Departures

The Margins

This taxi driver waits outside Cafe Naderi, a landmark in down-town Tehran and a place of gathering for writers, painters, poets, and students in the 1960s and 1970s. His taxi is a well kept white car, and he has obviously learnt through practice who needs a taxi most and who can afford his. He then approaches the person swiftly and politely offering his services at rates slightly above the norm. The following are the views he has arrived at.

> Just the other week I gave my daughter a lift to a party, and went and got her after midnight. I would rather do that; she won't take no as an answer in any case. This social life is not something I would have tolerated regarding my sister and my wife. Yet I do it for my daughter, willingly now. The truth is we have to keep our relations with our daughters sweet, they have new demands – needs even. I think it is important for her to have certain freedoms, so we have to develop a sense of trust. I have really changed my outlook through her. She is only in her last year at secondary school.

> Girls have more daring than ever before. Boys are different, potentially they become the breadwinner in the family. This weighs heavy on their shoulders. The fear of the future and unemployment troubles them, well it troubles girls too these days, it troubles us all. The danger of unsuitable friendships and drug abuse is worrying when it comes to boys. They don't establish a rapport easily. Besides, the army is there waiting for them.

The preceding Texts have illuminated Iranian women's intellectual preoccupations and aspirations including their personal critical and educational endeavours in everyday living, and their determining and articulating the dimensions of a shared horizon in society. As Saanaaz has expressed in Text Three 'the struggle for improving the condition of Self is ultimately the struggle for improving the condition of society'. We have further witnessed the range in women's vociferous activism as citizens who promote discourses of change, challenging both familial hierarchies and socio-political structures. Their campaigns are the pronouncement of their entitlement to a fully democratic civil society with equal rights especially in relation to the Family Law. The emerging over-arching narrative is one that possesses vitality and force, projecting complexities in perceptions, courage, and the profound desire to author their own fates despite restrictions.

In this Text I shall reference some of the predominant sources of inspiration and strength which I believe the new generation of women have drawn on to re-define their socio-political location. These culminate in the moment of reform, and in an atmosphere of optimism and hope in the post Iran-Iraq war period. With relatively inclusive cultural policies promoting a sense of belonging, cultural dialogue in the public sphere both nationally and internationally, and the inter-generational nurturing from female elders, whether present within the family, in educational institutions, or in the press and backstage politics. The Text will further create the moment to 'Meet Mehri'. Such reflexivity is in the first instance in solidarity and dialogue with the participants in Iran, but it is also an opportunity to acknowledge the interplay of their text and mine while authoring the narratives.

Reform through cultural dialogue

The memory of the ideas behind the 1979 Revolution, freedom, democracy and social rights for all citizens, were revitalized in the decade following the end of the Iran-Iraq war. The promise of peace, relative economic and political stability, regeneration and reconstruction created a period of critical political debate in the 1990s. There grew a rigorous and oppositional media with strong presence from the grassroots to which women made substantial contributions, setting examples for the new generation. By the late 1990s, there emerged a sharp increase in literary and socio-political publications and an internationally applauded cinema. Within the context of a free market doctrine, state control was reduced and non-governmental organizations were promoted.[99] These developments substantially influenced the election of Mohammad Khatami in 1997 which followed the lead from the grassroots, including women, and adopted a discourse of 'people's rule', and highlighted the need for the conceptualization of a civil society with a membership of the globe.

With a substantial and unprecedented majority vote from the youth and women, Khatami was elected as the fifth president of the Islamic

Republic on 23rd May 1997, or 2nd Khordad in the Iranian calendar. The '2nd Khordadists', his reformist secular and religious followers, thus became the pragmatic and visionary political faction in Iran's politics. A cleric trained in both Islamic and Western philosophy, rather than just Islamic jurisprudence, and equipped with a sound knowledge of Western political literature and an open face and smile, and impeccable dress sense, Khatami came with useful credentials and cultural know-how. As a former director of the National Library and Minister of Culture he had worked with secular intellectuals and artists who had instigated the cultural opening of the late 1990s.[100] As president, Khatami contained the growing popular discontent with the hardline factions in Iran's political system. He promoted a public discourse of inclusive national identity and political participation.[101] This was strengthened by an acknowledgement of the rule of law and Islamic *mardom saalaari*, or the rule of the people and democracy within Islam, with a promise of relaxing the state's ideological vigilance. In numerous speeches nationally and internationally, and in the UN specifically, Khatami spoke of the dialogue between cultures and civilizations. This frequently referenced the central position artists occupy in creating spiritual and metaphysical worlds alongside philosophers and poets. Crucially, specific focus was placed on creating an inter-generational dialogue with the youth, tolerating the coffee shop and internet cafe cultures and more widespread satellite television use on the one hand, and attracting them back into discourses of belonging with diverse and progressive cultural programmes on the other.

The Tehran Museum of Contemporary Art became a significant site for putting into practice the idea of cultural dialogue and art as education. This was echoed in cities such as Isfahan, Yazd, Mashhad, and Tabriz. In Tehran, under the directorship of Ali Reza Sami Azar, the Museum was given a carte blanche to further develop the already well-established arts community. Regular private viewings of uncensored material, art videos, art cinema from France and Japan and other locations around the world, scholarly research papers in these fields, and art-oriented documentaries, were held for invited guests from the artist and intellectual communities.[102] In turn, ideas were transported to the student body in numerous university art departments, nurturing their creative and emotional intelligence and giving birth to new ownerships in art forms. The reformist promise of regeneration and transparency thus manifested itself in the arts rather than politics, culminating in cultural policies which were as inclusive as they were rationally con-

ceived. In three consecutive national art festivals in 2001, 2002, and
2003 and under the banner of 'New Art', conceptual art was promoted
in dialogue with the country's youth. Large scale Installations and
newly addressed subject matter in art photography, video, and elec-
tronic art, as well as performance art and happenings manifested a
shift of focus in artistic imagination and expression. Young artists were
given the opportunity to exhibit alongside established artists. Young
women particularly submitted engaging and provocative works. With
distinctive local sensibility, the works presented depicted new perceptual and visual understanding of the world.

Learning about art at Tehran Museum of Contemporary Art

Cultural Centres in different quarters in the city were put in touch
with well-established art galleries in a series of site visits and meetings
in 2002 in order to exchange methodologies for bringing the arts to
the people. I was an observer on several of these visits. Iranian artists

from different disciplines were sent abroad to the United States, France, Britain, China, Bangladesh, Kuwait, and other locations, to show their work and share their sensibilities with others. The Barbican Art Centre in London witnessed a comprehensive display of Iranian Contemporary Art including masterly calligraphic paintings and video installations. The best of *Brit Art* was brought to Tehran in 2004 for Iranians to contemplate. The Museum's impressive Western art collection, unmatched in the East, was put on show in its entirety for the first time in 2005 before the end of Khatami's second term in office. Yearly national and international conferences with local and global perspectives in art and architecture, brought Eastern and Western scholars together, and I participated in several witnessing the enthusiasm with which these were received by tens of thousands of students and tutors.

The Second Biennale of Contemporary Painting in the Islamic World in 2002 offered a comprehensive show of Muslim visual heritage, its in-depth discussion and analysis, and the specificities in sensibilities from various Islamic regions such as Africa, Asia, and the Arab world. While some papers offered a re-reading of the diversities and complexities of expression in those regions, other research papers discussed the latest developments in the visual vocabulary and grammar of the arts of the Islamic world. Comparative studies between Islamic cultures and other cultures around the globe, analytical enquiries into tradition and modernity in Muslim societies through art, and research in museum collections in the Muslim regions, were also amongst the topics addressed.

It has been my sustained observation, as it has been consistent in conversations and interviews with the participants here, that the attitudes and policies briefly related above profoundly inspired the postwar generation in their teenage years. Despite the shortcomings, disappointments and the sense of betrayal the majority feel, during and after Khatami's two terms in office, Khatami's presidency recognized women as a growing socio-political force and generated selfconfidence amongst young women specifically. This air of confidence has encouraged young women to continue their search with probity and find means to articulate ideas regarding civil society, the membership of the globe, and the presence of Self.

Points of nurture

Any advance made by women in Iran at the beginning of the twenty-first century must be recognised as the collective journey of, at least three, generations of sustained activism and struggle. The mental development of the young women we have met has also drawn on the fervent sense of strife amongst the females at large around them. The longing, and nurture given by mothers, and the passion amongst female relatives to pass on social capital and competency have been intense and significant in this respect. Indeed they have set visible and perceptual examples. As related in Text Four, the work of numerous leading women political activists, in the press and judiciary, and in positions of opposition to current laws in the campaigns, have been without doubt sources of learning and guidance. Abbas Gholizadeh, Sadr, Sherkat, Amouzegar, and the 2003 Peace Laureate Shirin Ebadi are just a few examples where advocacy skills, legal expertise, entrepreneurship, academic ability, and human rights specializations are effectively adopted as methodologies to mobilize the vital elements any civil society movement requires to achieve its goals.

In dialogue with the above, I present short fragments from conversations with women who have intentionally engaged with daughters, nieces, and students to help them move forward. The fragments illustrate a sense of anticipation, profound integrity, and collective ownership of shared horizons and broadened territories of the mind. These women are the middle generation who experienced war directly as adults, and helped keep safe the young women we have met. Their brief narratives are also glimpses of the psychological consequences and cultural and political ramifications of war. I have marked the beginning of each woman's statement in bold letters.

I was in the last years of my secondary school when the Revolution started to take shape with a series of demonstrations in 1978. There was practically no schooling or teaching to speak of for months. The student body was unsettled and many older girls in my school would gang up and write anti-Shah slogans on walls, and sometimes windows would be smashed. Our school Head would send us home and after a day or two this would happen all over again. Those of us who were not activists would take advantage of the cancellation of classes and go to the cinema, or just hang out at the bust stop. My family had lots of revolutionary books banned by the government but easily available from the area around Tehran University. Many titles were related to the Russian and French Revolutions, hundreds of political books from around the world were available in translation, and many were written by a cadre of intellectuals from both the secular and religious-political background with anti-Shah rhetoric and an anti-monarchy stance.

Although the summer of 1979 was exciting because of radio and television programmes, the hostage-taking at the American Embassy created serious problems for our nation, and Islamic dress code became law. As if that was not enough, the closure of universities for political cleansing followed, and as if that was not enough, Saddam's army attacked Iran. What do you do when you are a young woman in that situation? Where do you go? I had been a judo trainee and would have been qualified as a trainer within a year with a brown belt when the regime banned this sport for women! I started teaching my niece at home, it was something to do. I also became addicted to the poetry of Forõugh Farokhzad [1935-1967] and recited them aloud.[103] She is the heroine, the legend, of my little life. She represented my passion and dare as a young woman, and that's why I have insisted my niece should know and recite her poems.

I am one of the female bus drivers from our university campus. We are called the 'service', and we collect our students from south Tehran neighbourhoods early in the morning, and return them again early in the evening. I trained as a bus driver after a period of two years mourning. I lost my husband in the Iran-Iraq war. There was no other way of earning money so I trained as a bus driver to be financially independent to bring up my baby girl. She was the gift my husband left behind and I wanted to provide for her education. Whatever I have not achieved in my life, I want her to achieve.

I had a gallery and a bookshop when the Revolution happened. I had to give up both because I published Shahrnush Parsipur's critical novel, *Women without Men*. I have had to re-established myself, taking my tools of pen and paper to the interiors of my study at home. I work as a translator and editor of art and academic books and I am also working with a group of international Muslim scholars based in Tehran to translate the Qoran, we want to create a new and alternative reading of it. I educated two of my children at home, they have turned out to be reasonable human beings. You know, my skin is tough, it has to be, I am a woman! My religious beliefs, looking at religion as a philosophy in a metaphysical sense, has helped me survive. I look to the future, to the possibilities of science at the end of the twenty first century, beyond geographical borders. Nations and nationhood become meaningless in that metaphysical space. Humanity will have to re-address and re-consider its thinking. I don't believe the rest of the world has any idea about secular and intellectual life in this country, as if they have forgotten this ancient mother culture. The heritage of painting, poetry, music, and ancient architecture in this land have survived for hundreds of years, and I have no doubt they will continue to do so despite the aggression we experience from governments here and in the West.

I live with my two sisters, my mother, and my brother who has been unwell for a long time. We did not marry because in the eight years of war marrying was the last thing on the minds of the men around us. My sisters and I have worked all our youth. I got my degree in psychology, returning to classes part-time while I worked in two places. My sisters eventually got theirs too. We have had to keep things going; surviving financially and emotionally. With life being so expensive, we have brought up my sisters' daughters as our own, we teach them what we know. The eldest niece has done very well in her education, and we hope she will become a doctor. That would be good because all of us have worked in doctors' surgeries in the evenings to pay the bills, and having a doctor in the family would bring joy.

I was enjoying being a student when the Revolution happened, we had such a good time as students, education was free and some of us who qualified got financial help to purchase our books and pay for our transport. But the universities closed down in the name of a cultural revolution. Luckily I had a fiance and I got married. There was no serious work to speak of if you did not wear the chador, and with the economic situation the way it was, and the war, the best thing for me was to marry. It was a sad time for many young women who either lost their intended in the war, or never found someone. The bombardments were horrific, I was pregnant in the latter part of the war, 1985, and walked everywhere with a blanket or a pillow in case we were hit. I was very naive, as if putting a pillow on my pregnant tummy would protect the baby. When she was born I would hold her and rush out of the room when the sirens went off, standing against the wall outside, as if that would protect the baby. Well, I thought at least she would be safe from the ceiling landing on her. My friend would stay indoors throwing herself over her baby. I always remind my daughter how lucky we are to have survived; I have told her I don't want anything from her other than being serious about education and not getting into trouble at university. No politics I said, I don't want you to disappear like the students who vanished in 1999, that's all. In a way she is living the future I wanted for myself. We do everything we can to help her continue with her studies as far as she can go.

My brother was killed in the war. Just as his term had finished and he was supposed to return home, he went to the front for a last time and that was it, he was killed by a large piece of shrapnel. I was not allowed to see him, but my mother says his front was completely intact but had no back at all. After a year, to make some happiness in the family I married a distant relative before finishing secondary school. This has been the biggest mistake of my life. I am still happily married but I never had the chance to think about further education. A ninth grade certificate is nothing these days, not even to work in a nursery school. I will not make the same mistake with my children, whatever we have we will give for their schooling, as far as they can take themselves. As for the memory of my brother, he is with us day and night, we all have large portraits of him in our hall as you enter the landing. 25 years after his martyrdom, we are tired of the black drapery around his photograph; we now celebrate the anniversary with a cake and candles and have replaced the black cloth with green. I have joined the One Million Signatures Campaign For Change and try to collect signatures.

My dear Dr Honarbin, when you were taking the air abroad, we were trying to survive the war here. That is what your British and American relatives did to us through Saddam Hossein. But humour aside, as an art historian I have tried to give my students what knowledge I possess, as if they were my own daughters. I draw them a vivid picture with words and alert their imagination. When I returned from my doctoral work in France, in the middle of war in 1984, I pledged to help our girls. I have written articles and travelled widely with some clerics to Switzerland, Turkey, and France in governmental delegations. When we have foreign dignitaries in my area of specialization I lead the discussions which surprises them. As for our young women, they are simply unstoppable, they have a mind of their own, we just aim to give them something through education.

I believe there is very little awareness and differentiation outside Iran between Iran and its neighbouring countries. The pictures from Iraq and Afghanistan, and our geographical proximity to them, and a number of other countries in the region do not help us at all. I have travelled extensively in Central Asia, Tajikistan and Turkmenistan, and know that things are different here despite the vast socio-economic and political challenges we face. We will not be servants to the Imperial hunger of the West, and this gets us into trouble. I am an educator, I have circumnavigated the world and arrived back here. In our youth, Cuba was the Left we wanted to know and emulate. I was in Washington at the time of the Iran-Iraq war working in a textile museum having finished my studies in London at Central St. Martins and at Chelsea Art College. One day my husband and I looked at one another and said let's leave this golden cage, this Washington. It was the most important decision of our lives and we do not regret it. We belong here. I have insisted on being autonomous in what I teach and I have written several courses. Because I have chosen to remain a sessional tutor I have some freedoms. I love being around my students, they give me energy, they are much wiser than we ever were at their age. I talk to them about their views and outlook in life. I get up in the morning and put my lipstick on and wear my headscarf and go to work, I need the income. I have supported my family financially all my married life and I am proud to have helped my students to go to Japan to do MA degrees, two of them have scholarships to do PhDs there. The West is not the only direction for us. I defy restrictions as much as I can, and refuse to apply self-censorship and insist on thinking freely, despite the head scarf. You cannot touch my mind.

The Author's critical and reflexive moment

I work across disciplines in fine art and social science with interest in gender. My work as an artist draws on observation and evidence, experience and imagination, and history and heritage, in order to express an emotional intellectual state also relevant to a wider cultural world. I believe I write in the same manner; I observe and engage with the material available to me and explore the message it posits. In turn, I reflect on how the essence of what has emerged might find resonance with sets of ideas and theories also available to others.

C Wright Mills' life history and influential work *The Sociological Imagination* have been a point of departure in my social scientific work. The dynamic interplay of the macro and micro is of interest to me, and his arguing for the understanding of the history of the individual in order to understand the society in which she lives resonates with my ideas. I have thus arrived at critical and reflexive approaches in ethnographic observation, placing attention on the lived experience of the individual. I have subsequently proceeded to tell or narrate the observed. This particular branch of ethnography echoes principles set forth by Clifford Geertz in *Available Light: Anthropological Reflections on Philosophical Topics*. He recommends that the perceived cultural, philosophical, and social-scientific boundaries between the researcher and the researched should be overcome. This resists Othering and validates interaction between the cultures and contexts of the researcher and the researched.[104]

The moment of reflexivity requires the further clarification of my political location while authoring the narratives from Tehran. I recognise that I live in the liberal West. However, I also see and experience on a daily basis that such liberalism is essentially conditional. Its structures practice prejudice, and frequently undermine the position of individuals and groups according to class, gender, and race. Such observations are strongly supported by academic research in education and social science. At best and at its head, this liberalism possesses and performs deeply rooted masculinist principles which strive to sustain power, and maintain economic hegemony at all cost. On a daily basis I witness how the policies of this brand of liberalism, and its greed machinery damage those of a different socio-political location and economic standing. A deep global rift has thus ensued, with desires for neo-colonialist principles, policies, and practices which devour those who do not wish to or cannot join in. This liberalism seeks to divide the world into simply the East and West and superficial categories of religion – the Christian world and the Muslims. It then attributes patriarchy and hegemony to the latter only. This liberalism relies heavily on what it refers to as the 'Christian values' and 'Western democracy'. The 'world' has thus come to mean the United States of America and Britain with a handful of other European countries thrown in. At best, the 'Christian values' are spoken about as if they were set by a gentleman banker named Jesus who played his guitar when roaming around somewhere West of Athens – when in fact Christianity belongs to the East as much as Islam does. I live in the liberal West, the allegedly 'non-tribal' world, and yet observe and encounter forms of tribalism throughout society routinely, whether political, religious, in sports, in the media, or in academia.

By necessity then, I turn to forms of theory and practice which decline binaries and adopt those conceptual trajectories which recognize the complexity of phenomena. Non-linear and non-absolutist Derridean deconstructive ethics, for example, have proved useful, and his notions of space and time have provided new points of arrival for understanding the emerging meanings in the data. Indeed I have considered the material to be autonomous, itself possessing deconstructive qualities and containing layers in meaning even if from the margins in society.[105]

With regard to my work as an artist, in 2002 the Tehran Museum of Contemporary Art invited me to show my studio work at The Artists Forum or *Khaaneh-ye Honarmandaan*. This took place in 2004 and was entitled 'The Archaeology of Self' with video and ceramic installations. The central thesis of this body of work was my experienced, felt and imagined psycho-geography. The body and clay share essential elemental qualities; they are as much about strength as they are about fragility. I see the body as a container and a metaphor manifesting a fluid language of formal ideas; I believe it to be a site for registering and remembering experience. Whether fragmented or imperfect the body possesses a physical/metaphysical and sensory presence. Similarly, clay as a material of 'the origins' possesses primal alchemy, warmth, and abstract qualities. Its inexhaustible physical potential and its response to touch I have found seductive.

I communicated such sensibilities through an installation of 33 sculptures of fragmented female forms suspended in an open cube structure (5 x 5 x 5m). Collectively, the sculptures interacted with time, creating dialogic rhythms and intervals in space which were ambiguous in nature, whether they were hung or dancing! Individually however, the sculptures were visual texts relating my creative identity. They externalized inner traces and residues of ideas narrating a cultural heritage from East and West in a visual and sensory language. 33 was a symbolic and emblematic representation of the strength of the collective body, and a metaphor for sets of ideas, including a fraction of the 99 names of God in Islam. I had frequently observed my grandmother holding rosaries made of 33 exquisite unfired clay beads strung in bright emerald green silks.[106]

Suspended ceramic sculptures: Archaeology of Self

Meet my grandmother

My first memory of observing a drawing takes me back to my early childhood sitting next to my grandmother from the Sangelaj area of old Tehran. She was a Qoranic scholar. She was also acutely attentive to the sound of the Qoran and would correct people's diction when they recited it, emphasizing the importance of the rhythm and music of every syllable and every phrase. She looked ancient and had a tall and slender physique with a slight limp. Although she never embraced us, her warm brown eyes welcomed us into her space and her fruitful pockets! Dried white mulberries, the tallest green raisins, and roasted chickpeas trickled out onto our palms. She had her red-hennaed hair in a single braid twisted into a bun, wore homemade dresses under her fitted jackets she bought on her travels to Karbala in Iraq, and she fastidiously tightened her dark thick stockings with a wide elastic band under her knees. She regarded television as having the ability to also see you and wore her flowery indoor chador in front of it. She carried her line of thin cigarettes in a silvery flat box, kept safe in a breast pocket if not in her bosom. She gave us a *shabnama*, or luminous snow globe, when she returned from her travels visiting important shrines in Iraq.

I was not yet of school age; she was holding a piece of charcoal in one hand and an egg in the other. As she drew with her charcoal, puffs of tiny black dots plunged into space. With concentration, she steadily and patiently organized the surface of the white egg as if it was a painter's canvas. She drew firm black vertical lines from pole to pole creating equal segments. She then placed her charcoal in the centre of the stripy form taking it around the egg to locate its equator. Parallel to this central line she drew more circles with exactitude, towards each pole, in order to create squares of similar measure. The marks she made rendered a formal pattern, and there emerged a series of fine black squares sitting on the surface of the white egg. Inside each of these she drew a circle. Finally, she divided each circle into equal portions by intersecting its diameters at right angles. To disperse bad spirits and to break the cycle of an illness, my grandmother would then call out the names of every member of the family, young and old, friends and relatives, while pressing down on the centre of each circle at the cross-section with a tiny silver coin. To my astonishment, at some point and with the name of a particular person the egg would shatter and hit the hard surface of the container beneath like a drop of weighty liquid!

I now understand that while rooted in talismanic-calligraphic illuminations found on objects as well as in the arts of the book, my grandmother's ritualistic drawing and performance has instigated in me sensibilities towards art, abstraction, and formal and visual ideas. I now see that the history of her quadrangles, circles, and their rhythms and cross sections go back further in time and space to the iconography of architectural form and ornament, tablets and seals, and clay vessels, found in Susa in Iran during the Elamite civilization in the 3rd and 4th millennia BC. They are related to a visual language in art which represent the heritage which forms the backbone of renowned international artists' works from contemporary Iran who were the founders of the Saqqa Khaneh Movement in the 1960s.[107]

In Tehran, many who visited my show stated that essentially the work belonged to Iran. They related the sculptures' ribbed and constructed surfaces to columns in Persepolis and the eroded landscapes around it with traces and residues from history. They recognised the 33 fragments of female body form to be emblematic of powerful presences, if also a comment on the fragile.

These observations were particularly interesting also because I knew I had produced the work during a period of one year in Canterbury, gripped by the aftermath of the September 11th tragedy, and the demonizing discourse of *the axis of evil,* and *you are either with us or against us* from the White House which was adopted by the media. I drew a connection between this and suddenly being isolated, and viewed as a foreign Other, experiencing the ransacking of my studio and drawings on campus, and at the receiving end of verbal abuse from a number of sources. In protest, and in order to overcome such an aggressive blend of ignorance, arrogance and resentment, I had engaged in intense cultural creativity in the studio. I had narrated a mindscape beyond borders and nations, becoming visible in my work. I had depicted the essence of common and shared experiences between myself and the women in Iran; a state of being which made us simultaneously live and function in our communities and feel as though in exile.

The narrative of women in Iran has thus been a march of self-realization of which I am part.

Notes

1. For insights into the lives of Afghani women in the last two decades see Rostami-Povey (2007), for insights into the lives of Iraqi women since 1948 see Al-Ali (2007).

2. Hersh (2007)

3. Amongst others, Noam Chomsky (2002), Arundhati Roy and Howard Zinn (2002), and Edward Said (2003a), outline the history of an expansionist US agenda since the late 1940s and 1950s and the American Framework of World Power.

4. Qom is also the site of the ancient shrine of her holiness Ma'soomeh, the daughter of the seventh Shi'ite Imam and the sister of the eighth, Imam Reza, and is visited by millions of Shi'ite Muslims from around the world. Whilst such characteristics are the reason for Qom to be a centre for spiritual gathering, outwardly expressed piety, and Shi'ite conservatism, it is also the site for a Theological Research University and a Medical Science University where both women and men may engage in educational research.

5. Amnesty International Press Release: AI Index: MDE 13/22/2007

6. The Office of the National Archives in Tehran in 2004-2005

7. Salehi-Isfahani (2008: 251).

8. Ibid.

9. http://www.accu.or.jp/litdbase/policy/irn/index.htm

10. Salehi-Isfahani (2008: 251).

11. Amongst these are Paidar (1997), Beck and Nashat (2004), and Amin (2005)

12. Bayat (1997: 109-126), Ansari (2006: 77-83), Afary and Anderson (2005: 1-10), Gheissari and Nasr (2006: 77-88).

13. Keddie (2003: 189), also Poya (1999).

14. For sanctions against Iran see:
    http://www.mafhoum.com/press3/108E16.htm,
    http://www.ustreas.gov/offices/enforcement/ofac/programs/iran/iran.shtm
    l, http://www.globalpolicy.org/security/sanction/indxiran.htm,

15. Diba (1999: 34).

16. Keddie (2003: 89).

17. Bayat (1997: 19-21, 25); also see Keddie (2003: 89, 153, 164).

18. Ansari (2006: 158-161).

19. This information is repeatedly used in the media in Iran. It is also referred to by Alavi (2005: 10).

20. Author's calculations based on the figures released by the Office of Iran's National Statistics in Tehran

21. Geertz (2000: 17).

22. Keddie (2003: 29).

23. An elderly relative of mine, 91 years old at the time of writing, was educated in the maktab system. Although she is an avid reader of the poetry of the 14th century Iranian Master Haafez-e Shiraaz, as well as the Qoran and other religious texts, she is unable to write words and sentences. She can take down a telephone number if really necessary.

24. Paidar (1997: 74).

25. Keddie (2003: 29).

26. Afary (1996: 182).

27. Paidar (1997: 69).

28. Dr Ali Shariati was a prominent figure in contemporary religious ideology in Iran. He published widely, and gathered substantial political and intellectual following in the 1970s holding regular meetings and seminars in Tehran. He was subsequently made isolated by the Shah's régime, imposing severe limitations on his activities which led to Dr Shariati's move to London in self-exile. He died there in 1977. Also see Afary and Anderson (2005: 59-62).

29. Paidar (1997: 104-106). She connects the official unveiling of women to a government reception for the students of Women's Teacher Training College in May 1935 and the founding of a 'Ladies Centre'. This was followed by an announcement in January 1936 outlawing the veil. However After Reza Shah was sent into exile in 1941, and with the backing of the clergy many women took up the veil again.

Although still firmly under the Shari'a Law, the Civil Code of 1931 and the Marriage Act of 1937 created new possibilities and interpretations for women's rights within the family, age of marriage, and certain circumstances for divorce. See Paidar (1997: 109-110, 153).

30. Ghamar-ol Molouk-e Vaziri is an iconic figure in Iranian classical music born in late nineteenth century. A singer during the last years of the Qajar (1785-1925) and early Pahlavi era (1925-1979), she was probably the first woman to perform in public to mixed, as well as all male, audiences in the theatres in Laaleh Zaar Street in Tehran in the 1930s. Like many aristocratic and highly educated women in Iran, she de-veiled well before the official and unofficial announcements in 1935-36. It is suggested that she accompanied the Iranian poet and wit Iraj Mirza (1874-1926) at gatherings in aristocratic circles and sang his poems. Ghamar-ol Molouk-e Vaziri is also remembered for her charitable and generous character sponsoring many economically vulnerable families of her time; ironically she is said to have died in abject poverty (private communications with Mr Ali Kamalvand who was a student in The Faculty of Literature at Tehran University in the 1930s).

31. For more detailed accounts see Paidar (1997), and Keddie (2003).

32. See Khosrowpanah (2003) where a typical advertisement for tailoring for ladies is illustrated.

33. Apart from the Bazar much of the financial affairs of the country had been dominated by the British prior to 1928 establishment of Bank Melli Iran (Ansari 2003).

34. The uses for the *biruni* and *andaruni* are varied. Essentially however the andaruni is the women's and the family's collective private space, whilst the biruni is the public space where males might gather and be entertained. The Web offers many links.

35. *Halal* is an Arabic term which means a permissible concept, form, or thing according to Islamic jurisprudence. In monetary transactions care must be taken that the inheritance of under aged children is not disinvested.

36. *Khanoom* means madam or lady, and *Aqa* spelt differently to the *Agha* meaning Sir or Master, indicates a further feminine seniority.

37. For a succinct analysis of these principles of conduct see Ghazali's ethics in Hourani (1976: 69-74).

38. A half circle piece of fabric which when placed over the head in its centre can cover the body from head to below the ankle. The outdoor chador was in thick black fabric, but indoors women wore light soft flowery ones over a white kerchief fastened under the chin. The most elaborate chador was formed almost like a cylinder, the lower part of which would be worn as if a wrap around skirt and the upper part would be pulled up to cover the head and arms; the latter is practically extinct.

39. *Bozorg* means senior, great or grand and it is interesting how it is different to titles such as *Agha* and *Mirza* mentioned earlier.

40. The Thousand Families consisted of the royal families, tribal nobility, military élite, upper clerics, and native landlords.

41. Afsaneh Najmabadi cites the first open and direct critical debate about the 'deplorable situation of women in Iran' in relation to the Hundred Sermons text written by 'Mirza Aqa Khan Kermani (1853-1896)'. He recognised female seclusion and the veil, polygamy and temporary marriages to be the root of Iran's 'social ills'. Mirza Aqa Khan Kermani contrasted Iranian urban women with their tribal sisters who did not veil and worked, and with European women (Najmabadi 2005).

42. The 13th century Iranian master of poetry and prose Sheikh Sa'di of Shiraz who travelled widely before returning to Shiraz and writing Boostan, the fruit garden, and Golestan, the rose garden, where he gives accounts of his experiences with people and discusses moral and social stories.

43. As related earlier the necessity of mass public education for women had been at the centre of social reform debate since before the Constitutional Revolution (1906-1911). In 1907 and 1908 specifically two schools were founded in Tehran to educate girls. 'Dabestan-e Dooshizegan' or School for Girls was founded by Bibi Khanoom Vazirof wife of Moosa Khan Mir Panj, and 'Maktab-e Dokhtaran' or Maktab for Girls. Neither lasted long but gradually and in the face of sever opposition by the clergy and reactionaries similar schools in Tabriz and Rasht and other locations were opened. By 1918 new taxes facilitated the opening of ten governmental primary schools for girls in ten different locations in Tehran. These were free and offered a common curriculum (Khosrowpanah 2003).

44. Taar is long-necked double bowl body carved from mulberry wood with a think membrane of stretched lambskin face. It is plucked and derived from the Central Asian rebab. It has become the chosen instrument of great masters of Persian Classical music since the mid-eighteenth century.

45. The Civil Code's articles on the family were supplemented in 1937 by the Marriage Act of Iran. Paidar (1997) analyses the articles in the new Marriage Act on page 111 of her book. It seems that they legal system remained largely patriarchal.

46. Kelileh-O-Demneh is an ancient book of fables brought to Iran from India before Islam but was translated into Arabic and back again into Farsi after Islam.

47. For wider discussions of the complex political dynamics of the abdication and exile of Reza Shah see Ansari (2003) and Keddie (2003).
http://www.iranchamber.com/history/reza_shah/reza_shah.php
http://www.iranchamber.com/history/pahlavi/pahlavi.php

48. *Tudeh* means the masses, and its leftist principles are linked to Russia from late 10th century. The law against communist and socialist collectivist propaganda was put into effect in 1931, and under this law over fifty people were sent to prison in 1937 (Keddie 2003: 88). These people were released from jail and joined with others to form the Tudeh Party in late 1941 after Reza Shah was forced to abdicate (Keddie 2003).

49. One of the most important political developments in the late 1940 and early 1950s Iran was related to the rise of Mohammad Mosaddeq and the achievements of his premiership and the nationalization of oil. He took Iran's case against to the UN and the International Court at the Hague defending Iran against the British claim to Iranian oil (Keddie 200: 131, Ansari 2006: 35).

50. Built on a 9th century site, the shrine of the eighth Shi'ite Imam, Imam Ali ibn Musa Al-Reza S.A. is the most significant place of pilgrimage for Iranians re-built in 15th century. It is estimated that around 15 million pilgrims, Iranian and no-Iranians from all over the world, visit the vast complex yearly.

51. From Arabic meaning a junior cleric with limited knowledge of religious texts.

52. Afari (1996:196-7).

53. Khosrowpanah (2003: 231-236) gives the date for Shokufeh's first publication 1911; Paidar (1997: 92) suggests 1913.

54. This type of title was given to those related to the monarch or his household, in this case it would be one of the Qajars (1785-1925). The last Qajar King Ahmad Shah was ousted by a coup d'etat by Reza Pahlavi who became Shah in 1925 (Keddie 2003: 80-81).

55. The Qajar censors were watchful of the slightest transgression by Shokufeh or other women's publication from domestic sciences and child-rearing. Women editors however ceased any opportunity they could to voice opinions. Sediqeh Dowlatabadi's Zaban-e Zanan was shut down because of her attack on the Qajar's 1919 Anglo-Persian Treaty (Amin 2005: 41-42).

56. Paidar (1997: 66-67).

57. An outspoken cleric based in Qom who profusely refuted secularism in the 1940s, and campaigned against women's suffrage and any form of emancipation. See Paidar (1997: 141-146). He became the leader of the Islamic Revolution in Iran in 1979.

58. Ansari (2003: 160).

59. Mir-Hosseini and Tapper (2006: 25).

60. Poya (1999: 78).

61. Rostami-Povey (1999: 138).

62. For a succinct summary of Shi'ism see Hujjatul Islam Sayyid Muhammad Rizvi http://www.jaffari.org/resources/alim.asp?id=16

63. Holliday, S. (2007: 31).

64. Paidar (1997: 232).

65. Paidar (1997: 234-236).

66. These come from my own experience when I was nearly arrested during a short visit to Tehran in 1985. I was circled by two armed soldiers and three ladies in Mohseni Square and was about to be taken to a *question and answer* session at the police headquarters. It was pointed out to me that my coat, which was just covering my knees over black trousers, was too short and I seemed to lack the modesty required of an Iranian woman during the difficult times of war with Iraq when the country was at mourning. I believe I just seemed too colourful because I had pushed up my coat sleeves showing their bright lining. Though I was taken aside in the street isolated from my relatives, they managed to shout out that I had just the night before arrived from England and that I was about to purchase an appropriate coat. Other incidents about the workplace have been discussed with me by my female friends and relatives who held senior positions at a number of ministries.

67. I follow the idea of social capital as analysed in Pierre Bourdieu's *Distinctions* (2006).

68. Diba (1978: 6).

69. Private conversation with the Museum's Director Dr Sami-Azar in 2005 in an international conference on the developments in contemporary art in Iran.

70. Amouie (2005).

71. *Jihad* is an Arabic word which simply means striving for betterment. *Jahad* is the Farsi pronunciation of the same word. The 'educational jahad' or 'jahad-e danesh-gahi' is a governmental organization that provides opportunities, and some financial assistance too if necessary, to vetted applicants. It creates an advisory/consultancy/tutorial space in almost any discipline. It has been particularly beneficial to re-habilitate many soldiers from the Iran-Iraq war to come into terms with their traumas and disabilities through education. This facility is also highly appreciated by many who have faced hardships through lack of opportunities; it has been part of the message of the Revolution to create such opportunities for the 'disadvantaged'. It is, however, generally understood that Jahad beneficiaries, at least outwardly and visibly, demonstrate their support for the government and its policies or stance on interpreting moral/ethical codes of behaviour. Participating in pro-government demonstrations, attending mass prayers and adhering to dress codes for women, in particular, are also implied.

72. *Sangak* means little pebbles, and *sangak* bread is one of the most loved and most traditional Iranian breads. It is made freshly with wholemeal flour, and baked on hot pebbles in large ovens three times daily in most neighbourhoods. It is flat and usually approximately 90 x 25cm, and decorated with sesame seeds.

73. This is an important date in the Shi'ite calendar. Processions of religious chants, forms of flagellation, and beating of drums are made in remembrance of the anniversary of the martyrdom of the fourth 'Shi'ite' Imam, Hossein the grandson of the Prophet Mohammad, over 1300 years ago in 680 A.D. in Karbala in Iraq. His martyrdom was because of the political/ideological differences between the courts of the Caliphates and those who wished to follow the descendents of Ali ibn Abou Taleb as the successor of the Prophet Mohammad. For a succinct and brief history see Chelkowski (1999). Although considered to be a tragic day and month of mourning and martyrdom, as children and young teenagers we were treated by my parents to watch these 'performances' of fabulously rich processions with extraordinary colourful emblems and banners from small balconies above the shops in the main street in Tehran Bazar. We were often given very good food and rosewater sherbets as alms as served to those in the processions.

74. Soldiers, but more importantly in contemporary life it means the Revolutionary Guards who support the hardline ideologies in the government. They often carry a baton and arrive at such occasions in grey minibuses and move in groups to intimidate and control crowds.

75. The 'axis of evil' was the unfounded term used by George W. Bush in 2002 in his State of the Union Address in Washington to brand Iran, Syria, and Korea as the countries threatening the destruction of the so called 'civilized world'.

76. I met Dr Rahnavard at the Visual Art Faculty at Tehran University where I observed her teaching the first year sculpture class. She arrived at the class in her chador, but removed it during the lesson and kept on her roopoosh and headscarf. Dr Rahnavard showed a video of world art with her own way of narrating the video making frequent use of vocabulary such as aesthetic paradigms and parameters, but the video was cleansed of any reference to female form. This appeared strange to me considering that the landscapes shown were of Greek and Indian antiquities where female form sets the canon for aesthetic and philosophical thought. Another occasion was when Dr Rahnavard received me in her office for a few minutes, she was in a roopoosh that had a large hole on the front of the right sleeve! I believe Dr Rahnavard intended to give an impression of down to earth modesty. However, in January 2007 we showed our work in the 8th Glass and Ceramic Biennale in Tehran, and Dr Rahnavard was very well made up under her black chador with thick powder and lipstick; this is contrary to her writings todate about the necessity of the modesty of a Muslim woman. Dr Rahnavard was an undergraduate stu-

dent in the Faculty of Art and Architecture before the 1979 Revolution and her miniskirts and theatrical activities are well remembered by her classmates and friends at the time.

77. The transition from the ustad-shagerd or master/apprentice traditions, leading to the naturalist style and institutional training stemmed from the reformist vision of Mirza Taqhi Khaan Amir Kabir (1807-1852), the first prime minister to Nasir al-Din Shah Qajar (1831-1896). He founded Dar al-Sanayi' or the art and craft institute in Sabzeh Meydan, and the Dar al-Funun or the first modern Polytechnic, where engineers, physicians, interpreters and musicians were trained. Painting classes at Dar al-Funun were given by Abu'l Hasan Ghaffari known as Sani'al-Mulk (c.1817-1866), court painter to Muhammad Shah Qajar (1810-1848). Continuity was maintained through the efforts of his great nephew Muhammad Ghaffari known as Kamal al-Mulk (1852-1940), court painter to Nasir al-Din Shah. He was trained at Dar al-Funun, and later at the Paris Beaux Arts. Kamal al-Mulk founded the Honarestan art secondary schools still in operation in Tehran, and more significantly the state funded Madraseh-i Sanaye'i Mustazrafeh or the fine art academy in 1911 situated on the grounds of Negarestan Palace. Following the realist style and the cannon of the academy in Paris and their implied liberal stance on the arts, the science of painting and stone carving were employed and recognised in institutional art training in Iran.

78. Spycket (1992: 183).

79. Keal (1989: 52-53).

80. Farhad (2000: 84), Hugo and Marjorie Munsterberg (1998: 75, 77), Fehérvári (2000: 95, 102).

81. Diba and Ekhtiar (1999).

82. The life class as a discipline within the university fine art curriculum and, as understood by art students in the contemporary period is a complex concept and subject to negotiation. Whilst drawing from the nude in the art class has never been entertained, even before the 1979 Revolution, its status as a relevant subject to the study of theory and practice in art, and as a tool to analyse and study formal and structural arrangements, has become problematic since the Revolution. Gradually, however, certain tutors have collaborated with the student body to re-introduce figure drawing as a subject to the curriculum. Tehran University students for example study form in the drawing class from plaster casts in the style of antiquity which depict the male torso.

83. http://news.bbc.co.uk/1/hi/world/middle_east/3570040.stm

84. Alavi (2005: 1).

85. This refers to the nationalism that came about as a consequence of nationalizing the oil during the premiership of Mohammad Mosaddeq, who was toppled by a CIA coup d'etat in August 1953.

86. Sadeq Hedayat (1903-1951) was a significant literary figure and founder of modern fiction in Iran in the twentieth century. He became the central figure in progressive circles in Tehran. He published novels, short stories and essays. He is the author of The Blind Owl, the most famous Persian novel both in Iran and in Europe and America.

87. Rostami-Povey (2001)

88. Van Engeland-Nourai (2004: 6).

89. Consult sites for Kanoon e Zannan e Iran, women's field:Meydaan.com, forequality@gmail.com, and http://www.wechange.info/spip.php?article48

90. Narggess continues as follows:

Another proposal is to change the age of criminal responsibility in articles 1210 and 49 in civil and Islamic laws respectively. This is based on puberty which is nine years of age for girls and fourteen years of age for boys. How can a child of nine bear criminal responsibility and be prosecuted as if an adult? This injustice has to stop. The inheritance and marriage laws too carry profound discrimination against women and you don't have to be a lawyer to understand these. The marriage law is profoundly flawed when it comes to the rights of brides. It is routinely in favour of men, whether in relation to the legal age for consent, the requirement of permission by a male blood relative, polygamy, the right to divorce, and the rights of mothers for access and equal custody for male and female children. It is truly nauseating how the majority of the clergy remain in favour of these laws and against change! The divorce laws for example allow men to ask for divorce any time they wish to, without having to produce a list of reasons. Women however, have to provide justifiable reasons and evidence of lack of financial support, violence, addiction, imprisonment, etc., which takes time and delays processes substantially. Often these lead to women having to forgo their dowry in order to get the husband to agree to a divorce. In a society where over sixty five percent of university students are female, where they are economic partners as well as important consumers in a capitalist economy, and where they practically hold the infrastructures of health and education together, the existing laws are shameful.

We operate within the framework of human rights and seek the social and legal wellbeing of women as citizens with equal rights. Even though there is always the danger of activists such as myself being arrested and charged with a criminal offence, we continue, and hope to raise the number of signatories to two million.

91. Rostami-Povey (2001: 68).

92. Amongst these are Shadi Sadr (lawyer and human rights campaigner), Shahla Lahiji (leading feminist publisher and writer), Elaheh Koulaei (MP, professor of political science, and campaigner), Mahboubeh Abbasgholizadeh (Chief editor of *Farzaneh* periodical, and political campaigner), Lili Farhadpour (journalist, peace campaigner, and author), and many more. These women have suggested both local and global dimensions to the Charter, maintaining a national dimension with regard to the specificities of laws in Iran, and an international overview in relation to the United Nations Charter of Human Rights. They have reflected on the fact that the latter and the One Million Signatures Campaign for Change are interconnected and can help locate knowledge about who they wish to be as a society. Narggess is but one of their many young trainees.

93. Connected to Susa in Khuzistan province and the Old Elamite Period around 2700 BC, this region has a vast material culture which links it to Mesopotamia, the Akkadian Empire, and Ur. For a succinct study of the regions' cultures and remaining sculptural, archaeological, and seals, see Harper et al, *The Royal City of Susa* (1992).

94. In a critique of Islam twelve cartoons depicting the Prophet were published in the Danish newspaper Jyllands-Posten on 30th of September 2005. These led to a series of protests within the Muslim world and the Danish Embassy in Syria. Muslim leaders worldwide denounced the publication of these cartoons around the world. See http://news.bbc.co.uk/2/hi/europe/4670370.stm

95. http://www.guardian.co.uk/iran/story/0,,1760745,00.html .

96. This is an award-winning weblog from Duetsche Welle Webblog Award in 2005.

97. This could be any of the *bassij, heraasat*, and *jihad-e danesh-gahi* forces. Bassij are a voluntary force who could work in the police and military to watch over the suitable conduct of individuals and groups. Heraasat are ethics guardians who would do the same as the Bassij if need be. Jihad-e danesh-gahi is an Educational Jihad facilitating the needs of the individuals towards joining the mainstream education systems.

98. Homi Bhabha (1994: xiv, xvi), Hall (1991: 34).

99. Rostami-Povey (2005: 46).

100. Gheissari and Nasr (2006: 130).

101. S.J. Holliday unpublished thesis (2008: Chapter 5).

102. Ibid.

103. She is an iconic literary figure in Iran
http://www.iranchamber.com/literature/ffarrokhzad/forough_farrokhzad.pp

104. Carspecken (1996).

105. Derrida (2002a).

106. Honarbin-Holliday (unpublished PhD thesis: Chapter Three), discusses these points fully.

107. See the breath-taking works of Hossein Zenderoudi, Morteza Momayez, Siah Armajani, Massoud Arabshahi, and the sculptures of Parviz Tanavoli

Bibliography

A Secret History of Clay from Gauguin to Gormley (Catalogue, London, Tate Publishing, 2004).

Abadan-Unat, N., 'The dynamics of women's spheres of action in rural Iran', in N. R. Keddie and B. Baron (eds), *Woman in Middle Eastern History: Shifting Boundaries in Sex and Gender* (New Haven, Yale University Press, 1991), pp. 195-214.

Abdul-Hossein, N., Zanan-e Iran dar Jonbesh-e Mashruteh (Iranian Women in the Constitutional Movement) (Germany, Navid Publications, 1989).

Abu Lughod, J., 'Going beyond global babble', in A. D. King (ed), *Culture, Globalization and the World-System* (New York, Palgrave, 1991), pp. 131-8.

Abrahams, N., 'Negotiating power, identity, family and community: women's community participation', *Gender and Society* 10/6 (1996), pp. 768-96.

Afary, J. and K. B. Anderson, *Foucault and The Iranian Revolution: Gender and The Seduction of Islamism* (Chicago, University of Chicago Press, 2005).

Afary, J., *The Iranian Constitutional Revolution, 1906-1911: Grassroots Democracy, Social Democracy, and The Origins of Feminism* (New York, Columbia University Press, 1996).

Afkhami, M., 'The women's organization of Iran: evolutionary politics and revolutionary change', in L. Beck and G. Nashat (eds), *Women in Iran: From 1800 to The Islamic Republic* (Urbana, University of Illinois Press, 2004), pp. 107-35.

Afshar, H., 'Women and reproduction in Iran', in N. Yuval-Davies (ed), *Gender and Nation* (London, Sage, 1997), pp.110-125.

Afshar, H., R. Aitken and M. Franks, 'Feminisms, Islamophobia and identities', *Political Studies* 53 (2005), pp. 262-83.

Aghaie, K. S., 'Introduction', in K. S. Aghaie (ed), *The Women of Karbala: Ritual Performance and Symbolic Discourses in Modern Shi'i Islam* (Austin, University of Texas Press, 2005), pp. 1-24.

Aghaie, K. S., 'The gender dynamics of moharram symbols and rituals in the latter years of Qajar rule', K. S. Aghaie (ed), *The Women of Karbala: Ritual Performance and Symbolic Discourses in Modern Shi'i Islam* (Austin, University of Texas Press, 2005), pp. 45-64.

Ahmad, A. *In Theory: Nations, Classes, Literatures* (London: Verso, 2008).

Ahmadi, H., 'Elements in Iranian national identity' (Unpublished paper, School of African and Oriental Studies, London University, 2004).

Ahmadi, H., 'The dilemma of national interest in the Islamic Republic of Iran', in H. Katouzian and H. Shahidi (eds), *Iran in The Twenty-first Century: Politics, Economics and Conflict* (Oxford, Routledge, 2008), pp. 28-40.

Al-Ali, N., *Secularism, Gender and The State in The Middle East: The Egyptian Women's Movement* (Cambridge, Cambridge University Press, 2000).

Alavi, N., *We Are Iran* (London, Portobello Books 2005).

Alizadeh, P. and B. Harper, 'The feminization of the labour force in Iran', in A. Mohammadi (ed), *Iran Encountering Globalization: Problems and Prospects* (Oxford, Routledge Curzon, 2006), pp. 180-96.

Al-Saltana, T. *Growing Anguish: Memoirs of a Persian Princess from the Harem to Modernity 1884-1914* (Washington, Mage 1993, trans. A. Amanat).

Amiet, P., N. Chevalier and E. Carter, (1992). 'Susa in the Ancient Near East', in P. O. Harper, J. Aruz, and F. Tallon (eds), *The Royal City of Susa* (New York, The Metropolitan Museum of Art, 1992), pp. 1-24.

Amin, C. M., *The Making of The Modern Iranian Woman: Gender, State Policy, and Popular Culture, 1865-1946* (Gainsville, Florida University Press, 2005).

Amin, C. M., 'Importing "beauty culture" into Iran in the 1920s and the 1930s: mass marketing individualism in an age of snit-imperialist sacrifice', *Comparative Studies of South Asia, Africa and The Middle East* 24/1 (2004), pp. 79-95.

Amnesty International Press Release, 'Iran: arrests of women may be an attempt to prevent International Women's Day calls for equality' (AI MDE 13/022/2007 (Public) News Service Number 044, 5th March 2007).

Amouie, B. A., '27 year import to observe Islamic dress code', *Kanoon-e Zanan-e Iran* (2005),
http://www.irwomen.net/news_en_cat.php?newsid=5

Anleu, S. R., 'Gendered bodies: between conformity and autonomy', in K. Davis, M. Evans and J. Lorber (eds), *Handbook of Gender and Women's Studies* (London, Sage, 2006), pp. 357-75.

Ansari, A. M. *Modern Iran Since 1921: The Pahlavis and After* (London, Pearson, 2003).

Ansari, A. M., 'Iran and the United States in The Shadow of 9/11: Persia and The Persian Question Revisited', in H. Katouzian and H. Shahidi (eds), *Iran in The Twenty-first Century: Politics, Economics and Conflict* (Oxford, Routledge, 2008), pp. 107-22.

Ansari, A. M., *Confronting Iran* (London, Hurst, 2006).

Ashraf, A., 'Irani boodan', in *Goft-e-goo* 3 (1373 AH), pp. 7-25.

Askarieh, M., 'A case for sustainable development of nuclear energy and a brief account of Iran's nuclear programme', in H. Katouzian and H. Shahidi (eds), *Iran in The Twenty-first Century: Politics, Economics and Conflict* (Oxford, Routledge, 2008), pp. 181-93.

Atabaki, T., 'From multilingual empire to contested modern state', in H. Katouzian and H. Shahidi (eds), *Iran in The Twenty-first Century: Politics, Economics and Conflict* (Oxford, Routledge, 2008), pp. 41-62.

Atai, F., 'A look to the north: opportunities and challenges', in H. Katouzian and H. Shahidi (eds), *Iran in The Twenty-first Century: Politics, Economics and Conflict* (Oxford, Routledge, 2008), pp. 123-35.

Balaghi, S. and L. Gumpert (eds), *Picturing Iran: Art, Society and Revolution* (London, I.B. Tauris, 2002).

Barsamian, D., N. Chomsky, E. Abrahamian, and N. Mozaffafari, *Targeting Iran* (San Francisco, City Lights, 2007).

Basmenji, K., *Tehran Blues: Youth Culture in Iran* (London, Saqi, 2005).

Bayat, A., 'A women's non-movement: what it means to be a woman activist in an Islamic state', *Comparative Studies of South Asia, Africa and the Middle East* 27/1 (2007), pp. 161-74.

Bayat, A., 'Islam and democracy: what is the real question?', *ISIM Papers* 8 (2007).

Bayat, A., *Street Politics, Poor People's Movements in Iran*. New York, Columbia University Press, 1997).

Beck, L. and G. Nashat (eds), *Women in Iran: From 1800 to The Islamic Republic* (Urbana, University of Illinois Press, 2004)Bourdieu, P., *Distinction: A Social Critique of The Judgement of Taste* (Oxford, Routledge, 2006).

Bhabha, H., *The Location of Culture* (London, Routledge, 1994).

Brah, A., *Cartographies of Diaspora: Contesting Identities* (Oxford, Routledge, 2005).

Brosius, M., *Women in Ancient Persia: 559–33BC* (New York, Oxford University Press, 2002).

Bulletin of The Volunteer Lawyers' Network 1 (2007).

Butler, J., *Gender Trouble: Feminism and The Subversion of Identity* (London, Routledge, 1999).

Carter, E., F. Hole, Z. Bahrani, A. Spycket, and J. Aruz, 'Prehistoric Susa', in P. O. Harper, J. Aruz, and F. Tallon, (eds), *The Royal City of Susa* (New York, The Metropolitan Museum of Art, 1992), pp. 25-46.

Carter, E., H. Pittman, A. Benoit, Z.Bahrani and M. W. Stolper, 'Proto-literate Susa', in P. O. Harper, J. Aruz, and F. Tallon, (eds), *The Royal City of Susa* (New York, The Metropolitan Museum of Art, 1992), pp. 47-80.

Carter, E., Z. Bahrani, B. André-Salvini, A. Caubet, F. Talon, J. Aruz and O. Deschesne, 'The old Elamite period', in P. O. Harper, J. Aruz, and F. Tallon, (eds), *The Royal City of Susa* (New York, The Metropolitan Museum of Art, 1992), pp. 81-120.

Chelkowski, P. J., 'Iconography of the women of Karbala: tiles, mural, stamps, and posters', in K. S. Aghaie (ed), *The Women of Karbala: Ritual Performance and Symbolic Discourses in Modern Shi'i Islam* (Austin, University of Texas Press, 2005), pp. 119-138.

Chelkowski, P., 'Popular arts, patronage and piety', in L. S. Diba, with M. Ekhtiar (eds), *Royal Persian Paintings* (London, I. B. Tauris Publishers, 1999).

Chomsky, N., *The Emerging Framework of World Power* (Audio recording, Ford Hall Forum, Blackman Auditorium, North-Eastern University, Boston Ma. 2002)

Code, L., 'Women knowing/knowing women: critical-creative interventions in the politics of knowledge', in K. Davis, M. Evans and J. Lorber (eds), *Handbook of Gender and Women's Studies* (London, Sage, 2006), pp. 146-166.

Coffey, A., *The Ethnographic Self* (London, Sage, 1999).

Croke, T., *Cross-Cultural Education: Arab Women Studying a Non-Traditional Subject* (unpublished PhD Thesis, English and Language Studies Department, Canterbury Christ Church University, 2007).

Cronin, S. (ed), *The Making of Modern Iran: State and Society under Riza Shah 1921-1941* (London, Routledge Curzon, 2003).

Dabashi, H., *Iran: A People Interrupted* (New York, The New Press, 2007)

Davis, K., 'Feminist politics of location', in K. Davis, M. Evans and J. Lorber (eds), *Handbook of Gender and Women's Studies* (London, Sage, 2006), pp. 476-80.

de Bellaigue, C., *In The Rose Garden of The Martyrs: A Memoir of Iran* (London, Harper Perennial, 2005).

de Bellaigue, C., *The Struggle for Iran* (New York, New York Review Books, 2007).

Derrida, J., *Positions* (London, Continuum, 2002).

Derrida, J. *Derrida* (DVD, Jane Doe Films, 2002a).

Diba, D., 'Reflexions sur l'architecture contemporaine en Iran', *Architecture D'Aujourd'hui* 195 (1978), pp. 2-4.

Diba, L. S. and M. Ekhtiar (eds), *Royal Persian Paintings: The Qajar Epoch 1785-1925* (London, I. B. Tauris, 1999).

Diba, L. S., 'Images of power and the power of images: intention and response in early Qajar painting (1785-1834)', in L. S. Diba and M. Ekhtiar (eds), *Royal Persian Paintings: The Qajar Epoch 1785-1925* (London, I. B. Tauris, 1999), pp. 30-49

DiPalma, C. and K. E. Ferguson, 'Clearing ground and making connections: modernism, postmodernism and feminism', in K. Davis, M. Evans and J. Lorber (eds), *Handbook of Gender and Women's Studies* (London, Sage, 2006), pp. 127-145.

Eberly, D. E., 'Introduction', in Don E. Eberly (ed), *The Essential Civil Society Reader* (Maryland, Roman and Littlefield 2000), pp. 3-32.

Edadi, S., *Iran Awakening* (London, Rider, 2006).

Einhorn, B., 'Insiders and outsiders: within and beyond the gendered nation', in K. Davis, M. Evans and J. Lorber (eds), *Handbook of Gender and Women's Studies* (London, Sage, 2006), pp. 196-213.

Elahi-Ghomshei, M., 'Identity and classical Persian literature' (Unpublished paper, School of African and Oriental Studies, London University, 2004).

Elkins, J., *What Painting Is* (London, Routledge, 1999).

Esfandiari, H., 'The role of women members of parliament, 1963-88', in L. Beck and G. Nashat (eds), *Women in Iran: From 1800 to The Islamic Republic* (Urbana, University of Illinois Press, 2004), pp. 136-62.

Etemad Moghadam, F., 'Women and labour in the Islamic Republic of Iran', in L. Beck and G. Nashat (eds), *Women in Iran: From 1800 to The Islamic Republic* (Urbana, University of Illinois Press, 2004), pp. 163-81.

Ettehadieh, M., 'The origins and development of the women's movement in Iran, 1906-41', in L. Beck and G. Nashat (eds), *Women in Iran: From 1800 to The Islamic Republic* (Urbana, University of Illinois Press, 2004), pp. 85-106.

Etzioni, A., 'Communitarianism and the moral dimension', in D. E. Eberly (ed) *The Essential Civil Society Reader* (Maryland, Roman and Littlefield 2000), pp. 123-42.

Evans, M., 'Getting real: contextualizing gender', in K. Davis, M. Evans and J. Lorber (eds), *Handbook of Gender and Women's Studies* (London, Sage, 2006), pp. 474-5.

Farhad, M., 'Ceramics from the Islamic world', in L. A. Court, M. Farhad and A. Gunter (eds), *Asian Traditions in Clay: The Hague Gifts* (Washington D. C., Smithsonian, 2000), pp.57-89.

Farhi, F., 'Crafting a national identity amidst contentious politics in contemporary Iran', in H. Katouzian and H. Shahidi (eds), *Iran in The Twenty-first Century: Politics, Economics and Conflict* (Oxford, Routledge, 2008), pp. 13-27.

Farokhzad, F., *Khaneh Siah Ast* (DVD, Safarian, n.d.)

Fehérvári, G., *The Ceramics of The Islamic World in The Tareq Rajab Museum* (London, I. B. Tauris, 2000).

Fisher, J., *Global Visions: Towards a New Internationalism in The Visual Arts* (London, Kala Press, in association with The Institute of International Visual Arts, 1994).

Flaskerud, I., '"O, My Heart is Sad. It is Moharram, the Month of Zaynab": the role of aesthetics and women's mourning ceremonies in Shiraz', K. S. Aghaie (ed), *The Women of Karbala: Ritual Performance and Symbolic Discourses in Modern Shi'i Islam* (Austin, University of Texas Press, 2005), pp. 65-92.

Galloway, D., *Parvis Tanavoli, Sculptor, Writer and Collector* (Tehran, Iranian Art Publishing Co, 2000).

Geertz, C., *Available Light: Anthropological Reflections on Philosophical Topics* (Princeton, Princeton University Press, 2001).

Ghaissari, A. and V. Nasr, *Democracy in Iran: History and The Quest for Liberty,* (Oxford, Oxford University Press, 2006).

Ghorashi, G. R., 'Economic globalization and the prospects for democracy in Iran', in A. Mohammadi (ed), *Iran Encountering Globalization: Problems and Prospects* (Oxford, Routledge Curzon, 2006), pp. 77-85.

Gombrich, E. H., 'In conversation with Anthony Gormley', in A. Gormley, *Anthony Gormley* (New York: Phaidon, 2000), pp. 6-29.

Gormley, A., 'An act of embodiment', *The Guardian* (22nd April, 2004), pp. 10-16.

Gormley, A., *Anthony Gormley* (London, Phaidon Press Limited, 2000).

Goverde, H., P. G. Serne, M. Haugaard and H. Lentne, *Power in Contemporary Politics: Theories, Practices, Globalization* (London, Sage, 2000).

Greene, M., *Variations on a Blue Guitar* (New York: Teachers College Press, 2001).

Griffin, G., 'Gendered cultures', in K. Davis, M. Evans and J. Lorber (eds), *Handbook of Gender and Women's Studies* (London, Sage, 2006), pp. 73-91.

Groom, S., 'Terra incognita', in A *Secret History of Clay from Gauguin to Gormley* (Catalogue, London, Tate Publishing, 2004), pp. 14-23.

Gubrium, J. F. and J. A. Holstein, 'Analysing interpretive practice', in K. Denzin and Y. Lincoln (eds), *Handbook of Qualitative Research. 2nd Edition* (London, Sage Publications, 2000), pp. 487-508.

Hall, S. 'The local and the global: globalization and ethnicity', in A. D. King (ed), *Culture, Globalization and the World-System* (New York, Palgrave, 1991), pp.19-40.

Hall, S. 'Old and new identities, old and new ethnicities', in A. D. King (ed), *Culture, Globalization and the World-System* (New York, Palgrave, 1991), pp.41-68.

Harper, D., 'Re-imagining visual methods', in K. Denzin and Y. Lincoln (eds), *Handbook of Qualitative Research. 2nd Edition* (London, Sage Publications, 2000), pp. 717-767.

Harper, P. O., J. Aruz and F. Tallon (eds), *The Royal City of Susa* (New York, The Metropolitan Museum of Art, 1992).

Harrison, C. and P. Wood (eds). *Art in Theory: 1900-2000, an Anthology of Changing Ideas.* (London, Blackwell, 2003).

Hersh, S., *An Interview for The New Yorker* (6th October, 2007), http://www.newyorker.com/online/video/festival/2007/HershRemnick

Hillenbrand, R. (ed), *Persian Painting From the Mongols to the Qajars.* London, I. B. Tauris, 2000).

Hillmann, M., 'An autobiographical voice: Forough Farrokhzad', in A. Najmabadi (ed), *Women's Autobiographies in Contemporary Iran* (Cambridge Mass., Harvard University Press, 1990), pp. 33-54.

Holliday, S. J., 'The politicisation of culture and the contestation of Iranian national identity in Khatami's Iran', *Journal of Studies in Ethnicity and Nationalism* 7/1(2007), pp. 27-44.

Holliday, S. J., Discourses and Counter-Discourses of Iranian National Identity during Khatami's Presidency (1997-2005), (unpublished PhD Thesis, Exeter University 2008).

Honarbin-Holliday, M., 'For the love of oil', *Red Pepper*, June Issue (2007a), pp. 22-4.

Honarbin-Holliday, M., 'Experience and imagination', *The Middle East In London* 4/3 (2007b), pp. 6-7.

Honarbin-Holliday, M., Art and identity: an ethnographic investigation into art education in the Islamic Republic of Iran with the researcher as a participant ceramic artist in Canterbury (unpublished PhD thesis, University of Kent, 2005).

Honarbin-Holliday, M., 'Locating the evolutionary journey of institutional art training in the processes of transition and continuity', in H. Keshmirshekan (ed), *Between Shadow and Light: Contemporary Iranian Art and Artists* (London, Saffron Books, 2008), pp. 60-72.

Hopkins, D., *After Modern Art, 1945-2000* (Oxford, Oxford University Press, 2000).

Hourani, G. F., 'Ghazali on the ethnics of action', *Journal of The American Oriental Society* 96/1 (1976), pp. 69-88.

Institute for the Secularization of Islamic Society (ISIS) Newsletter, www.secularism.org. separation.secularization.htm

Interview with Dr Sami-Azar, *Etelaat International* (3rd Mordad 1380/2001).

Interview with Dr Sami-Azar. The cultural section, Tehran Museum of Contemporary Art (12th Dei, 1380/2001).

Issa, R., R. Pakbaz and D. Shayegan (eds), *Iranian Contemporary Art* (London, Booth-Clibborn Editions, 2001).

Jafari, A., 'Two tales of a city: an exploratory study of cultural consumption amongst Iranian youth', *Journal of The International Society of Iranian Studies* 40/3 (2007), pp. 367-383.

Jahanbagloo, R., *Iran and The Problem of Modernity* (Tehran, Goftar, 2001).

Kar, M., 'Women's political rights after the Islamic revolution', in L. Ridgeon (ed), *Religion and Politics in Modern Iran* (London, I. B. Tauris, 2005), pp. 253-79.

Karshenas, M., and Hassan H., 'Managing oil resources and economic diversification in Iran', in H. Katouzian and H. Shahidi (eds), *Iran in The Twenty-first Century: Politics, Economics and Conflict* (Oxford, Routledge, 2008), pp. 194-216.

Katouzian, H., 'Iran and the problem of political development', in A. Mohammadi (ed), *Iran Encountering Globalization: Problems and Prospects* (Oxford, Routledge Curzon, 2006), pp. 7-23.

Katouzian, H., 'The significance of economic history, and the fundamental features of the economic history of Iran' in H. Katouzian and H. Shahidi (eds), *Iran in The Twenty-first Century: Politics, Economics and Conflict* (Oxford, Routledge, 2008), pp. 273-90.

Katouzian, H., *State and Society in Iran: The Eclipse of the Qajars and The Emergence of The Pahlavis* (London, I. B. Tauris, 2006).

Katouzian, H. and H. Shahidi, 'Introduction', in H. Katouzian and H. Shahidi (eds), *Iran in The Twenty-first Century: Politics, Economics and Conflict* (Oxford, Routledge, 2008), pp. 1-12.

Kazemi, F., 'Moderns or Iranian politics, the road to the Islamic Revolution, and the challenge of Civil Society', *World Politics* 47/4 (1995), pp. 555-574.

Keal, E., 'The Art of the Parthians', in R. W. Ferrier (eds), *The Arts of Persia* (New Haven, Yale University Press, 1989), pp. 49-59

Keddie, N. R., 'Introduction: deciphering Middle Eastern women's history', in N. R. Keddie and B. Baron (eds), *Woman in Middle Eastern History: Shifting Boundaries in Sex and Gender* (New Haven, Yale University Press, 1991), pp. 1-22.

Keddie, N. R., *Modern Iran: Roots and Results of Revolution* (New Haven, Yale University Press, 2003).

Keddie, N. R., 'Women in Iran since 1979' (Women Living Under Muslim Laws Organization, 2001). http://www.wluml.org/english/pubsfulltext.shtml?cmd[87]=I-87-90862be92116ceddae

Keshmirshekan, H., 'Contemporary Iranian art: the emergence of new artistic discourses', *Journal of The International Society of Iranian Studies* 40/3 (2007), pp. 335-66.

Khatami, S. M. *Ain va Andishe dar Dame Khod-kamegi* (Tehran, Tarhe-hno, 1379/2000).

Khosrowpanah, M. H., Hadafha va Mobarezeh-ye Zan-e Irani: Az Enghelab-e Mashrouteh ta Saltanat-e Pahlavi (Tehran, Payam-e Emrooz, 1382/2003).

Kian-Thibaut, A., 'From motherhood to equal rights advocates: the weakening of patriarchal order', in H. Katouzian and H. Shahidi (eds), *Iran in The Twenty-first Century: Politics, Economics and Conflict* (Oxford, Routledge, 2008), pp. 86-106.

Leonard, D., 'Gender, change, and education', in K. Davis, M. Evans and J. Lorber (eds), *Handbook of Gender and Women's Studies* (London, Sage, 2006), pp. 167-182.

Lotfian, S., 'Nuclear policy and international relations', in H. Katouzian and H. Shahidi (eds), *Iran in The Twenty-first Century: Politics, Economics and Conflict* (Oxford, Routledge, 2008), pp. 158-80.

Mahbaz, E., Zanan-e Iran: Cheraghi dar Dast Cheraghi Dar Rah (Anga, Baran, 2005).

Mahdavi, S., 'Reflections in the mirror – how each saw the other: women in the nineteenth century', in L. Beck and G. Nashat (eds), *Women in Iran: From 1800 to The Islamic Republic* (Urbana, University of Illinois Press, 2004), pp. 63-84.

Mahdi, A. A., 'Iranian women: between Islamicization and globalization', in A. Mohammadi (ed), *Iran Encountering Globalization: Problems and Prospects* (Oxford, Routledge Curzon, 2006), pp. 47-72.

Mernissi, F., Scheherezade Goes West: Different Cultures, Different Harems (New York, Washington Square Press, 2001)

Milani, F., 'Veiled voices: women's autobiographies in Iran', in A. Najmabadi (ed), *Women's Autobiographies in Contemporary Iran* (Cambridge Mass., Harvard University Press, 1990), pp. 1-16.

Mills, C. W., *The Sociological Imagination* (Middlesex, Penguin Books, 1970).

Mir-Hosseini, Z., 'Sexuality, rights, and Islam: competing gender discourses in post-revolutionary Iran', in L. Beck and G. Nashat (eds), *Women in Iran: From 1800 to The Islamic Republic* (Urbana, University of Illinois Press, 2004), pp. 204-17.

Mir-Hosseini, Z., *Islam and Gender: The Religious Debate In Contemporary Iran* (London, I. B. Tauris, 2000).

Moallem, M., *Between Warrior Brother and Veiled Sister: Islamic Fundamentalism and the Politics of Patriarchy in Iran* (Berkeley, University of California Press, 2005).

Moaveni, A., Lipstick Jihad: A Memoir of Growing Up Iranian in America and American in Iran (New York, Public Affairs, 2005)

Moghadam, V. M. (ed), *Gender and National Identity* (London, Zed Books, 1994).

Moghadam, V. M., 'Islamic feminism and its discontents: toward a resolution of the debate', *Journal of Women in Culture and Society* 27/4 (2002), pp. 1135-1171.

Mohammadi, A., 'Iran and the globalized world', in A. Mohammadi (ed), *Iran Encountering Globalization: Problems and Prospects* (Oxford, Routledge Curzon, 2006), pp. 5-6.

Mohammadi, A., 'The sixth majles election and the prospects for democracy in Iran', in A. Mohammadi (ed), *Iran Encountering Globalization: Problems and Prospects* (Oxford, Routledge Curzon, 2006), pp. 228-244.

Mottahedeh, N., 'Ta'ziyeh: a twist of history in everyday life', in K. S. Aghaie (ed), *The Women of Karbala: Ritual Performance and Symbolic Discourses in Modern Shi'i Islam* (Austin, University of Texas Press, 2005), pp. 25-44.

Munsterberg, H. and M. Munsterberg, *World Ceramics: From Prehistoric to Modern Times* (New York, Penguin, 1998)/

Najmabadi, A., *Women with Mustaches and Men Without Beards: Gender and Sexual Anxieties of Iranian Modernity* (Berkeley, University of California Press, 2005).

Nashat, G., 'Introduction', in G. Nashat and L. Beck (eds), *Women in Iran from The Rise of Islam to 1800* (Urbana, University of Illinois Press, 2003), pp. 1-10.

Nashat, G., 'Introduction', in L. Beck and G. Nashat (eds), *Women in Iran: From 1800 to The Islamic Republic* (Urbana, University of Illinois Press, 2004), pp. 1-36.

Nashat, G., 'Marriage in the Qajar period', in L. Beck and G. Nashat (eds), *Women in Iran: From 1800 to The Islamic Republic* (Urbana, University of Illinois Press, 2004), pp. 37-62.

Nashat, G., 'Women in Pre-Islamic and Early Islamic Iran', in G. Nashat and L. Beck (eds), *Women in Iran from The Rise of Islam to 1800* (Urbana, University of Illinois Press, 2003), pp. 11-47

Nashat, G., *Women in the Middle East and North Africa: Restoring Women to History* (Bloomington: Indiana University Press, 1999).

Paidar, P., 'Zanan va asr tamadon-e bozorg', *Goft-o-gu* 37 (1380/2001), pp. 91-135.

Paidar, P., *Women and The Political Process in twentieth Century Iran* (Cambridge, Cambridge University Press, 1997).

Pakbaz, R., Y. Emadian and T. Maleki (eds), *Pioneers of Iranian Modern Art: Charles-Hossein Zenderoudi* (Tehran: Mahriz Publications, 2001).

Pakbaz, R., Y. Emadian and T. Maleki (eds), *Pioneers of Iranian Modern Art: Massoud Arabshahi* (Tehran: Mahriz Publications, 2001).

Parsi, T., 'Israeli-Iranian relations assessed: strategic competition from the power cycle perspective', in H. Katouzian and H. Shahidi (eds), *Iran in The Twenty-first Century: Politics, Economics and Conflict* (Oxford, Routledge, 2008), pp. 136-57.

Pink, S., *Doing Visual Ethnography* (London, Sage, 2004).

Poya, M., *Women, Work and Islamism: Ideology and Resistance in Iran* (London, Zed Books, 1999).

Price, M., 'A brief history of Iranian women', *Iranian Online Magazine* (2000).

Prins, B., 'Mothers and Muslims, sisters and sojourners: the contested boundaries of feminist citizenship' in K. Davis, M. Evans and J. Lorber (eds), *Handbook of Gender and Women's Studies* (London, Sage, 2006), pp. 234-50.

Rogoff, I., Terra Infirma: Geography's Visual Culture (London, Routledge, 2000).

Roohbakhsh, R., 'Miras-e ayatollah borujerdi', *Goft-o-gu* 37 (1380/2001), pp. 7-35.

Rostami-Povey, E., 'Feminist contestations of institution domains in Iran', *Feminist Review* 69 (2001), pp. 44-72.

Rostami-Povey, E., 'Workers, women and the Islamic Republic', *International Socialism* 105 (2005), pp. 43-62.

Rostami-Povey, E., *Afghan Women: Identity and Invasion* (London, Zed Books, 2007a).

Rostami-Povey, E., 'Khorasani, Noushin Ahmadi', in M. R. Fischbach (ed), *Biographical Encyclopedia of The Modern Middle East and North Africa* (Gale Cengage, 2007b), pp.443-4.

Rostami-Povey, E., 'Alaee Taleghani, Azam', in M. R. Fischbach (ed), *Biographical Encyclopedia of The Modern Middle East and North Africa* (Gale Cengage, 2007c), pp. 35-37.

Rostami-Povey, E., 'Sadr, Shadi', in M. R. Fischbach (ed) *Biographical Encyclopedia of The Modern Middle East and North Africa* (Gale Cengage, 2007d), pp. 680-2.

Rostami-Povey, E., 'Abbas Gholizadeh, Mahboubeh', in M. R. Fischbach (ed), *Biographical Encyclopedia of The Modern Middle East and North Africa* (Gale Cengage, 2007e), pp. 8-10.

Roy, A. *Come September: in conversation with Howard Zinn* (Audio recording, Lensing Performing Arts Centre, Santa Fe. Lannan Foundation, 2002).

Sadig Al-Ali, N., *Iraqi Women: Untold Stories 1948 to The Present* (London, Zed Books, 2007).

Sadri, M. and S. Ahmad, 'Three faces of dissent: cognitive, expressive and traditionalist discourses of discontent in contemporary Iran', in H. Katouzian and H. Shahidi (eds), *Iran in The Twenty-first Century: Politics, Economics and Conflict* (Oxford, Routledge, 2008), pp. 63-85.

Saeed-Vafa, M. and J. Rosenbaum, *Abbas Kiarostami* (Urbana: University of Illinois Press, 2003).

Safarian, N., Saad-e Sabz, a Film of Farokhzad's Life (DVD, n.d.).

Said, E. 'Preface to Orientalism.' *Al-Ahram Weekly Online* 650 (7-13 August 2003a) http: weekly.ahram.org.eg.2003.650.op11.htm

Said, E., 'A monument to hypocrisy.' *Al-Ahram Weekly Online* 625 (13-19 February 2003b) http: weekly.ahram.org.eg.2003.625.op2.htm

Said, E., *The Last Interview* (DVD, London, Drakes Avenue Pictures, 2005)

Salehi-Isfahani, D., 'Human resources: potentials and challenges', in H. Katouzian and H. Shahidi (eds), *Iran in The Twenty-first Century: Politics, Economics and Conflict* (Oxford, Routledge, 2008), pp.243-72.

Salehi-Isfahani, D., 'Human resources in Iran: potentials and challenges', in H. Katouzian and H. Shahidi (eds), *Iran in The Twenty-first Century: Politics, Economics and Conflict* (Oxford, Routledge, 2008), pp. 243-72.

Sanasarian, E., *Religious Minorities in Iran* (Cambridge, Cambridge University Press, 2000).

Sanctions against Iran website,
http://www.ustreas.gov/offices/enforcement/ofac/programs/iran/iran.shtml, http://www.mafhoum.com/press3/108E16.htm, http://www.globalpolicy.org/security/sanction/indxiran.htm

Serpentine Galley Press Release on Shirin Neshat, Exhibition 28 July-3 September (2000).

Shirazi, F., 'The daughters of Karbala: images of women in popular Shi'i culture in Iran', K. S. Aghaie (ed), *The Women of Karbala: Ritual Performance and Symbolic Discourses in Modern Shi'i Islam* (Austin, University of Texas Press, 2005), pp. 92-118.

Shirzanan Iran, http://www.shirzanan.com/

Shuster, W. M., *The Strangling of Persia* (Washington, D. C., Mage, 1987).

Song, M., 'Gender in a global world', in K. Davis, M. Evans and J. Lorber (eds), *Handbook of Gender and Women's Studies* (London, Sage, 2006), pp. 185-195.

Soudavar, A., *Persian Courts, Selections from The Art and History Trust Collection* (New York: Rizzoli, 1992).

Spivak, G., 'Diasporas old and new: Women in the transnational world', in A. Kumar (ed), *Class Issues: Pedagogy, Cultural Studies, and the Public Sphere* (New York, New York University Press, 1997), pp. 87-116.

Spycket, A., 'Popular Art At Susa', in P. O. Harper, J. Aruz and F. Tallon (eds), *The Royal City of Susa* (New York, The Metropolitan Museum of Art, 1992), pp. 183-196.

Supporting Iraq to attack Iran website,
http://www.gwu.edu/~nsarchiv/nsa/publications/iraqgate/igdoc 1.html,
http://www.gwu.edu/~nsarchiv/nsa/publications/iraqgate/iraqg ate.html,
http://www.gwu.edu/~nsarchiv/nsa/publications/iraqgate/iraqg ate.html#SDT

Szuppe, M., 'Status, knowledge, and politics: women in sixteenth century Safavid Iran', in Guity Nashat and Lois Beck (eds), *Women in Iran from The Rise of Islam to 1800* (Urbana, University of Illinois Press, 2003), pp. 140-169.

Takeyh, R., *Hidden Iran: Paradox and Power in The Islamic Republic* (New York, Henry Holt, 2006)

Tapper, R. (ed), *The New Iranian Cinema: Politics, Representation and Identity* (London, I. B. Tauris, 2002).

Time Zones: Recent Film and Video (Catalogue, London, Tate Modern, 2004).

Tohidi, N., 'Peyvand-e jahani-e jonbesh-e zanan-e Iran', *Goft-o-gu* 38 (1382/2003), pp. 25-49.

Torab, A., *Performing Islam: Gender and Ritual in Iran* (Leiden, Brill, 2007).

Van Engeland-Nourai, A., 'Iran: civil society versus judiciary, a struggle for human rights', *Cornell Law School Papers* 3 (LLM Papers Series, 2004), http://lsr.nellco.org/cornell/lps/clacp/3.

Walmsley, J., 'Iranian women take to the field', *BBC News* (3 March, 1999)
http://news.bbc.co.uk/1/hi/programmes/crossing_continents/2 84262.stm

Weitz, R. (ed), *The Politics of Women's Bodies: Sexuality, Appearance and Behaviour* (Oxford, 2002).

Whitehead, L., *Democratization: Theory and Experience* (Oxford, Oxford University Press, 2003).

Winter, B., 'The social foundations of the sacred: feminists and the politics of religion', in K. Davis, M. Evans and J. Lorber (eds), *Handbook of Gender and Women's Studies* (London, Sage, 2006), pp. 92-108.

Wise, S. and L. Stanley, 'Having it all: feminist fractured foundational-
    ism', in K. Davis, M. Evans and J. Lorber (eds), *Handbook of Gender
    and Women's Studies* (London, Sage, 2006), pp. 435-56.
Yuval-Davies, N., 'Theorizing gender and nation', in N. Yuval-Davies
    (ed), *Gender and Nation* (London, Sage, 1997), pp. 1-25.
Zanghaneh, L. A., *My Sister, Guard Your Veil: My Brother, Guard Your
    Eyes: Uncensored Iranian Voices* (Boston: Beacon Press, 2006).

Index